The Paranormal

STAN GOOCH

WILDWOOD HOUSE LONDON

For
BILL DUFFY

First published 1978
© Stan Gooch 1978

Wildwood House Limited
29 King Street
London WC2E 8JD

ISBN 0 7045 0307 7

Typeset by Supreme Litho Typesetting, Romford, Essex
Printed and bound in Great Britain by
Redwood Burn, Trowbridge and Esher

Contents

Note Occasionally the names of people and locales have been changed
in the interests of those not wishing for publicity.

Introduction

A book about the paranormal should open with a sense of wonder and delight. Therefore I am deliberately leaving my more critical comments for later in the book. Chapter 1 takes us without preamble straight into the astonishments of the 'alternative universe' — that breathtaking world which somehow exists in complete contradiction to the universe our normal senses discern around us. The alternative universe is in fact not part of this objective universe. It is somewhere else.

The notion of 'somewhere else' is very hard for us to grasp, let alone to define. Still more difficult is the fact that while we are very definitely in and part of this present objective universe, we are also, fitfully, in touch with that other universe. So in some sense, apart from being here, we are also simultaneously there as well.

Nevertheless, it is not the case that the alternative universe is mysterious in itself. It is mysterious only *to us*. For our nervous system is poorly equipped to understand the paranormal. As I sometimes remark, it is not that god is inexpressible, it is only that we are incapable of expressing him.

The alternative universe — I should really say universes — of the paranormal do have their own laws and their own coherent existence. It is the case, however, that these in no way resemble those of the objective universe. They simply bear no relation to the rules of every day. This, in brief, is why the application of science and the scientific method to the paranormal not only produces no results, but rather literally causes the phenomena to disappear.

In a dark room the face of a luminous watch glows at me in mid-air. I switch on the light — and the watch face disappears as does the watch itself in a jumble of objects. The watch face is the paranormal and science is the light.

Just one look at this point at my harder comments in later parts of the book.

Years ago as a very young child I saw a gardener at work in a garden. He was pruning a large rose bush in the centre. He went on snipping and cutting and snipping. After a while I realized he was trying to kill the rose bush, but I wondered why he just did not dig the whole thing up. In the end all that was left was a mutilated stump. The next summer a glorious bush, filled with roses, appeared on that spot.

What the gardener did for the rose bush I hope to do for the paranormal in this book.

My image of the rose bush is a metaphor. But perhaps I need also to spell out my intention in plainer language. Part II of this book, then, does contain some rather severe criticism of paranormalist beliefs and attitudes. This section does not contain only criticism, by any means, but it is the criticism which may initially predominate in the eye of the sensitive believer.

So it is most important for me to emphasize that I am not engaged there in any task of destruction, but in a work of reconstruction. I indicate the shakiness of some paranormalist thinking simply in order to build more surely from a stable base in Parts III and IV. I believe the edifice I construct there will satisfy the largest appetites for creative vision — but importantly, with the added knowledge that we build on a sure and certain foundation.

It is no longer the question whether science will recognize the paranormal. It is rather a question of allowing science to apologize with as little loss of face as possible. But still there is a last price for the paranormalist to pay for his victory — and that is the price of putting his own house in order. The paranormalist and the psychic must demonstrate to the scientist that they too are willing to act responsibly and as adults, not expecting all that glitters to be gold, nor to be right always, all of the time.

I cannot too strongly state my belief that paranormalists gain absolutely nothing by extravagance or by adopting standards in respect of the paranormal that they would never for a moment tolerate in their social and economic lives. They not only do not gain — they lose. Why on earth (or in heaven) should we trade this priceless possession, the paranormal, for the momentary, spurious gains of extravagance, euphoria and wishful thinking?

The paranormal is the most glorious gift that life has to offer. This book is in affirmation of that fact.

PART I

ONE

Mysterious Midlands

At the age of twenty-six I went to become a teacher in Coventry in the English Midlands. The year previously I had spent as a management trainee in the scrap-metal business, but had found the commercial world not really to my taste. Prior to that, I had spent some years obtaining a degree in Modern Languages. In Coventry I taught not Modern Languages, but general subjects in a secondary modern school.

I had no acquaintances in that part of England. After the day's marking and preparation was done, the choice really was between watching television with my Irish landlord or going to a film. An occasional variation was the once-a-week dance, or the once-a-week concert, or a visit to Coventry repertory theatre.

To fill the series of empty evenings I enrolled for three sets of evening classes. Two of them involved folk-dancing, one of them gymnastics. The gymnastics was needed also for another reason — I had to teach it to my class.

I was, and remained, in the beginner's class in gymnastics. One evening in the changing room, however, a member of the advanced class struck up a conversation with me. He subsequently told me that his 'spirit guide' had instructed him to do so. The following week he and I had a cup of tea in a buffet near the Institute after the classes.

In due course he told me he was a Spiritualist and himself a medium. He suggested I might like to go along to the church service the following Sunday, on the far outskirts of Coventry. I did so that week, and also for several weeks subsequently.

I found the unadorned simplicity of the church (apart from the habitual enormous basket of fresh flowers in front of the altar), the service itself and the people very appealing.   It was quite unlike anything I had seen in frankly miserable Christian churches.   The hymns were especially delightful, many of them written by spiritualists. The service was always followed by a display of clairvoyance. This I found completely fascinating, but to my disappointment I myself never got a 'message'.

Eventually Peter (as I will call him) suggested I might like to attend a seance at his parents' house.   Apparently all his family were psychic to some degree.   I had in fact already met the family — very genuine, rather rough-and-ready people, who ran their own greengrocery business.   They lived outside Coventry in a rambling house, parts of which were several hundred years old.   It had once been a public house, and the room in which the seances were held was the old taproom.

This was an extremely atmospheric building and an extremely atmospheric room.   We — some eight or ten of us gathered on that evening — sang one of the simple Spiritualist hymns, and the presiding medium gave a short prayer.   We were not sitting in a circle nor at a table, but on ordinary hardback chairs facing the medium.   In the distance the house-dog, Bruce, barked and wailed dismally from the room in which he had been shut.

At this point I became aware of a certain light-headedness. And then suddenly it seemed to me that a great wind was rushing through the room.   In my ears was the deafening sound of roaring waters.   Together these elements seized me and carried me irresistibly forward.   As I felt myself swept away I became unconscious.

As I have written elsewhere, the great force and the abruptness of the onset very much conveyed the impression of a dam or barrier having suddenly collapsed.   Something, perhaps, could flow through which had previously been denied.

When I regained consciousness I was standing in front of the chairs, my face covered with tears, and the medium was holding my two hands and talking to me.   It seems, as I was told later, that several 'entities' had spoken through me — one of them, apparently, a cousin of mine of the same name as myself, who had been killed during the Second World War. I will speak later of mediumistic trance and what it is that I think then occurs. For the moment, the upshot was as follows. The presiding medium told me that I was myself a strong natural medium and that I ought to develop the gift. She suggested that I attend her own weekly circle, which consisted entirely of mediumistic individuals.

These weekly seances proved the gateway to wonders.

There would be seven or eight people, of whom Peter was one. Apart from an occasional change, it was always the same people. The purpose of these seances was to develop further individuals who had already shown evidence of strong psychic powers, and to explore, as a joint force, the farther reaches of the spirit world. The people involved, aside from their actual gifts, were straightforward, uncomplicated individuals — a shopkeeper, a railway porter, a secretary and so on. These seemed to have no difficulty in reconciling the mundaneness of their everyday existence with the marvels which occurred in the small suburban room.

The room was lit by a very small lamp with a slightly yellowish, but almost white bulb. This was not, therefore, the standard red light recommended for these occasions. We could actually see quite well, once our eyes became accustomed to the low intensity of light.

Aside from physical light there was also a less tangible form of 'electricity' in evidence. That is, we often felt that the air, or at any rate our skins, tingled. This sensation was, I think, physical, and not psychological. I think it was not just 'in the mind'. The others assured me it was a manifestation of the psychic power which we collectively generated. Some claimed to be able to see it sparking about the room. I never saw it myself, though sometimes I did see the faint auras of individuals. Years later I experienced the same (or at least a similar) power, much more strongly, in the presence of such gifted psychics as Jan Merta and Marcel Vogel.

Each member of the group was, on different occasions, the

vehicle for an evening's work. Sometimes the meeting consisted of an address from one of the 'higher guides' speaking through a particular member of the group in trance. On some other occasions we had a rescue circle.

A rescue circle is where the spirit guides bring into the circle the spirits of individuals who, allegedly, have died but do not realize they are dead. These spirits are said to wander about in darkness, attached to the Earth and to those they cannot forget. The idea is then for the members of the circle gently to educate the lost spirit in the facts of death.

It is a strange experience to be possessed by one of these lost souls — stranger even, that is, than 'normal' possession by the more conventional spirit guides. Normal possession is certainly amazing enough. Although some mediums go into deep trance (or full unconsciousness) and remember nothing of what has transpired on waking, it is possible to learn to remain conscious while the possession occurs and unfolds. Subjectively, one withdraws one's consciousness to a place apart. It is as if one steps aside from one's body, although the expression is incorrect — for one does not then occupy another space in the physical sense. One is in a somewhere else that is nevertheless still within oneself.

Then it seems, again subjectively, as if another being 'materializes' or arises within one's body and pervades it. The sensation, surely enough, is of someone else putting on your body as you yourself might put on clothes. There is a very clear and definite sense of another person within you. You now have — or rather *are* — the body of an old man, a young girl or whatever. You feel, for instance, the arthritic joints. Fingers become gnarled and twisted — or fine and slender. You grow tall, or short, or fat. You now stand and walk in a way that is *characteristic* of someone else. You begin also to have other memories — though these are sketched in rather than fully drawn. You have a sense of being the person you have now become, and this person is not you. Your voice, when you speak, if it is that of a young girl, has no trace of falsetto, no unnaturalness. This is someone else's *own* voice.

When one experiences, or becomes, a lost spirit in a rescue circle, experience goes yet further. You feel the agonizing pain of broken legs, the bursting lungs filled with water, the flesh hanging in shreds after a road accident.

These were some of our seance evenings. On yet others, events took a turn of their own. The most memorable occurrence of this kind for me was as follows.

We had not long been settled into our seats, and the presiding medium was talking quietly to us about 'the work', as she often did, when we became aware of a figure in a corner of the room.

This was a crouching, ape-like shape, which became clearer as the moments passed. I guess it approximated to most people's idea of what an ancient cave-man would look like. Yet one could not make out too much detail — the eyes were hidden, for example. It stood half in shadow, watching us, breathing heavily as if nervous. I must say, though, that I sensed rather than heard the breathing. I could not decide whether our visitor was wearing the skin of some animal, or whether it had a rough coat of hair of its own.

After a time the group leader addressed the creature. Did it want to tell us something? Would it like to come into the circle? Could we help it in any way? There was no reply, and very little reaction. After a while the image of the creature simply faded — and our seance continued. I was quite breathless with delight. The others seemed to take it calmly enough.

After each seance I always said very little and never anything that would 'lead' any of the other witnesses. I waited instead to see what the others had to say. In this way I could compare their reactions and perceptions with my own, without having fed them information which could modify or add to their reports.

On another occasion the presiding medium announced we were to have a lecture from a very highly-evolved spirit indeed. The lecture began. The spirit speaker told us that his message was coming to us from the highest realms of light, not far below the Highest One of all. The light of the message, he said, was beaming down to us through many layers of spirit, a gorgeous radiance beaming down, down through the darkness of matter. A wondrous radiance, beaming to us the love and compassion of the highest-evolved spiritual realm.

This basic theme was repeated by the speaker in different words over and over again. And then, finally, the centre of our circle grew bright as if a light shone down from the ceiling, and for a while a radiance illumined even the dark corners of the room.

It was clear that these events we occasionally saw were *at the very least* collective hallucinations. There was, in other words, considerable general and detailed agreement in the reports each individual gave. Yet even the minimal 'explanation' of a collective hallucination is a happening unheard of in modern psychology.

It should not be imagined that there was actually very much discussion after a sitting — in fact no *discussion* in any sense, just casual conversation. One would think that after such experiences a room would be filled with the babble of excited conversation. But not at all. My fellow sitters reacted to the miraculous happenings of the seance in much the same way as they might have reacted to seeing a more or less interesting film.

Later in this book I shall be talking about what I think underlies the mediumistic experience. For the moment I will just say that, in my opinion, the manifestations of our seance room were not physical materializations. That is, I do not think that any of the happenings would have registered on a photograph of the scene. These were psychological, that is, *parapsychological* events. But even though I describe them as psychological, you can search, as I did in the years ahead, all the psychology textbooks of the Western world and find no mention whatsoever that such things as I witnessed and underwent could even take place — much less, therefore, any attempts to account for them.

As regards the figure of the cave-man, which so very much impressed and haunted me both then and afterwards (in a wholly agreeable way, I must add) — I had and could not have had any inkling that one day I would write books about Neanderthal man. For those familiar with these matters, I wonder if it was classic Neanderthal I saw that evening.*

* See *The Neanderthal Question* (Wildwood House, London, 1977).

Meanwhile, outside the seance room, my 'education' in other aspects of psychic affairs continued.

On the negative/sceptical (though never destructive) side, I kept, for instance, a mental note of the names and addresses which the 'lost souls' of the rescue circle sometimes gave us. I wrote to all these addresses, and sometimes visited the locales described. None of these places or addresses existed. I said nothing of this to anyone.

On the positive side, I had many talks and walks with Peter.

He took me once to a dark, deep lake, the bottom of which he said had never been fathomed, and where a number of people had committed suicide. He said that if one opened oneself to the experience, one could sense the dead souls in the water. It is true that on doing as he instructed I felt a great and indefinable sense of melancholy.

Thereafter I would sometimes go to country graveyards and isolated, ruined houses. It seemed to me then that in such places one did make contact with some kind of presence — I even felt I learned something of the emotional history of the houses in question. But I at no point followed up or checked on any aspect of these particular situations.

When I knew him better, Peter offered rather condescendingly (he was always very full of his own mediumship) to let me have a private session with his own spirit guide. The guide was a former Red Indian. I cannot today remember whether he was called Grey Owl or Grey Hawk, but I think it was the second.

Accordingly we went to the house of one of Peter's relatives, well out in the countryside. Around the back of the house was tethered a goat. I was astonished to hear that Peter's aunt made her own milk and cheese. As a city boy of working-class antecedents, such situations and antics amazed me.

Peter and I sat in a darkened room. Outside, and within, all was completely peaceful (the reason why we had come). Peter went into trance. Gradually, as he did so, his dim face and profile became those of a non-European — of a story-book Indian in fact. In dim light I have often since observed faces in trance take on the features of the guide or

spirit in question and many others report the same experience. It is not just the face, but the very bone structure
which appears to alter.

Grey Hawk gave me a long lecture on the nature of spirit.
He disliked being interrupted (very much like Peter!) and
clearly did not really want me to ask him any questions.
The lecture was nevertheless very moving in a quiet, poetic
kind of way. Grey Hawk said that spirit incarnated in matter
is like the ripple one sees on the surface of a lake when the
breeze touches it. After the breeze goes the lake is still
again. The invisible and elusive breeze is spirit.

I have since heard talks by many guides and have read
books 'dictated' by them. I do not deny that there is a
certain poetic quality in the best of them. Yet all of them
remain a kind of intellectual candy-floss. This is not to
imply that they are sweet or sickly — I mean that when you
try to chew on these utterances, there is nothing there. The
mouth is empty.

Peter also went in for spirit painting and automatic writing. In spirit painting the medium, using a conventional
easel and paints, allows spirit forces to paint through him. I
thought Peter's work was rather good, with an ethereal or
out-of-this-world quality. I have since seen other spirit
paintings and find in all certain common qualities. (I do not
think that the painters are copying each other or conforming
to an accepted style, in that sense.) The paintings have many
curved lines and few or no straight ones. There is great use
of colour, but often pastel shades — unsaturated colours, I
believe the term is. The subject matter is often 'angelic' or
'heavenly-pastoral'.

Although I was never personally attracted to the idea of
spirit painting, I tried automatic writing for myself as soon as
I heard of it. After only one or two attempts my hand began
to write vigorously and fluently.

To perform automatic writing one is usually advised to sit
somewhere quiet, in not too strong a light. One holds a
pencil or pen in one's hand, which rests on a writing pad or
a sheet of paper. One then relaxes or 'meditates', trying as
far as possible to pay no attention to the hand and certainly
not attempting to use it in any normal, conscious way.

After a few sessions, perhaps even in the first, the hand will begin to twitch occasionally of itself. Marks and scribbles may be made. In time many people can progress to a hand that writes coherently by itself.

This is a slightly daunting — though of course exciting — experience, at first. However, one gets used to it quickly enough. I can produce automatic writing at will at any time in any circumstances (as, in fact, I can go into full trance at any time in any place in any circumstances). At the time of which I am speaking, automatic writing seemed to me to offer an invaluable method of investigating aspects of the paranormal without the agreement or assistance of any other person.

Just as in the full mediumistic trance, all kinds of 'personalities' express themselves in automatic writing. At first respectful of the 'communicators', I soon became more cavalier with them. Long conversations with my hand more and more firmly dissuaded me of the idea that any real, disembodied spirit was talking to or through me.

Sometimes the hand produced the solemn, soulful tones of the spirit guide. At other times the naughty remarks of the 'impish spirit'. And occasionally the cursing and filth of the true demon or devil. But I discovered that I could cause the tone (and the style of writing generally) to switch from one form to another in an instant, simply by a mental command — *not*, of course, by any deliberate, physical action. I could also lead the conversation in any direction I chose. I could easily catch out the communicant by causing him or her to contradict something said earlier. There was here much food for thought.

Also on this more negative side, I observed that in the seances where a guide or spirit spoke a foreign language known to me, it was never more than a meaningless copy of the real language. I myself was once possessed by a medieval monk, who chattered on a bit in 'Latin'. It was nothing of the kind — just a plausible-sounding imitation. And finally, when guides or communicants spoke with a foreign accent, as they quite often did, *it was the foreign accent as the Englishman mistakes it*, not the accent of the true foreigner.

Nevertheless, genuine wonders remained in plenty.

Towards the end of my stay in Coventry, Peter took me to visit a friend of his who was a psychometrist. Psychometrists are individuals who by holding an object belonging to a person can paranormally ascertain facts about that person's past or future.

This particular psychometrist was a rather elderly lady, not long for this world, I thought. I gave her a ring of mine, which she held in her hand for a while. Then she began to give a string of generalizations about my future, to none of which I paid much attention, precisely because of their generalized vagueness.* That was by the way. The important event was as follows — and now we begin to touch material of the kind I shall discuss in the next chapter, 'Footprints in the Sand'.

The psychometrist said that I would soon meet a girl with whom I would have a rather significant relationship. Now, such an event is commonplace and likely enough in the life even of a rather neurotic young man — so I asked the psychometrist whether she could give me some sign whereby I could identify the event when it came, something specific. She thought for a moment and said: 'Her blue eyes.'

I was completely unimpressed with this remark, as indeed with the whole session.

A few weeks later I left Coventry and spent a month on a farming camp before returning to London. On my third day at the camp a party of German girls arrived. My attention was immediately caught by one of the group, a most unusually attractive girl. She had the largest and most striking eyes I have ever seen, of a blue that was close to true violet. She was blonde, but had thick black eyelashes. The young Elizabeth Taylor was lucky never to have found herself in the same room as this girl.

* She did say that I would one day speak from public platforms to large audiences of people. I think, looking back, that the inclusion of the word 'public' was important. It made the prediction less of a vague generalization. She could, after all, have said 'you will address groups of people', an occurrence that could readily happen to a teacher, say, talking to parents. At the time I had not the slightest idea of entering public life in any sense, or that I would find myself one day addressing international conferences.

It genuinely did not occur to me until I had been keeping company with this girl for several days — and then abruptly it did — that this was the girl with the blue eyes. Of course, so far a sceptic could not unreasonably plead mere coincidence — perhaps aided by an unconscious impulse on my part. But the next day I received a letter from Peter, whom I had not contacted in any way since leaving Coventry. His letter began: 'How is the girl with blue eyes? A little bird tells me you've met her.'

(To round off the incident, the girl was actually from East Germany. In those days, before the Berlin Wall was built, if they were prepared to take the risk, it was possible for East Berliners to cross into West Berlin, change East marks illegally into West marks, and travel abroad. This the girl and her friends had done. After she returned home we corresponded, and the affair was serious enough for me the following spring to go to Berlin and cross not just into East Berlin, which was legal for a foreigner, but into East Germany — a silly risk to take. In the end, there proved too many such difficulties in our way.)

This, then, was my Coventry experience, though there remain a few important details to bring out later.

I returned to London fully determined to follow further this trail to wonderland I had discovered. I joined the Society for Psychical Research, the Marylebone Spiritualist Alliance (as it was then) and enrolled in a psychic development class at the College of Psychic Studies. In Coventry I had read Joan Grant's marvellous autobiography, *Time Out of Mind*, and I now prepared a full reading list of relevant books. I in fact read a good many, yet I found no other book that impressed me so deeply as *Time Out of Mind*.

Further Developments

The Society for Psychical Research was a disappointment. I had great schemes for experimental programmes, and though the Society did publish one of my papers, its initial enthusiasm for my ideas suddenly waned. I also felt, reading the Society's *Journal* and books published by its members, that these people had very little real grasp or understanding of psychic phenomena. My opinion has not changed since.

The Marylebone Spiritualist Alliance was a disappointment in a different way. People there seemed to display exactly the same uncritical attitude as the mediums and psychics in Coventry. It was the mixture precisely as before, sense and nonsense rolled into one unquestioned ball.

Progress came via the College of Psychic Studies. I had applied for and obtained a place in one of the development classes then operating there. During my initial interview with the class leader, he said in the course of conversation: 'You have recently lost someone. I get a strong impression of whiteness and the name Alma or Anna.'

As it happened, my father had died a few weeks before. He and I had not been close in any emotional sense (though I have since come to understand him better). His death had not really affected me. I do not believe I displayed any outward signs of grief and certainly I had no black tie or armband. Still, possibly my face might have given something away that could register, at any rate unconsciously, with a sensitive observer. There was, however, far more to this communication.

As a very young child I had been taken to see the body of my grandmother (my father's mother) whom I had seen living only twice before in my life. She lay in a white coffin, but to me the striking thing was that she herself was absolutely white, as if drained of all blood. I was paralysed by the whole situation, but was nevertheless forced by the adults present to kiss the corpse. My grandmother's name was Alma. My mother's name is Annie.

It is interesting – and perplexing in terms of trying to understand what is going on in psychic communication – to see how various elements are jumbled together in the paranormal 'message'. Often quite diverse elements are woven together to form a totally spurious story-line. This aspect of mediumistic communication strongly reminds us of dreams, and of what Freud called the dream-work.

This particular event, incidentally, was also picked up by another medium many years later. She said: 'I get a strong impression of whiteness; and this person was someone you were not close to, but in later life you thought you would like to have been close to.'

The actual development class comprised seven or so students, plus the class leader. This was not intended as a class for trance development. Trance and possession were in fact firmly discouraged. The medium who led us took the view, common among more intelligent psychics, that the so-called guides and spirits of the average medium are nothing of the sort. Only a few gifted mediums are considered to have 'real' guides and genuine contact with the true spirit world. No one, however, can tell you what are the essential differences between pseudo and true guides! I do not myself believe that there are any.

At any rate, this class was not concerned with possession and trance. Instead, during some three-quarters of an hour, we sat together attempting to obtain information about each other paranormally. The particular exercise which the leader recommended, though he did not mind if one devised a strategy of one's own, was as follows. We were to close our eyes and then mentally lift ourselves as it were above our own physical bodies, and with the mind's eye and in fantasy see what other members of the group did.

The method was surprisingly effective. For example, performing the exercise as instructed, I 'saw' the group leader go over to a glass-fronted cupboard and take out and examine some crystal goblets and decanters. When I later reported this to him, he said that he had a set of valuable crystal goblets, which he had decided to sell because he needed capital. He had already placed an advertisement in the press.

On another occasion I 'saw' one of the female members of the group constantly stand up, turn around, and adjust her cushion. (In actuality, none of our chairs had cushions.) When I reported this to her she told me that she suffered quite severe back pains — and during her favourite pastime of watching television she would continually have to re-arrange the cushions around her to ease the discomfort.

I was by now also pursuing a course of teacher training at the London Institute of Education, having decided, after some actual teaching, that I ought to be better prepared. At the Institute I met Dr John Read, the counsellor to the students there and at the London School of Economics. I discussed with him my experiences of the paranormal and my wish to discover what it all really signified. He himself felt there was something real involved in the paranormal, but that it was wrapped in a good deal that was not. Someone was needed who had experienced the phenomena at first hand, but who also had a firm critical sense. Dr Read's encouragement was actually invaluable to me, and to him goes some of the credit for the genesis of this book.

Despite all the activity I have been describing, it was nevertheless clear to me after six months that my involvement with the paranormal had now lost some of its impetus, and certainly a lot of its excitement. This was all dull stuff indeed compared with the atmospheric richness and the sense of wonder of my year in Coventry. Here in London there was no sense of a psychic community. Nature herself was far away. On all sides was a frenetic rush to get somewhere — while in that suburb of Coventry people had been happy just to 'be' somewhere.

Yet what was I to do? There could be no going back to the simplistic level of my early mentors. On the other hand, here in London, intelligent people, in particular my fellow teachers and students, had no interest in the paranormal except as an occasional game. From another point of view I now realized how altogether ill-informed I was about the normal mechanisms of the human personality. I had no normal background against which to measure or compare the paranormal. How could I square the mental mechanisms involved in parapsychology with normal psychology, unless I first understood normal psychology?

The passing of another six months saw me installed as Head of Department in a London grammar school. In addition I had now registered for a degree in Psychology at Birkbeck College. And I had also begun a personal psychoanalysis.

In the last case Dr Read again proved invaluable. I had discussed the matter of having analysis with him and he had asked me what kind of psychoanalysis I wanted, so that he could make the necessary arrangements. Without an instant's hesitation I replied 'Jungian'.

This answer was in itself remarkable. Although I had by

now made the acquaintance of the Freudian school of psychoanalysis (via Karen Horney and the neo-Freudians) and was an enthusiastic admirer of Freud's ideas, Carl Jung was nothing more to me than a name. Yet the issue was not in doubt for a moment. It is possible that from some over-heard chance remark I had unconsciously grasped the idea that Jung was a champion of the paranormal, while Freud detested it ('the black tide of mud of occultism' as he called it). Yet, I think not.

The years that followed at first and in one sense took me ever farther away from the direct experience of the para-normal. But the movement was what geometrists call a parabola — a curved path which surely and inevitably led me back to my departure point. Or rather, as with a spiral — a circular movement which also rises — I found myself returned at a higher level and with a greatly extended overview. In the intervening years I gave up my post at the grammar school and began teaching maladjusted children. Ultimately I became Senior Research Psychologist at the National Children's Bureau. I was also married and divorced. So there were events enough to take up my days.

Looking always for further knowledge about the human condition, I was at the same time prospecting for a frame-work which could accommodate all the information that was accumulating. I thought perhaps the problem was that nobody had yet used a broad enough canvas. They had tend-ed always to treat religion as religion, politics as politics, science as science — and of course largely to ignore the paranormal altogether. Might it be possible, on a giant canvas, to create a set of terms, a theoretical framework, in which all aspects of human existence could be considered simultaneously?

Not only did I feel such an attempt to be desirable — I felt it to be absolutely essential. For I was quite clear, first, that such apparently divergent individuals as Freud, Marx, Christ, Nietzsche, Jung, Skinner, Pavlov, Russell, Darwin (and many others) had all been talking about one and the same human being — you and me. Second, that these individuals, far from being variously uninformed or misguided, were all extremely gifted and insightful men. Instead, then, of saying that all, or all but one, of these thinkers were wrong, I took the opposite view and said that all must be right. Every one of these seemingly differing views must be incorporated in any would-be universal statement of man.

So gradually a schema began to emerge. I began, principally, to discern an enduring and persistent duality in all of man's activities, in everything he is and does. This central duality or dualism seemed to offer the hope of a framework both of adequate dimensions and of adequate explanatory powers. My list of dualities always grew. In time I began to consider that all the items on the left-hand side of the short list below had that in common which could be used to explain all of them — and that those on the right (the polar opposites of those on the left) had, similarly, that in common which could define their central nature.

spiritualism	psychic research
psychoanalysis	academic psychology
unconscious	consciousness
religion	science
psychic phenomena	materialism
dreaming	waking
magic	logic
child	adult
the left hand	the right hand
female	male
Neanderthal man	modern man

Between 1969 and 1976 I set down an outline of my general theory of the human personality in a trilogy of books.[34-6] With that task finished, I knew I would then be free to write about the paranormal directly and in detail — although of course the paranormal had also formed part of the earlier work. The result of my freedom is the present book.

TWO
Footprints in the Sand

In Defoe's novel *Robinson Crusoe*, the tale of a man marooned on a desert island, Crusoe is one day walking along the beach, when he comes upon the imprint of a naked human foot.

At this moment Crusoe does not require the services of a statistician. He does not need a second opinion. He knows, without any argument, that there is now another person on the island.

There are many, many events in the annals of psychic phenomena which are instances of such footprints in the sand. They do not require debate. They are far beyond the reach of any coincidence — just how far I shall try to say in later sections. To deny the validity of such instances, and the relentless implications that follow from them, is to take up a position actually *far more unreasonable* than the 'unreasonable' belief in psychic phenomena.

Let us at once look at some examples. These are the tiniest sample of many hundreds of such cases. Those that I have selected often involve animals, for reasons I will explain in the next chapter.

In the late 1930s, Osbert Wyndham Hewitt was living in Headington, near Oxford. He owned a cat named Mitzi, of whom he was extremely fond. At the time of the incident which follows Hewitt was away from home, staying with friends in London. He and they spent the evening after dinner hotly debating the rights and wrongs of the Spanish Civil War. All went to bed late. Once asleep, Hewitt began to dream. In his dream Mitzi came into the room dressed as a volunteer for the Spanish war and very badly hurt. She cried and sobbed and begged him to kill her, because the pain she was suffering was more than she could bear. As is the way with dreams, Hewitt was not surprised that Mitzi could speak and did his best to comfort her, telling her he would take her to hospital. His assurances had no effect, however, and Mitzi went on screaming and sobbing. Hewitt awoke very distressed at 4 a.m.

Next morning at breakfast he told his hostess of his dream. He had just finished his account, when the phone rang. The hostess answered it. On the line was the housekeeper in Headington. She wanted to report that Mitzi had been badly hurt. Mitzi had come into the house via Hewitt's bedroom window around 4 a.m., waking the household with her howling. She had been found crouched on his pillow with one ear torn nearly off. Hewitt at once returned home, taking a vet with him, and in due course Mitzi recovered fully from her wound.[48]

Among all the significant detail of this event we should not overlook the circumstance that Mitzi came to her master's bed, suggesting that she was actually attempting to find him — so that there is an intention. Then from the point of view of dream analysis we note also that the dream 'logically' makes Mitzi into a soldier. She had, of course, been fighting.

A similar story concerns a Mr Grindell-Matthews, an inventor of some reputation.

In the autumn of 1924 Matthews was given a six-month-old kitten. Owner and pet rapidly became devoted to each other. Then one evening the cat fell from the roof of Matthews's house in Hanover Square in London. When examined she had lost one tooth and appeared to have a broken back. A vet, after consultation, advised putting her to sleep as the only possible course of action. However, the cat clung so affectionately to her master — and moreover was in no apparent pain — that he decided to have her X-rayed. A fracture of the spine was confirmed. The cat could live, but would probably not walk again. Matthews made his decision — now undertaking, among other things, to feed the animal every two hours with a drip-feeder for several weeks. In due time the cat did recover and resumed its engaging ways, occasionally walking on four legs, but more usually dragging her hindquarters.

About a year after the cat's injury, Matthews had to go to New York on business. The cat was left in the care of the housekeeper.

One early morning three weeks later, in New York, Matthews awakened from a nightmare, sweating profusely. In his dream he had seen his cat struggling in the hands of a man wearing white clothes. The man had had a goatee beard. Though now fully awake, it seemed to Matthews that his room reeked of chloroform. This smell haunted him for the next ten days, though no one else was able to detect it.

Later during that morning of the nightmare Matthews cabled to London for news of the cat. He received no reply. Full of unease, and cutting short his trip, he set off to London ten days later.

On his arrival home the housekeeper — who had been afraid to reply to his telegram — told him that she had had the cat put down. It had refused to touch food after his departure and was starving to death. The sight of the paralysed cat dying of starvation had been too much for her. She had called the vet and had the animal put to sleep. The vet had not been previously known to Matthews. He had a goatee beard. The time of the cat's actual death coincided with the time of Matthews's nightmare.[30]

The details of this story again speak more than adequately for themselves. Among the points I shall emphasize later is the enormous distance involved — several thousand miles — and the hallucination of the smell of chloroform.

The last of this trio of examples concerns the novelist Rider Haggard.

On the night of July 9th, 1904, Haggard had a long, vivid nightmare. During it he experienced what he describes as a sense of awful oppression and a desperate, terrified struggle for life. He was aroused from this nightmare by his wife — but the dream then continued briefly.

Haggard, as he woke, now thought/dreamt that his black retriever, Bob, was lying on its side among brushwood by water. The writer tells us: 'My own personality in some mysterious way seemed to me to be arising from the body of the dog . . . In my vision the dog was trying to speak to me in words and, failing, transmitted to my mind in an undefined fashion the knowledge that it was dying.' Once Haggard had awakened properly, his wife asked him why he had been making those weird and horrible noises. In her own later testimony Mrs Haggard described these moans as not dissimilar to the moans of an animal.

These events took place around 2 a.m.

Next morning the tale was told to the rest of the family at breakfast. A complete joke was made of it, with the usual ragging about what not to eat late at night, and so on. No attempt at all was made to look for the dog, because all knew perfectly well that he was in the yard with the other animals. That evening, however, the youngest daughter of the family, whose special job it was to feed Bob, reported that she could find no trace of him anywhere.

The next day a fruitless search of the neighbourhood was made and continued on subsequent days. Not until the following Thursday did Haggard and his manservant, Charles Bedingfield, discover the dead body of Bob in the Waveney river, floating against a weir and very severely mutilated. Their first thought was that the dog had been deliberately destroyed by a person or persons unknown. On their way home, however, they were hailed by two plate-layers employed by the railway. These said that they had found a torn dog's collar (which proved to be Bob's) together with some flesh and black hair on a railway line on a bridge over the river, some distance away. They further said they had observed the dog's body floating among the rushes below the bridge on the previous Monday.

The vet who subsequently inspected the body of the dog was of the opinion that its injuries (forepaws cut off and the skull smashed) could have been caused by the impact of a train, which could also have had the effect of flinging the body clear of the bridge and into the water. The vet was, however, of the opinion that the dog must have died almost instantly. A knowledge of the infrequent trains, the time of the plate-layers' discovery of the traces on the line and so forth at first allowed the firm conclusion to be drawn that the dog had been struck and killed on the Saturday night, around 11 p.m. Subsequently, news that the train in question had been running late, due to defective carriage lights, moved the time of death on by an undetermined amount.[45]

I think once again we can let this story speak for itself. A point of special interest, though, is the continuance of Haggard's dream after waking — only a brief hallucination, unlike Matthews's enduring one of the chloroform. But this kind of evidence will enable us to connect these psychic dreams both with traditional mediumship and many other trance states.

We ought to note, in these stories, the very high reputation of the individuals concerned. These are highly respected and respectable professional people. They have no partisan connection with the field of psychic phenomena. In every instance the testimony of several independent and reliable witnesses is involved. The Haggard incident was actually printed in full in *The Times* and was the subject of exhaustive public debate.

The aspect of 'public debate' is well worth emphasizing. Not all psychic events happen behind closed doors in dark rooms. They can occur in the full glare of the public eye — as the following account (by Immanuel Kant) shows even more clearly.

In the year 1759, towards the end of September, on Saturday at 4 p.m., Swedenborg arrived at Gothenburg from England, when Mr William Castel invited him to his house, together with a party of fifteen persons. About six o'clock Swedenborg went out, and returned to the company quite pale and alarmed. He said that a dangerous fire had just broken out in Stockholm, at the Södermalm, and that it was spreading very fast. He was restless, and went out often. He said that the house of one of his friends, whom he named, was already in ashes, and that his own was in danger. At eight o'clock, after he had been out again, he joyfully exclaimed: 'Thank God! The fire is extinguished; the third door from my house.' This news occasioned great commotion throughout the whole city, but particularly among the company in which he was. It was announced to the governor the same evening. On Sunday morning Swedenborg was summoned to the governor who questioned him concerning the disaster. Swedenborg described the fire precisely, how it had begun and in what manner it had ceased, and how long it had continued. On the same day the news spread through the city, and as the governor thought it worthy of attention the consternation was considerably increased; because many were in trouble on account of their friends and property, which might have been involved in the disaster. On Monday evening a messenger arrived at Gothenburg, who was despatched by the Board of Trade during the time of the fire. In the letters brought by him, the fire was described precisely in the manner stated by Swedenborg. On Tuesday morning the royal courier arrived at the governor's with the melancholy intelligence of the fire, at the loss which it had occasioned, and of the houses it had damaged and ruined, not in the least differing from that which Swedenborg had given at the very time when it happened; for the fire was extinguished at eight o'clock.[57]

Do we *really* appreciate what happened here? On a day in 1759 (long before telephones or any other method of communication over distance) a public figure of considerable note and reputation (Swedenborg was special assessor to the Royal College of Mines), travelling from Britain, arrives at 4 p.m. in Gothenburg, Sweden. At 6 p.m. he announces that a large fire has broken out in Stockholm. Stockholm is 250 miles away on the *other* side of Sweden. At 8 p.m. Swedenborg announces that the fire is over and has halted three doors away from his own house, although the house of a friend has been completely destroyed. The next day, Sunday, the news of Swedenborg's vision spreads through the whole town. It is only on *Monday* evening that the first messenger arrives from Stockholm, bringing confirmation of all Swedenborg's claims.

This story came to us from Immanuel Kant, a contemporary of Swedenborg's and, of course, one of the world's outstanding philosophers.

The accounts in this chapter are not given with a view to talking anyone into acceptance of the paranormal — although certainly with a view to carrying him or her towards it. I believe that *acceptance* of the paranormal can only come through one's own personal experience of it. The more modest aim in quoting these stories is to show *how absolutely unreasonable is the position of those who are absolutely sure that the paranormal does not exist.* When we meet people who still maintain that a *first case* has not been made out for the existence of the paranormal, we necessarily have to take the inquiry into the psychological state in which these individuals find themselves.*

We are not tied to anecdotes and reports from the past. We have any number arising at the present time.

Dr Fernand Méry is a vet of more than thirty years' standing, living in Paris. He has published a book relating many incidents from his working life, entitled *Our Animal Friends*.

I must emphasize that Méry's book contains only one instance of a paranormal event. For, once again, Dr Méry is no occultist. He is one of the large majority of individuals who give little thought to the paranormal, beyond perhaps that of idle curiosity, until the possible moment when it so dramatically touches their lives.

A friend of Méry's, prior to going abroad, had given Méry his cat, Timmy, a pet the friend had had since it was a kitten. A year passed, during which Méry's friend made no contact at all either by letter or telephone. Then a letter came. In it the friend apologized for not having written for so long a time. He said that he was only writing now on account of a dream he had had the three nights previously, on October 10th and the two nights thereafter. In the

---

* In passing I will just mention here Friedrich Schiller's remark in a similar context, where he said that he could no more call a man free who lived under the compulsion of objective thought than a man who lived under the compulsion of an emotion. Schiller's actual words were: 'I call a man tense when he is under the compulsion of thought, no less than when he is under the compulsion of feeling. Exclusive domination by either of his two basic drives is for him a state of constraint and violence, and freedom lies only in the cooperation of both his natures.'[92]

dream he had seen Timmy with bandages all round his head. The cat kept climbing up at his window to get in, but always fell back.

On the night of October 10th, and the two subsequent nights, Timmy was dying of meningitis, with his head wrapped in bandages.

This story never fails to move me, but it also never fails to fill me with anger — anger towards my 'half-witted' scientific colleagues and their empty prattle of statistics and coincidence.

From the point of view of evidence it is of course a marvellous story, beautifully concise, with no loose ends and a wealth of significant agreement. But once again we see also the influence of the dream-work. Dreams not only usually, but habitually, transmit their information by the use of symbols, not by words. The state of mind which Timmy was transmitting was something like: 'I need my master, but I cannot reach him'; or 'but he does not help me'. Therefore the window is shut, the master does not open it, and the cat always falls back from his attempts to get in.

The symbolism is perhaps clearest from the master's point of view — and it is of course his dream. The window is shut because he has 'shut out' Timmy from his life (and, incidentally, his friend Méry also). There is a great deal of guilt in this dream. Quite aside from the paranormal element, it is a perfectly reasonable dream for someone to have who knows he has behaved badly. The otherwise normal functioning of the dream and its wholly acceptable symbolism in terms of standard dream analysis should, I think, help some otherwise sceptics to accept this dream in its paranormal entirety.

Can we accept an animal as the 'sender' of the message — or was the sender Méry himself? Can animals form (not in words, of course) concepts as sophisticated as 'I need my master, but he does not come', or 'I wish a particular person were here', or whatever?

The answer is yes, but it is by no means the foregone conclusion that most animal lovers imagine it is. Virtually all examples of so-called animal intelligence (such as the sheep-herding activity of the sheep dog, for instance) really involve pre-programmed, instinctive actions that are *entirely* mindless.

These actions exist as 'printed circuits' in the animal's brain, and are triggered instinctively and compulsively by the presence of certain stimuli. This is not intelligence. However, I have myself for some time been collecting examples of the ability of the rare, gifted individual animal to form concepts, analyse situations and devise solutions to self-posed problems. These are given in Appendix II (pp. 289–94).

What of the animal as *receiver*?

Writing in the correspondence columns of the *New Scientist* (which, to its credit, printed the letter) Dr W. J. Tarver, chairman of the Veterinarians' Union, made this comment:

> Not many people have experienced, as I have, the noise of kennelled dogs who have been settled for a week or two, become wildly excited around the exact time when their owners commence the journey back from holiday ... It does not seem to matter how far away the owners have been, the message still arrives.[99]

We have also a great many accounts of animals reacting violently to the actual distant *death* of their owners. Here is one that touches such accounts and that of Dr Tarver.

A dog was quartered with a local vet while its owners were away on their holiday. One morning at 10 a.m. this dog began howling and barking in an alarming fashion. He kept this behaviour up for an hour or so. Then abruptly he stopped. He did not display such behaviour on any other occasion during his stay. The vet naturally examined the animal carefully at the time, but could find nothing wrong with him. When the family returned from holiday the vet reported the incident. The couple reacted with astonishment. At 10 a.m. on the morning in question they had been caught in a flash flood, and had climbed on top of their car as a last resort. They were rescued at 11 a.m.[68]

So common are accounts of paranormal communication between people and animals in danger (or of course simply between human beings) that any general theory of the paranormal must have a sub-section concerning what I call this 'love and mayday' element. ('Mayday', the international distress signal used by shipping, comes from the French *m'aider*, meaning 'help me'.) At the moment of death, and in times of great danger, the chances of the occurrence of a paranormal event are greatly increased. The individuals between whom paranormal communication then occurs almost invariably have close emotional ties — the 'love' aspect of my equation.

The emotions generally are heavily involved in the paranormal, as are dreams. Such observation will lead also to the question, what parts of the nervous system must therefore be involved?

THREE
The Psychic Universe –
Minor Key

The psychic experiences we have looked at so far have carried an obvious sense of significance. We have been, as it were, in the deep end. But there is also a shallower end to the psychic pool and the shallow end is actually far more extensive. As a fairly firm rule, psychic experiences are rarely of great or even of any significance in terms of their content. In content the large majority are trivial. There is not the slightest point in denying that fact, as many wish to do. Actually the question why triviality of communication should be the rule (when there is so much of importance we would dearly like to know) is a very intriguing one.

While still acknowledging the general triviality of much psychic communication and intercommunication, we can nevertheless legitimately suspect in at least some instances a hidden subjective significance. As Freud showed in the case of dreams, apparently trifling or incidental elements are often the most significant. When we follow the associative trail from some 'unimportant' dream item, it often leads us quite quickly to the heart of the real problem or significance. Such might be the case also with psychic experiences. In general psychiatry, also, it is frequently the trivial or chance remark or behaviour which reveals the true position. Charles Berg, the psychiatrist, reports the following incident. A young man had been referred to him by a doctor, and for an hour Berg and the young man talked about every subject under the sun, without the psychiatrist noticing anything wrong. Then, right at the end of the interview, when Berg had decided there must have been an administrative mistake, the young man remarked that the bus conductress had felt his arm as he got off the bus. 'Why did she do that?' asked Berg. 'To see if I had been masturbating.'

This single, casually delivered remark demonstrated that the young man was in fact undergoing a severe psychotic breakdown.[4]

So we have two points. One, that the objectively trivial may nevertheless be subjectively important. Two, that a trillion rational events or statements do not wipe out the significance of one that is not. And in the last context we touch on the most important aspect of all.

In one of the programmes in a British television series, 'Leap in the Dark',* a report was made on a man — Lord Kilbracken in fact — who for a time as a student dreamt the winners of horse races. Fortunately in some cases he confided his foreknowledge to independent witnesses. The day after the programme a reviewer in one of the national newspapers asked what did it matter if someone did dream the winners of horse races? Surely the programme should have been concerned with something important.

Here we see the obtuseness of the vast majority of the allegedly intelligent and thinking population in respect of the paranormal. The reviewer, like so many others, could not grasp that *what* one foresees is the least important aspect. It is the fact that a person can paranormally foresee *any* future event of any kind whatsoever that is of supreme and final importance. A person dreams that a man with a red tie sneezes five times in a restaurant. The next day that essentially meaningless event actually occurs. This one tiny pebble then suffices, alone and all by itself, to slay the mighty Goliath of Einsteinian—Newtonian physics. All the armour and edifice of science is of no avail against it. With this one stroke the materialistic universe, as a *total* explanation of events, lies in ruins.

The point here cannot be made too strongly. It is a completely different one from the otherwise valid point that the actual content or information of the paranormal event often has little significance at all in intellectual and objective terms.

* Compèred by Colin Wilson.

These lines of reasoning, then, form part of the backdrop to the subject matter of this chapter. It deals, as I said earlier, with the 'shallower' end of psychic experience: the paranormal as it affects the day-to-day lives of psychic individuals. It could perhaps be called 'an everyday story of psychic folk'.

In the late summer of 1974 I walked one morning down to St John's Wood in northwest London from Swiss Cottage, to collect a small sum of money due to me. I walked partly to save the 5p fare, because I was broke, a common enough experience even for the 'successful' writer. I duly got my sum of money and the main thought in my head was to get speedily back to Swiss Cottage to buy myself a celebration breakfast. However, at the back of my mind I had the slight feeling of tension that I have learned to attend to.

From where I was standing there was a direct, short walk of less than a hundred yards to St John's Wood Underground station. Yielding, however, to the impulse that was directing me away from the station, I set out on a much longer, circular walk via side streets that actually at first led away from the Underground. It took me some ten minutes to reach the station by this route. I have to emphasize that I did not 'feel like a walk' – I had had my morning's walk.

When I reached the top of the station escalator a train was just pulling out. Had I gone direct to the station I would have been on that train. I was mildly irritated, knowing that I might have to wait some time for the next one. When I boarded the next train, after a wait of ten or fifteen minutes, I found myself facing an acquaintance I had not seen for well over a year, a freelance picture researcher, Susan Pincus. We had a 'how's business' conversation about this and that.

A few days later Susan rang me to ask if I was interested in doing some proof-reading for a few days. She was too busy to handle it herself – and it was very urgent, starting that same afternoon – and probably well paid. The 'few days' work turned into two months' work and it *was* very well paid. It was proof-reading a national leisure guide. This work was a life-saver, the first real money I had earned for months.

The sequence of events did not stop there. Towards the

Christmas of the same year a publisher was looking for an author to write a book on animals and ESP. He asked Susan if she knew of anyone. She put him in touch with me. As a result I was in fact commissioned to write the book. For two months I was able to devote myself full-time to paid research, during which work some of my ideas on the paranormal were further clarified. Then, alas, like so many other people, the publisher ran into increasing financial difficulties.

None the less, from my point of view the two months had been a complete bonus. Part of this present book is indebted to the thinking and research of that period.

A further incident concerns Roy Grant, a business and sports journalist whom I have known for many years. He does not consider himself in the least psychic, though he has a fairly strong interest in the subject, mainly perhaps on account of his sister. She occasionally has psychic premonitions, many of which have the stamp of apparent authenticity.

Roy's only claim to a psychic experience of his own was having a dream in which he saw the interior of the Edinburgh Royal High School, which he has never visited, although himself from Glasgow. A week or so later he was watching a television programme when a shot of the interior of the school was shown — it is to become the Scottish Assembly. He now recognized many details from his dream. Certainly Roy himself would be the first to admit that he might at some time have seen pictures of the interior of the High School. But he does not remember ever having seen any.

One evening Roy and I went to see Claude Lelouche's film *La Bonne Année*. That day and the previous day I had been working on an article about ESP, and I needed a good example of the general inconsequentiality of many psychic experiences. I could not precisely recall an example of what I needed — that is, not in the kind of detail that is required if one is going to write about it — and so was resigned to making a trip to one of the paranormal library collections to refresh my memory.

Towards the end of the Lelouche film, which is set in a French city and is as French as any film could be, there is an unexpected shot of a man reading the *Guardian* newspaper. For a British audience this was especially amusing, but in any case a brilliant film director was reminding us suddenly that other frames of reference still coexist within (or without) any frame of reference we happen to be involved in at a particular moment.

After the film, Roy embarrassedly 'confessed' to me, in a more than usually gruff version of his generally gruff manner, that at the beginning of the film the absurd idea had entered his head that before the end of the film someone in it would be reading the *Guardian*. Here was the example I had been in need of! I had been consciously in pursuit of such an example (though Roy did not know that) and I do happen to be a reasonably-endowed psychic. Probably, therefore, I triggered the experience.

But the incident is consequential also from a quite different angle. As it happens, Roy is a journalist and the occurrence involved a newspaper. The associational point raised here will be raised again later on in a wider context. The point is that very often a paranormal event also has some reasonable, that is, *associational* connection with the person who experiences it. What we see in this and many other examples are actually the entirely acceptable functions of associative psychology at work. Such normal aspects of the paranormal situation cast, so to speak, a ray of validity on the occurrence as a whole. In a similar way, we saw in Chapter 2, especially in the Méry incident, the normal functions of standard dream-work operating alongside the paranormal element of a dream. The paranormal is found embedded in the normal, in the way the miraculous pearl is found in the commonplace oyster.

The next incident comes as near to an experiment as one can get in respect of psychic phenomena, and as near as I would in any case let myself get to one. It also illustrates what is possible in these areas when genuinely psychic individuals are involved.

One afternoon I was at the house of Simmona de Serdici in London. I had not known beforehand, but now she told me that she was expecting a visitor, a male visitor, whom she thought I would be interested to meet. Then, on impulse, and in a teasing way, she asked me if I could tell her what he looked like.

I closed my eyes and described the person I saw. Short, thick-set, with straight fair hair. 'What colour eyes does he have?' asked Simmona. I replied that I could not say, because he had his eyes shut. However, as we spoke, I was becoming more and more impressed with the man's muscularity. I said as much to Simmona, namely that I thought he was quite a powerful person. I could see his muscles standing out under the black fisherman's polo-necked sweater he was wearing.

Then, as I still watched, the muscles began to bulge rather grotesquely and oddly, and suddenly I now saw before me a figure very like the Michelin man in the Michelin tyre advertisements. This man was wearing just such a pneumatic outfit. However, I did not say this to Simmona, because I thought my 'vision' was now breaking up and drifting off on some associational track of its own. How wrong I was.

The visitor who was coming was Jan Merta, the well-known psychic (though I must add that at that time the name meant nothing to me). Those who know Jan will appreciate the accuracy of my description of him. Probably the first thing that strikes one is his powerful bright blue eyes — and it is interesting that in my picture of him the eyes were closed, a kind of 'negative' view of this aspect. In case I sound as if I am trying to make my vices into virtues, or my misses into hits, let me finish the story. I did not know, and could in no way have guessed given a hundred normal tries, that Jan was currently working as a diver for a North Sea oil company. Hence the 'fisherman's sweater' and then the more explicit 'Michelin man' — which of course was Jan in a diving suit.

The examples I have given so far have all had at least some kind of positive aspect or direction. Now an instance of a negative or *counter-productive* influence.

Some years ago I had a protracted involvement with a girl (whom I shall call Miriam) which lasted for two or three years. Apart from an initially happy few months, from my point of view the affair had gone from bad to worse, until finally we broke up completely. During the affair, and because of it, I made a number of important decisions which materially affected the course of my life. So it was no trivial business. At the time of the incident described below

I had heard little about Miriam since, except that she was now married.

For the purpose of this story it is important also to know that I was born and raised in London. Apart from one or two spells abroad and the period in Coventry I have never lived anywhere else. I know the inner stations of the London Underground railway as well as I know my own front garden. I could probably find my way around them blindfold.

On a particular late afternoon about a year and a half ago, I was travelling by Underground train from Swiss Cottage to Knightsbridge. I was reading a book. I often do read in the train, but even without paying attention have little difficulty sensing where we are — any regular traveller on any fixed route does the same. However, I looked up from my reading and saw that we were at Piccadilly Circus, where I had to change trains. I got out. Now we begin to have a measure of the experience that was starting, for I had walked some way down the platform, and the train I had been on was moving out, before I realized that this was not Piccadilly Circus, but Oxford Circus.

A trifle nettled at my error, I decided to turn the mistake to some possible advantage. Instead of waiting for the next train to take me to Piccadilly Circus (there to change to the Piccadilly Line) I would go down to the Victoria Line and go on to Green Park instead. About four minutes later, however, I emerged on to the eastbound *Central* Line platform. I was too surprised to be irritated. Marvelling at my ineptitude, I set off once more to the Victoria Line. Several minutes later I emerged on to the other platform of the Central Line. Such a thing, of course, could not happen to me. I set out yet again, as calmly as my growing annoyance would allow. Three minutes of walking now deposited me back on the Bakerloo Line platform where I had originally left the train by mistake.

I was now feeling extremely disoriented. But more than that I realized that I was in the grip of a psychic episode. I was not scared — I am never disturbed by the paranormal — but I was now warily expectant. A trifle grimly, therefore, I headed once more for the Victoria Line, pig-headedly determined not to be thwarted in my intentions.

I was quite numbed to emerge at the *other* end (which made a change) of the eastbound Central Line platform. I now stood for a while leaning against the wall, wondering what I should do next. Only then did it occur to me that I might not be being led *to* somewhere or something but *from* something. Vague ideas of a train crash went through my mind. Heartened by this positive view of events, I set off down the platform – and ran straight into Miriam.

We stood looking at each other more or less speechless. She then asked how I was. In desperation for something to say I asked if she had any children yet. This comment touched some raw area – because she flared out at me that there was plenty of time for having children – why was I asking *that*? We stared at each other for a moment longer, and then each walked on.

I had no further difficulty finding the Victoria Line.

It is probably impossible to convey the feeling of this incident, in words, on paper. Though I rate it as one of my most vivid and impressive psychic adventures, nothing whatever came of the incident. It was without consequence.

The only other time I ever mistook or, more probably, hallucinated aspects of a station in a lifetime of travelling by Underground was also fairly certainly a psychic incident. This time I alighted at St John's Wood, one stop before my own home station of Swiss Cottage. I was not reading a book or even a newspaper. Near the top of the escalator an elderly man in front of me lost his balance and fell back. I was two steps below him and easily able to catch him as he fell. There were only one or two of us on the escalator and the next person was several steps lower down. Had I not been where I was, the man would necessarily have taken a nasty fall. Only when the incident was over did I then realize that I was at the wrong station.

If the Miriam incident is, to me, one of my most striking psychic experiences, the most striking of all, ranking first equal with the Neanderthal vision in Coventry, concerns Marcel Vogel. Marcel Vogel is Senior Chemist at I.B.M. in California, a powerful psychic and a devout Catholic. He is the only person so far who appears able to duplicate Cleve

Backster's results with plants, and has taken this work considerably further. Vogel, however, believes that the plant registers the states and moods of the individual relating to it, rather than possessing these in any true sense itself, as Backster believes.

I first saw Marcel Vogel in 1974 at the first series of May Lectures in London, where he was one of the speakers. I had been hired by a publisher to attend the series to consider if these were worth publishing in book form. Simultaneously I was hired by the organizers of the series to edit the rough lectures into some kind of shape for possible book publication. Neither of these two principals objected to my working for the other.

In the course of his lecture, Vogel gave us an astonishing demonstration of his psychic powers. My comments on this demonstration were eventually included in the published form of the lectures, and I reproduce them here as they appeared in that book.[11]

Some ten minutes after the start of his lecture, Marcel Vogel announced that he was going to give us, the audience, proof of the tangible reality of thought by projecting a thought image into our minds. My instant reaction was: 'No, don't — don't attempt that.' For although no stranger to telepathy, I had never yet met anyone who could produce results to order. I felt Vogel was putting his head on the block quite unnecessarily. He then asked us to close our eyes. More in sorrow than in anger — that is to say, very half-heartedly — I did so. Vogel then announced that he was beginning the transmission of the image. In my mind's eye (and apparently somewhere around the middle of my forehead) I 'saw' at that point a triangle, on which seemed to be superimposed a rather less clear circle. I opted for the triangle. Vogel then said he was giving the image a colour. At first it seemed to me that the triangle was blue — then it became red — and I opted definitely for red. Vogel said we should now open our eyes. He asked how many of us had had an image. Some fifty people or so raised their hands. I must confess that I did not

bother to raise mine. Vogel pointed to one of the
volunteers — 'You, sir, what did you get?' His answer —
a triangle. At this point I almost literally fell off my
seat. Further shock was however already on its way.
Vogel told us that he had projected the image of a triangle enclosed in a circle. First he had coloured it
yellow, but then after a moment had switched the
colour to red. I spent the rest of that lecture in what
I can only describe as a state of joy. At the close the
audience clapped enthusiastically. But why did they
only clap? We should have stamped and shouted and
broken the chairs in honour of this world-beater.

Marcel Vogel is clearly out of the ordinary, even for a
psychic. He appears to have made the remarkable step of
acquiring a degree of control over his gifts. I have not had
the opportunity to speak to Vogel, so I do not know whether
he reserves his demonstrations for occasions when he is
among sympathizers (as he was at the May Lectures) and
other psychics, or whether he attempts them also before
audiences of sceptics. (I do not say that he should. There is,
as we know, a prevalent type of sceptic who claims victory
when a psychic fails, or, if he or she succeeds, at once sets
about finding out how the 'trick' was done. It is better in
my opinion simply to avoid confrontation with such
individuals.)
    From the possibly sublime to the more mundane. I have
recently discovered a name for an ability I have always
possessed — the ability to generate unearned income when
life becomes really desperate. Richard Kirby tells me this is
known as 'ready-money karma'. Because the discussion of
this phenomenon is protracted and takes us into areas a little
away from the main drift of the book, I have placed it
separately in Appendix I (pp. 279—88).
    While the paranormal undoubtedly exercises a pervasive
and continual influence in the life of the psychic individual,
it is *continual*, but not *continuous*. That is, it comes and
departs as it deems fit. In the words of the sage, the paranormal is a spirit that bloweth where it listeth. One rarely
knows where it will strike next or in what context.

A week or two ago from the time of writing the following incident occurred. I knew that Colin Wilson was working on a new book called *Mysteries*, a sequel to his previous book, *The Occult*. One afternoon it came into my head to wonder if he was going to include in it discussion of Robert Temple's *The Sirius Mystery*. It suddenly seemed urgent to me that he should. I also simultaneously realized how well Colin and Robert would get along together — and that they ought to meet. So I sat down immediately and wrote to Colin, urging on him *The Sirius Mystery* and enclosing Robert's address. That same afternoon (it is impossible to say whether it was the same moment) Colin, in far-off Cornwall, was sitting down writing to Robert, care of his publisher.

Robert Temple is himself a generator of paranormal events. He has dreams in which he is specifically instructed or invited to take precise courses of action, often ones which he has been considering consciously. In the early part of 1975 he had a dream in which a voice told him to go and ask to review books for *Time Out*, the London leisure magazine. Robert himself lives in Warwickshire. Accordingly he went without preamble to *Time Out* (this was long before the publication of *The Sirius Mystery*, incidentally) and offered himself as a reviewer.

Matt Hoffman received the request affably, went over to a large cupboard, unlocked it, and asked Robert to select any books from it he would like to review. After a while Robert came up with two books, both of them mine (*Total Man* and *Personality and Evolution*). Apparently Hoffman said that these were the two he had hoped Robert would pick.

Occasionally the psychic individual finds himself playing the role of the Ancient Mariner. That is, he feels impelled to give a particular individual what the Spiritualists call a 'message'. About six weeks ago I found myself giving the following 'message' to a young lady I had just met, who was in the company of a male friend of mine. I said that she stood at a crisis point in her life, and that the choice for her was between being extremely happy or extremely unhappy. I said that she was at the end of a stage, which had already gone on long enough, and that she should be planning the next stage as a matter of some urgency. She said she could understand what I meant, and pressed me for details how she could make the choice. But I was unable to help her on this.

I later learned that the girl in question, Mary, was twenty-seven years of age — I had thought her to be twenty-three or -four — and that she was in the habit of going around with her younger sister of twenty-two and her set. Mary was (and is) able to get away with this behaviour. Yet — as she subsequently admitted to me — she realizes that she ought to be thinking, for example, about a more settled career. She is now a little worried, too, that none of her relationships has so far resulted in marriage. She was about to go off on holiday, by herself, and though she was looking forward to the break (to 'getting away', as she put it — with, I think, the appropriate double meaning of somehow cheating) she could not see much that was positive ahead of her after that. She thought perhaps she ought to live abroad again — and so on.

The kind of profile presented by this young woman is a common enough one, as far as the psychological counsellor is concerned. The point is that I had only just met this girl, knew nothing about her, and assumed her to be significantly younger than she actually was. 'Significantly', because I think it is fair to say that there is a good deal of difference for a single girl between the early twenties and the late twenties. My initial impression was of a genuinely happy-go-lucky girl, not in any special difficulty. So my impulse was really purely psychic.

From the objective standpoint then, paranormal occurrences, even for the psychic individual, are rather rare, on the whole trivial and usually inconsequential. This statement is not a devaluation or criticism of the paranormal. It is simply a description of its nature, from an objective point of view. This just happens to be how manifestations of the paranormal are. As Freud remarked to a critic in another not dissimilar context: 'As to the indistinctness of dreams, that is a characteristic like any other. We cannot dictate to things their characteristics.'[28]

The statement on rarity, and triviality for that matter, applies even to the output of the full-time, practising medium.

Most of the content produced during a mediumistic sitting is 'filler' or padding. It is as if we would wrap up a small or cheap present in an elaborate or expensive wrapping paper. (But the medium's urge is not any form of cheating — it is only the work of the unconscious mind, as I will show.) Most mediumistic material consists of vague, rambling, generalized statements — good wishes and so forth 'from the beyond' — and other such-like matters. The percentage of genuinely paranormal content is very tiny. Sometimes there is none at all.

The rarity of the truly paranormal, both in mediumistic communication and generally (say, in dreams), resembles that of the element radium, discovered by Pierre and Marie Curie. The very richest ores of this element produce only a quarter of a gramme of radium per ton of ore. Some produce only one three-hundredth of a gramme per ton. Yet a small piece of this ore suffices to make an impression on an ordinary photographic plate. In a similar way the paranormal penetrates and impresses itself upon the fabric of our normal universe. Its general rarity (as with radium) is no argument whatsoever against its existence. But like radium, the paranormal is easily overlooked.

I have been trying as we have gone along to emphasize certain points about the paranormal. These points include its rarity, its brief life when it does occasionally appear, its frequent irrelevance to the aspects of life that we consciously and logically think are important. None of these, of course, at all recommends it either to the scientist or the materialist. There is one further very important aspect — that of subjectivity. It seems that the paranormal is closely interwoven with purely personal aspects of our lives, the workings of our own unconscious minds in particular, with *existence* in the subjective sense of *being*, and with relationships.

In brief, I believe that ESP is a subjective experience or state that can in no way be approached by the detached, cold, objective, controlling methods of science. On the contrary, I believe that all the scientific approach can do is to take us away from the paranormal. The experience and 'control' of the paranormal is a quite different one. It is, on the contrary, a yielding and a willingness to accept paranormal events on their own terms, as they arise — much in the same way as a surf rider can only ride a wave if and when it appears, and must adapt *his* strategy to the *wave*, and never expect the *wave* to accept *his* strategy.

None of this at all means, however, that we have to abandon either our common sense or our grip on reality.

PART II
Matters Arising

Matters Arising

CONSPIRACY

Conspiracy theory is traditionally indulged in by individuals and by groups — philosophical, religious, political, social and so on — that have failed to make any real impression; or, in some cases, have failed to make a *universal* impression. These last groups are not content with a small empire. Their wish is to express and control everything in their own terms.

A reasonable person in the face of such failure to convince might wonder, under the circumstances, whether his views had any real interest or value after all. Or that his views were perhaps *part* of the answer but not the *total* answer. But many will not let matters rest there. They insist that there is a conspiracy — by government, by authority, by opposing groups, by private but powerful or wealthy individuals — to make sure that their views are not heard, and their final, triumphal victory postponed.

So believers in the existence of flying saucers hint darkly, or state openly, that the authorities are well aware of the existence of genuine flying saucers — even have in their possession the wreckage of crashed saucers — but are keeping this knowledge from the people.

The Christian has invented the Devil to explain Christianity's failure as a world movement, and in its full purpose, altogether.

Many left-wing sympathizers believe that Conservative Members of Parliament are in the direct pay of industrialists and millionaires, and that this fiendish alliance is the reason that the great Socialist revolution is not fulfilled. Many right-wing sympathizers believe that the trade-union movement in this country receives large quantities of finance and encouragement from Russia — which is why the British economy is being destroyed, and the British working man is discontented.

Most scientists believe that there is only one kind of truth in the universe, namely scientific truth. Far from being willing to consider calmly and reasonably any evidence there might be to the contrary, they resort instead to mockery and underhand tricks, to censorship and to smear tactics (see especially p. 62).

Sometimes there is a grain of truth at the heart of conspiracy theory, just enough to make it one-tenth of the way plausible to a person who wants it to be true anyway. But often — and this is always true to an extent — it is the twisted psychology, the neurotic compulsions and inadequacies of the individual who considers himself conspired against that fuel and maintain conspiracy views.

There seems to me clear evidence that conspiracy theory is at work *both* on the part of the scientist and on the part of the paranormalist. One result is that neither side will ever accept as proven anything which damages their case — nor conversely accept as unfounded anything which helps it. The outcome is no outcome. Everything stays where it is. Genuine progress and the resolution of the difficulties involved is out of the question.

There is, it seems to me, nevertheless a way out of this stalemate, and this book, like all my other books, is an attempt to describe what that is.

GOING GA-GA AND FLIEING

The verb 'to flie' is an invented word of my own, hence the rather odd spelling. It is a combination of the verbs 'to fly' and 'to lie'. I invented it to deal with a very common happening in the paranormal field.

When a person is 'flieing' his feet, certainly, have begun to leave the ground — though only metaphorically, not literally. At the very least he has begun to exaggerate, just as when a man who has won £80 on a horse tells his friends he has won £100. The figure is 'rounded up', for convenience perhaps. But it is never rounded down. This type of exaggeration is the minimum definition of flieing.

Even in the more intense phases, the individual concerned is not telling a hundred per cent lie. But flieing does also cover the situation where a person tells a lie on a *second* occasion to assist what was genuinely true on a previous occasion. Dr W. J. Levy provides us with an example of this particular behaviour (see p.153). Flieing is a progressive disease. In its worst form the person begins telling supportive lies to assist what was only *perhaps* true the first time and what the person hopes is true. The motto is: 'If this isn't true, it should be.'

In all forms of flieing, for whatever reason or reasons, somewhere along the road the truth is lost.

'Going ga-ga' is a colloquial phrase that already exists in the English language. It signifies the losing of one's grip on reality. For example, a car salesman who begins taking unsecured cheques in payment for his cars has gone ga-ga. The man who goes on holiday leaving his front door wide open, in the belief that no one will rob him, has gone ga-ga.

In going ga-ga a softening of the critical faculty occurs. Judgment is impaired. Basic common sense goes out of the window. Importantly, evidence *contrary* to the position one has taken up is ignored.

This affliction is very common among those who become involved in the paranormal.

At a paranormal seminar in London I shared a lift with a physicist, a man with several important patents to his credit. I remarked that the trouble with some people in this business was that if you said to them that you had spent last weekend on Venus they would say: 'Oh, how was it?' The physicist turned away from me in icy contempt.

In all seriousness, I believe that among the dangers of the occult against which so many fairy stories and legends warn is this weakening of the hold on objective reality. It is true that what we might call the 'uncritical faculty' is often much praised in religious contexts. The English word 'silly' means 'holy', for example, and we have the general concept of the holy fool.*

I think myself there is little doubt that paranormal abilities are favoured by this state of mind, that is, by unreasoning acceptance. But I think also it is too high a price to pay for the paranormal — producing an individual who is merely crippled in an opposite way to the materialist. It is a price which we do not have to pay.

By championing the cause of the paranormal unreservedly, that is, by never being critical, I know that many paranormalists think that they are performing a positive service. But in fact, just as our hypothetical car salesman would soon go bankrupt, so the uncritical approach here leads rapidly to the bankruptcy of the paranormal. I for one am not prepared to see this prince — the paranormal — reduced to beggary either by well-intentioned fools or by outright charlatans.

The opposite state of mind — that of unrelenting scepticism — is equally of no use. It is no less a one-sided, crippled development. What we need instead of two kinds of one-sidedness is the genuine synthesis of the best in each viewpoint.

Casualties

I regret to number three quite outstanding individuals among those who have fallen victim to what I call softening of the critical faculty: Professor John Taylor, Dr Lyall Watson and Dr Andrija Puharich. In the first two named the condition I propose is only incipient — so that I believe these can (and I hope will) without much difficulty resume the true, narrow path. In the case of Dr Puharich matters seem to me to have deteriorated more seriously. I think he has a very long and difficult period of restructuring ahead of him.

Professor John Taylor has been engaged for the past three years in the investigation of a number of children, who can allegedly produce so-called physical phenomena — spoonbending of the Geller variety and the like. The spectacular

* This figure is the most important and powerful of all the Tarot trump cards. He survives as the Joker of the conventional playing-card pack.

early results have not stood up at all well to a rather more
critical look — but I am not mainly concerned here with the
genuineness of the results.

The point, rather, is this. Professor Taylor is an outstanding scientist, a Professor of Mathematics (in one of the most
important chairs in the country) and an Emeritus Professor
of Physics. We need not hesitate to describe him as brilliant.
Yet lately he seems to call an experiment what a strict
scientist would not even call a controlled observation. For
example, Professor Taylor would give a child a sealed tube
containing a piece of metal and allow the child to take the
tube out of the room for several hours — even to keep the
tube in his possession at home for several days. During this
time the tube was, of course, out of observation. As it
happens, the Amazing Randi, a professional conjuror, has
shown that the seals of the tubes Professor Taylor used can
be by-passed without detection, and the material inside
then be bent by normal means. So apart from allowing the
tubes to pass out of his view, which in scientific terms ruins
the observation, Professor Taylor had not made sure of his
apparatus. (Often, actually, the metal object concerned
was not even *in* such a tube.) I am myself, as will become
clear, no champion of the experimental method as a means
of investigating the paranormal. But if you *are* going to do
an experiment it has to *be* an experiment.

At a conference where I shared the platform with him,
Professor Taylor showed me (and the conference) a rather
beautiful little model of a dog, made entirely from paper-
clips. He said that one of his 'paranormal' child subjects
could put a handful of ordinary paper-clips in a box, shake
it, and by so doing after a while produce the model.
Professor Taylor told me that the boy's mother is an artist.
He remarked that the boy had obviously unconsciously
inherited his mother's talent. I must say that quite another
explanation occurred to me, as perhaps it will to the reader
— that the boy's mother, or the boy himself, had made the
model in a perfectly normal way. I am of course not saying
that either of them actually *did*. I am saying that this
explanation also presents itself as a *possibility*. Given the
less than perfect observation that went on in respect of the

previous metal-bending, can we have complete faith in the model dog?

Finally, in his book *Superminds*, Professor Taylor prints a large number of photographs. Some are simply a pictorial record of the results of 'observations' of the children. Others are Victorian photographs of various spirit manifestations and materializations. There are pictures of mediums exuding ectoplasm — a mystical substance allegedly produced from the medium's body which can supposedly form itself into human features and hands, and even complete figures. It should, in my opinion, worry Professor Taylor enormously that not one fragment of ectoplasm has ever been available for public inspection; and that in contrast to the dozens of mediums in the past who could apparently produce the phenomenon, there does not seem to be one today. But Professor Taylor does not warn his reader that some or all of these old photographs may be forgeries. I myself do consider all of them to be, and would very much question the wisdom of presenting them in a scientific text at all, except as curiosities or subjects for debate.*

Dr Lyall Watson is a slightly more serious case. He, too, is a highly-trained and skilled scientist — a biologist. He was an assistant of Dr Desmond Morris (author of *The Naked Ape*) and prior to his interest in the paranormal he himself wrote a book called *The Omnivorous Ape*. He then wrote two extremely readable and perceptive books dealing with aspects of the paranormal, *Supernature* and *The Romeo Error*. Of the usefulness of these two books there is not the slightest doubt — I refer to the second of them later in this book.

However, having subsequently heard Watson lecture on several occasions, I started to fear that the suggested 'softening' had begun. His lectures had now lost their scientific quality and gained a religious one. There is nothing wrong

---

* There is better news however. In a recent interview (*New Scientist*, July 14th, 1977), Professor Taylor admitted he is now much less sure that there even *is* a metal-bending effect. The powers of the 'super-children' have apparently declined in direct relation to the tightening of experimental conditions.

with that as such — the real point is that his words had lost their edge. He seemed to be reaching the point where 'anything goes', where something is true *because* you say it is. It is enough just to say it.

Let us look at a short extract from Dr Watson's latest book, *Gifts of Unknown Things* (p.109).

Cattle in a field choose to lie down in one particular area despite the fact that it many times offers no apparent advantage in the form of food, shade or shelter. They may well be responding to stimuli too subtle for us to appreciate, but it is also possible that we could be underestimating our own sensory capacity. *Very often the cattle congregate in that part of a field already selected at some earlier time by man for the erection of a standing stone or the construction of an old mound or barrow.* [my italics]

What is the basis for the last sentence in particular? How many times has Dr Watson observed how many cattle congregating around some (real or alleged?) old human site? How many times has Dr Watson seen (or not seen) *other* cattle congregating, or not congregating, in parts of a field where there is no human site? Moreover, if the stone or mound is still visible, might not that object itself in some way focus the cattle's attention?

The reader comes away from the paragraph I have quoted with the feeling that something has been *proved*. But there is no proof in the paragraph. There is only speculation. If I myself were forced to categorize Dr Watson's book, which he himself considers to be a scientific text, I would call it a novel.

Turning back to lectures, I was already a little worried, for instance, by Dr Watson's absolutely whole-hearted support of the Philippine healers (see pp.111—18). He issued them with a complete clearance certificate on every count. (I wonder if he is still so convinced following Mike Scott's second documentary — see pp.114—15.) There was nothing to prevent him offering such endorsement, of course, if that was his opinion. The next matter, however, was and is rather more worrying.

At the May Lectures in London in 1974, Dr Watson told
us of a boy he met in India who could drink water into his
body through the palms of his hands. He said that he had
film of the boy doing this. I wondered at that moment why
Dr Watson was not showing us the film — it certainly would
have been fascinating. Now, as I have mentioned before
(p.37), I was hired to do the rough edit of the Lectures for
publication. Working with the tape transcript, I left in the
reference to the film, as we shall see in a moment. But when
the book appeared, the reference was missing.

What had happened? Had Dr Watson lost the film? (These
things sometimes happen.) Or has he personal reasons for
not wanting to show the film? Or what?

Here, for comparison, is the section as I submitted it to
the main editor, followed by the passage as it appears in the
book.

> . . . the boy picked up an earthenware jug of water,
> poured some into his hand and drank it, not by lifting
> his hand to his mouth but by sucking the water in
> through the pores of his skin. It gurgled briefly on his
> hand and then was gone. I asked if he would do it
> again. He did, using the other hand, and I filmed it.
> That day was a major turning point for me . . .

> . . . the boy picked up an earthenware jug of water,
> poured some into his hand and drank it, not by lifting
> his hand to his mouth but by sucking the water in
> through the pores of his skin. It gurgled briefly on his
> hand and then was gone. I asked if he would do it
> again. He did, using the other hand. That day was a
> major turning point for me . . .

This kind of thing does worry me enormously. At very best
it is a form of slipshodness which those in public life cannot
permit themselves. As I said, films do get lost, or things go
wrong for any of a dozen reasons. But let us then *say* that
they have.

Dr Andrija Puharich seems to have lost the ability to
distinguish between audio-visual hallucinations, such as

mediums (and I myself) sometimes experience (see pp.72–6), and the objective world.

By professional origin, Dr Puharich is a respected neurophysiologist, who was for many years employed by an American university. He holds over fifty patents in the field of medical electronics. As a result he is a man who is independently wealthy.

All of the foregoing statements are important. They reveal a highly-qualified, gifted individual, a man both respected and respectable. Perhaps above all his comfortable financial position renders meaningless the charge we can make against some others — that they are purveying the fantastic in order to make money. In view of his very real achievements in science, we also can hardly assume that Puharich is chasing pseudo-achievements in order to compensate for some kind of personal failure, as again I believe some do.

In more recent years, Puharich has become involved in the paranormal, and now devotes himself to its study full-time. As is well known, he has attached himself to and worked closely with Uri Geller. An upshot of this co-operation was Puharich's biography of Geller. It is this book, *Uri*, which we now talk about.

Some have challenged the extravagant claims of Puharich in *Uri* by pointing out how very few of the miraculous happenings — sightings of UFOs, materializations, levitations and so on — have happened in the presence of witnesses. I agree that this is a weak point — but it is not my own main line of criticism. (However, given that others present at some alleged happenings saw nothing — like the soldiers who failed to see the red light over Mount Sinai, visible to Puharich and Geller — I think myself that we need not worry too much about whether the happenings were *objectively* real.) Some, again, find it highly suspicious that virtually all the physical evidence of the reported miracles conveniently vanished subsequently (that is, dematerialized) — the vast majority of the photographs, and all the tape-recordings, for example. Again, I am personally inclined to think that these items of evidence never existed objectively in the first place.

My own doubts, and my final view of the Puharich–Geller

affair, are based on internal aspects of the story.

Puharich claims that he and Geller have been contacted by beings from outer space far in advance of us scientifically, and presumably culturally. Among other things, they are able to travel in time. They are allegedly observing human development at intervals of 6000 years.

As in all 'mediumistic' communication — which is all, at very best, that the Puharich affair can involve — throughout the whole of Puharich's book there is given *not one single objective fact that we do not know already*. Professor John Taylor himself has pointed out that there is only one scientific formula in the book — and that already known. Would it not have been possible for the 'Spectra' forces to have given us just one tiny hitherto unknown scientific fact as proof of their existence? It could be argued that this information was withheld because these beings do not want to influence or interfere with our development in any way. But they have already done that by contacting us! Puharich, in fact, has allegedly been specifically entrusted with the task of convincing humanity of the existence of the super-beings. One tiny scrap of objective evidence would have made all the difference. Instead we are left with the standard non-outcome of 'mediumistic' communication.*

It would seem to me that Puharich ought to read some science fiction. Had he done so not only could he have asked the Spectrans (who apparently 'really' live several million years in the future) to resolve some of the well-known philosophical paradoxes of time travel, but he would have realized that the situation he apparently found himself in could not have arisen in the first place. For if the super-beings are due to visit us in 6000 years' time — then they have already done so! All parts of time are equally and instantaneously accessible to the time traveller.

---

* I do not think we can draw a parallel here with the Devil asking Jesus to prove that he was the Son of God by performing a miracle to order. That (alleged) situation was different psychologically and in many other ways. That was rather like asking a lover to *prove* that he or she loves you — to give in to the demand is to agree by implication that there is room for doubt. Such is not the case here — there is *every* reason to doubt the existence of the super-beings!

Of course, these remarks apply to 'pure' time travel — the kind where you arrive back home at the same split-second in which you depart, without 'real' time having elapsed. One can, certainly, hedge a little and argue that the same amount of 'real' time elapses while one is away as one uses up in the past. Still, that difficulty is easily dealt with. A bunch of us, say, aged thirty, volunteer to spend a year in the past. When we come back (we are now aged thirty-one) the current crop of thirty-year-olds sets off. Roughly speaking, if a million of us volunteer every year, the investigation of the past proceeds at the rate of one million years for every year of elapsed time.

I must resist the temptation to get any further involved in these fascinating issues — for this book is not specifically about them. Instead I recommend the books and stories given in the footnote,* and many others, where writers have tackled these issues in fictional form. I leave the reader with one comment to think about, which I have already hinted at — namely, that if time travel were ever going to exist, it would always have existed.

What a pity, then, that Puharich put none of these and other of the many paradoxes of time travel to the Spectrans for their view. I suspect he would have received no worthwhile answer — because these answers do not exist in Puharich's mind. (Or in fact in anybody's mind. They are paradoxes by the very nature of the terms they are couched in — like the square root of minus one and the constructs of non-Euclidean geometry.)

Reverting to generalization for a moment, and anticipating the subject matter of later sections, I have personally never yet met a spirit guide or control that was more intelligent than the medium concerned. In fact I have never met one who was *as* intelligent as the medium concerned. Puharich's 'guides' in particular are as unintelligent as any I have come across. For me their utterances are just more of the endless ramblings of the seance room, whose *face-value content* leads

* *Poor Little Warrior* (Brian Aldiss), *Command in Time* (James Blish), *Flux* and *Behold the Man* (Michael Moorcock), *The Seeds of Time* and *Time to Rest* (John Wyndham).

nowhere, and comes from nowhere, except from the personality of the medium. I have italicized the words 'face-value content', because in the trance material are sometimes embedded, as we shall see, fragments of the genuinely paranormal — though it seems there are none in Puharich's.

Assuming Puharich and Geller are telling the truth about the voices from space and the psychic lights (and without doubt Geller has in the past been guilty of deception — see p.148) then we would have to agree that Puharich and Geller are both powerful mediums. Their working together would redouble their powers, and could lead to the production of sustained and integrated hallucinations. That such things are possible in principle we need not doubt.

I take Puharich to task — in the event of the episodes he describes being genuine — because of the loss of his once-considerable powers to distinguish between objective and subjective reality. This is of course not a crime, in that wilful sense, but it is a fatal weakness. 'Fatal' in the sense that the individual concerned ceases to be of any direct use in the investigation of the paranormal. He can no longer make a meaningful contribution. The individual who has been magicked out of his normal senses is as valueless to the study of the paranormal as the most obtuse, insensitive sceptic.

Slovenliness spreads ever more relentlessly through the person infected by flieing. *Uri*, the book written by this once-careful scientist (although he believes he has been entrusted with the task of converting the world), does not even have an index.

More Sinning than Sinned Against?

When Gilbert Anderson, Secretary of the National Federation of Spiritual Healers, says in public, as I have twice heard him do, that he has seen a medium's hands dematerialize and rematerialize inside a patient, I am willing to accept that he has taken a hallucination to be objective reality. I do not doubt his sincerity.

It is not easy to keep one's balance in the paranormal field. It is only too easy, even when doing one's best to be reasonable, to be driven on the defensive by the persistent obtuseness and sneers of, say, the scientific establishment. Sometimes in sheer self-defence one makes statements that are more definitive, more dogmatic than they should be. This, at least, is a sin we can forgive and overlook.

Even so, there are some claims which I find it hard to excuse.

In his lecture to the 'Health for the New Age' conference in 1974, Alan Vaughan, an editor of *Psychic* magazine, stated that he, personally, can deflect a laser beam with the power of his mind. This statement was thrown into the lecture casually, as if a matter of no consequence. He did not go on to tell us when he had done this, or how often, or under what conditions, or in the presence of which witnesses. Possibly this remarkable event has been front-page news in some section of the psychic or scientific press. If so, then I have missed it. For the moment I am still anxious for further details.

However, more was to come. Vaughan then went on to say that he had been in a car with Uri Geller and some other people (not named) *when the car and its occupants dematerialized and reappeared eighty yards further down the road.* Apparently the car had at this point met an accident or a traffic jam (in New York, I believe) blocking further progress. The car and its occupants, according to Vaughan, psychically jumped the impassable barrier.*

Clearly, this is not a story that can easily be proved or disproved, in the normal sense of the terms. It would help a great deal if Vaughan (and Puharich and others) could produce reliable independent witnesses of the miraculous events he describes. In fairness, however, it is not always

---

* Though the lectures were due to be published, in fact they never were. I checked on the details of the story with a couple of friends subsequently. Interestingly, we all had a slightly different memory of the distance involved and the cause of the traffic block. Such variance is a phenomenon well known to psychologists — you cannot trust the *details* you recall after seeing, or hearing, an event once. All agreed upon the main point, however, that, supposedly, the car and its occupants had literally dematerialized, and rematerialized at a point further on.

easy to find witnesses, even in respect of such straightforward incidents as car crashes or robberies. So we must not become unreasonable in our demands. Nevertheless, the lack of independent witnesses on these very dramatic occasions is regrettable. In the circumstances and in general, the truth of Vaughan's statements remains therefore purely *a matter of opinion*.

Matters of opinion must be treated as something less than matters of fact.

Conclusions

The general literature of the paranormal is riddled with fraud, lies, errors, exaggerations and general silliness, in the way an old house is riddled with dry rot.

In an article in the *Sunday Times* (September 15th, 1974) devoted to Erich von Däniken's book, *In Search of Ancient Gods*, Jacquetta Hawkes, remarking that it was hardly worth picking out examples of gross factual carelessness from the general anarchy of the author's thought (although she actually gave several) added that von Däniken's illustrations 'include more than forty reproductions of well-known forgeries'.

Do the publishers of von Däniken's books not know that many of his illustrations are forgeries? Are they very careless? Are they not careless, but simply indifferent? Or what are they?

Does von Däniken not know that many of his illustrations are forgeries? Is he very careless? Is he not careless, but simply indifferent? Or what is he?

In its programme *The Case of the Bermuda Triangle* (1975) the B.B.C. exposed much of the myth of the so-called 'Devil's Triangle' as did further the *New Scientist* of July 14th, 1977. This triangle is an area in the neighbourhood of Bermuda (so sometimes called the 'Bermuda Triangle') where allegedly a great number of unexplained disappearances of ships, aeroplanes and people occur. The programme and the *New Scientist* showed how such a legend grows by distortions of the truth — omissions, biased reporting, the favouring of hysterical witnesses over sober witnesses, the continued retailing even of discredited facts, and so on. For example, one book carries a report of aeroplanes disappearing in mid-afternoon on a clear day. But in fact an airport radio log shows that the planes were still flying several hours later, after dusk, in rapidly deteriorating weather conditions. None the less, in such cases it is the incorrect or more sensational version (which arises often we do not know how) which continues to be used by subsequent authors.

Of course, some disappearances of aircraft and shipping always remain unaccounted for — and this is true in all parts of the world. But the following story is very instructive.

On December 29th, 1975, the *Berge Istra*, a new super-tanker, was reported missing in the Pacific. No trace of her could be found — no wreckage, no oil slicks. No distress call had been received. How could this giant modern ship simply disappear without warning and without leaving a trace? On January 14th the air force officially called off its fruitless search. On January 19th, when hope had gone, two survivors were found drifting on a raft. They reported that three sudden explosions aboard ship had broken the *Berge Istra*'s back and that she sank almost immediately.

What excellent material this story could otherwise have made for some occultists. But, on the contrary, what a salutary lesson it gives all of us. Is it not at least possible that some such prosaic explanation lies behind all the mysterious disappearances of ships and planes?

A word or two of clarification about what I am *not* saying here. I am not at all saying that speculation is not permitted about possible mysteries, such as apparent traces of visitors from outer space, unexplained disappearances of craft, or strange animal sightings. On the contrary, I make not dissimilar speculations myself. Speculation is something we always need in every field — and that comment applies equally to pure science. But we must have *responsible* speculation. If there are conflicting accounts of an event, for example, we must give both of them. If one is sure of some items and less sure of others, the distinction between these has to be made clear. What is not acceptable is for writers to throw everything, reliable and unreliable, into one great stewpot and say to the reader in effect: 'Here, you sort it out.' For the reader is rarely in a position to do any such thing. He is necessarily relying on the writer to do this for him. But all too often there is a quite deliberate dereliction of duty on the writer's part.

What happens as a result? Here is one of the things which happens.

The myth of the magical Philippine healers in Manila has been very largely exposed by Mike Scott's second documentary on the subject (see pp.114—15 for details). But one of the 'explanations' offered by believers in the work of the healers was that in that area of the world around Manila, there was (is) a concentration of psychic forces — perhaps somehow connected with the geophysical structure of the planet. Others had already said much the same about the Bermuda Triangle. The upshot was that one began to find people in the paranormal field speculating about patterns of psychic forces and beginning to draw maps of the 'psychic globe' — using Manila and Bermuda as focal points.

However, since many of the stories of the Bermuda Triangle and many aspects of reports on the Philippine healers are manifestly unreliable, then the assumption of psychic forces in these areas is still less founded. But we can see how the situation readily escalates. The first round of confusion gives rise to a second and still more complex layer of error. The whole affair now begins to get out of hand to the extent that it becomes completely uncontrollable — and so completely without value.

While we are on this subject: I am by no means dismissing out of hand theories from individuals like John Michell (in *View Over Atlantis*, for example) that there may be 'lines of force' on our planet which orthodox science has not yet discovered. One theory is that oracles and ancient shrines may be placed at junctions of such lines. However, these views are for the moment only speculation. At some point we will need to demand hard evidence of the existence of such lines of force — actually see them in operation. (John Michell himself believes they were harnessed to move objects.) Meanwhile, though, for many paranormalists saying is once again believing. If you say it — then it is true.

What price here too the stories of flying saucers allegedly from Mars and Venus, now that we actually know that on Venus the surface temperature is 980 degrees Fahrenheit — hot enough to melt lead — while it rains sulphuric acid, and that on Mars the surface temperature drops to minus 160 degrees Fahrenheit, the planet being buffeted meantime by winds of 300 miles an hour? What price the stories of those who claim to have been on these planets? If my experience of the individuals concerned is anything to go by, they will claim that of course they meant not Venus, but Alpha Centauri. A golden rule of many occultists has always been: when in a corner, change your story.

The follies of paranormalists of all persuasions are legion. It seems to worry no one — at least, not in the way it should — that out of all the seas of words produced by mediums and paranormal communications of all kinds (and that includes 'reincarnation' memories) *not one single statement of objective fact emerges that is not already known to us.* Only misinformation emerges — 'facts' about life on other planets, for example, which, as we have just seen, the actuality in no way bears out.

Much of the folly escapes notice altogether, because so few in the movements seem capable of thinking critically in these matters. One small example. The names of the spirit guides of mediumship, who are drawn from all manner of strange lands and past times, are always readily pronounceable in English! The repeated incidence of certain names — and there are not more than a few dozen all told — further exposes what I consider to be this cliché of the unconscious mind, which can only generate its ideas from what you have in some sense experienced yourself (see the later section 'Trance States', p.76). Thus a high proportion of 'Chinese' guides are called Chang.

I was present at a lecture given by a noted American medium, who was asked by a sycophantic yet perceptive (though not perceptive enough) member of the audience why so many spirit guides were called Chang. Did this not suggest that the 'guides' of many simple mediums were spurious? Alas, the name of the visiting American's guide was also Chang.

Perhaps we ought also to pay tribute to the delicate sensibilities of the guides in choosing names which do not offend our good taste. For let us hope that a certain South Korean prime minister does not come back in spirit form. His name was Bum Suk.

Anti-ga-ga

If there is an overwhelming 'will to believe' in most paranormalists, this has its opposite counterpart on the other side of the fence.

Among sceptics generally and orthodox scientists in particular there is a fear of the paranormal, which leads to a stubborn refusal to listen even to reasonable evidence, and the punitive hounding of the paranormalist. This paranoia — no milder word will do — of the scientist in the face of the paranormal is a particular aspect of the general paranoia of the human Ego when faced with aspects of the human Self. (These more general matters are discussed in Chapter 5.)

Compulsive 'anti-ga-ga' is every bit as serious an illness as flieing. It leads to incidents like the following.

In July 1975 the *New Scientist* dispatched the professional magician, the Amazing Randi, to the offices of the Spiritualist newspaper *Psychic News*, with instructions to pass himself off as a physical medium. While at the offices of *Psychic News* Randi, by trickery, put back clocks, bent forks and so on 'paranormally'.

The result was that in their next issue *Psychic News* ran banner headlines proclaiming the advent of a new Uri Geller. Then only did *New Scientist* disclose its part in the affair.

This thoroughly disgraceful behaviour on the part of an allegedly responsible journal, the *New Scientist*, towards the kindly and well-meaning (though, as I also think, misguided) staff of *Psychic News* requires no condemnation from me. Certainly there is a great deal of naïvety among paranormalists and certainly this needs drawing attention to — but this is not the way to go about it. If it is clever to deceive someone who trusts you without question, then the *New Scientist* was clever. If it is praiseworthy to steal from a house in which you are an accepted guest, then the *New Scientist* should be praised. It is in such terms that this incident must be judged. Science, not the paranormal, emerges the lesser from the affair.

DREAMS

Dreams, in my opinion, make the single greatest contribution of all to our understanding of paranormal phenomena. They, by themselves, provide conclusive evidence of an 'alternative consciousness' which itself constitutes a major step towards the idea of an 'alternative universe'.

It was Freud who first demonstrated conclusively that dreams and the unconscious operate under laws of their own, laws entirely different from those of conscious, logical thought.[27] Dreams are associative and wholistic; logical thought is linear and compartmentalized. Jung for his part subsequently went on to show how dreams and the unconscious also touch the paranormal.[56]

It is to me absolutely astonishing, in the face of the mountain of this and other evidence, that we find leading modern psychologists and physiologists treating dreams as if they were mere by-products or accidents of the nervous system — as if they were trivial, incoherent and irrelevant to life.

Chris Evans (for whom in other respects I have a great admiration) has suggested that dreams are only the brain 'computer' processing the day's information. Dreams are incoherent and meaningless, he suggests, because the procedure of sorting and coding the information necessarily involves jumbling it. Ian Oswald, an authority on the psychology and physiology of sleep, considers dreaming to be simply the by-product of chemical processes in the brain. The processes themselves are important, but the dreaming is not.

I often want to ask such individuals whether they have ever actually had a dream — just as on a more general level I often feel like asking most psychologists if they have ever met a human being.

In fact, however, it really is the case that people of the dream-denying type spend a smaller proportion of their sleeping time in dreaming, and dream less vividly. On waking they recall less of their dreams and tend to attach little importance to them.[46]

This factual situation goes some way towards explaining the attitude of these psychologists to dreaming. But only some way. So sweeping is their denial not only of normal dreaming, but of all paranormal and psychic phenomena (despite the overwhelming evidence for the significance of the one and the existence of the other) that we have to examine closely their own personal, psychological state. We have seen already in the case of the uncritical individual that 'anything goes'. Conversely, in the case of the extreme critics we are now discussing, 'nothing goes'. Both of these extreme mental states are equally undesirable, and equally significant, though for entirely opposite reasons.

My own experience of dreams and dreaming is very different from the accounts and descriptions of Evans, Oswald and like-minded others.

During times of reduced activity or monotony in my life, and in times of emotional or financial deprivation, my nervous system supplies me with 'adventure dreams'. It is as if there is some compensation mechanism at work. These adventure dreams appear to last most of the night — or, more accurately, to take up a whole night's dreaming time. It is quite often the case that if I wake in the night and then go to sleep again, the dream resumes where it left off. Sometimes on being woken by the alarm clock in the morning I have deliberately gone to sleep again in order to continue an interesting dream.

These adventure dreams possess not only continuity, but an objective coherence and reasonableness for which dreams are not usually noted. For example, individual characters tend to maintain their role and functional integrity throughout. This is not to say that fantastic things never happen in the course of the adventures — but they are comparatively rare. It is in a sense 'fantastic' that I should, in the dream, be a spy working for a government. What I mean rather is that in the dream anyone who is killed remains killed, for instance. I remember one dream where I myself was shot dead — and that was the end of the dream.

Apart from adventure dreams, though clearly not entirely unconnected with them, I have on occasion dreamt the plots of short stories. I even dream jokes. Sometimes I laugh so much at them that I actually waken. There is no pleasanter feeling in the world than to wake up laughing. I should add that while the short stories stand up rather well, the jokes, in the light of the following morning, usually do not. They are a more subjective phenomenon — 'fairy gold' that will not bear the examination of the day.

While it is not uncommon for writers and other artists to dream matters which they subsequently incorporate in their work (see also pp.86—7), it is of the greatest interest, and in principle far more unlikely from a rationalist point of view, that scientists sometimes dream scientific discoveries. Nils Bohr, the Nobel Prize winner, reports, for example, that he dreamt his model of the atom. Von Stradonitz attributed his interpretation of the ring structure of the benzene molecule to a dream, as did Otto Loewi the experiment with frogs' nerves which contributed to his eventual Nobel Prize.

So there is some strong connection between dreams and the creative process generally. We shall also see that not only dream life but artistic creativity has a close connection with the paranormal.

In Chapters 2 and 3 we had several examples of dreams with a clear and strong paranormal element. Not only are dreams relatively frequent carriers of paranormal information, but for a great many individuals, their one and only paranormal experience occurs in a dream. We could say that in a sense it is the ability to carry the dream state into waking life which constitutes being psychic.

A paranormal dream of my own was at the same time precognitive. In this dream I was standing talking to Isaac Asimov (a man I have never actually met, though I am a great admirer of his books). When I say 'talking', we were in fact not talking at all. I was desperately racking my brains to think of something he had written, in order to start a conversation. I knew we were at a party, though in fact no one else was present. On the contrary, he and I were floating in a grey mist suspended in space. I suppose it was the fact that we were each holding a drink that made it a party. Floating alongside us was an old-fashioned hot-water radiator, an item to which I have since been unable to attach any significance. I noticed that Isaac Asimov was taller than myself. I do not know if he actually is. That was the dream, and this was a Wednesday night.

A few days previously I had written a letter to the *New Scientist*. I was not at all sure they would publish it – there is always enormous pressure on letter space in any journal. Moreover, the editor had already published a previous letter of mine on the same subject. Finally, even when letters do get published, they do not by any means necessarily appear in the issue directly following receipt. All in all, I had no great hopes of seeing my letter in that Thursday's edition of *New Scientist* (August 1st, 1974).

In fact that Thursday's copy carried my letter, and in the column next to it a letter on a totally different subject from Isaac Asimov.

As I see it, the interpretation of the dream is as follows. The grey mist was the printed page. Asimov and I were standing next to each other in the dream as the two letters stood in their two adjacent columns. Asimov was taller than I because his letter was longer than mine. The party or gathering was all the letters of the letter section. Asimov and I had nothing to say to each other – our letters were on totally different subjects.

My letter was about dreaming. Asimov's was about there being too many people on the planet – overpopulation. Risking the charge of special pleading, I think that the over-population theme of Asimov's letter was reflected oppositely in the underpopulation of the dream (see p.81 on opposites). My own letter was about dreaming, and the paranormal experience came as a dream.

I hope the *New Scientist* will not be too put out at finding itself involved in a paranormal event.

As a life-long gambler, I regret that I can report only once dreaming the winner of a horse race. This dream repeated itself twice in the same night, already a slightly unusual occurrence. The first version of the dream was in black and white, the second in colour. In the dream I and some friends were queueing to see a film. We were all enthusiastic about the event. However, the name of the film was not mentioned. We eventually got into the cinema and the film began. At this point the dream ended. Subsequently the dream repeated itself. Once again a crowd of us were outside the cinema. Now, however, there was a greater sense of urgency and the details of the dream were sharper. Once inside the cinema, the name of the film was given. It was *Showman's Fair.* Then the actual film began, in colour. The plot of this film was not at all clear — but nevertheless our general feeling was that the film was a marvellous experience, entirely living up to our expectations of it. We said as much to each other.

Next morning, during breakfast in a local café, I was surprised to see that a horse called Showman's Fair was running that day. I do not consciously recall ever having seen the name of the horse before. It had no recent form. It was an elderly horse — eleven years old, by which age most horses have been long retired. My guess was that it had been out of circulation for some time and had been brought back for one last season. Despite all these actual and hypothetical circumstances, Showman's Fair was none the less third favourite in the ante-post betting. I mentioned the dream and the fact that the horse was running to Roy Grant, a business and sporting journalist (see Chapter 3) who happened to be in the café at the time.

Not without some misgivings I went to the bank, drew out £5, and that afternoon placed it on the horse. It started second favourite and won at 7 to 2. A week or two later the horse ran again. I only bet £1 on it on this occasion, but again it won, this time at 5 to 2. The horse was never subsequently placed, and I believe it was then permanently retired from racing.

For me to 'see' the horse as a film (in my dream, that is) was perfectly appropriate in terms of my background — I was at one time a script reader for Paramount Pictures, and films have always been a passion of mine.

The appropriateness of this dream has a strong relevance
to an article written by Thelma Moss in *Psychic* magazine.
Thelma Moss is a medical psychologist and Assistant Professor at the Neuropsychiatric Institute of the University of
California. Her article is entitled 'Dreaming Winners at the
Races'. This contains authenticated accounts of three people
who have dreamt winning horses. The three individuals are
known personally to the author in connection with her work
as a psychologist.

The first story concerns an educational psychologist. This
woman dreamt the winners of races three or four times a
week for about four months. Her dreams were vivid and in
full colour. In these dreams, as the leading horse crossed the
line, the announcer gave the horse's name loud and clear over
the speaker system. The woman had no interest in racing
herself, and could not consciously recall ever having heard
the names of the horses before. She told her husband,
however, and he began to bet on these horses — for which
he first had to scour the racing papers, since the locale of
the race was not given in the dream. Probably the husband's
confidence and the size of the bets gradually increased.
Eventually he in fact amassed considerable winnings and
decided to buy a new car. With the purchase of the car,
the dreams abruptly ceased.

Another woman, a devout Catholic and, interestingly, an
accountant, likewise saw the end of a race in her dreams.
She heard no sound, however, but instead saw clearly the
number on the side of the horse. She told her husband of
the dreams and he was able with research to locate the horses
involved, which duly won. However, the couple did not bet,
this being against their religious beliefs. Nevertheless, the
woman woke one morning and told her husband that if they
bet the daily double that day they would make $1000. They
decided to make this bet and to give the money to charity.
The two horses she had dreamed for the daily double were
both long shots. Both of them won, however, and the Tote
Double that day paid $964 per ticket.

The third report is still more interesting, not least by
reason of its conclusively involving a large number of
independent witnesses. The man involved, a television

producer, had only one dream, in colour. In his dream he was watching a race on television. The commentator of the race grew very excited. There were three horses neck and neck as the end of the race approached. The names of these horses were repeated several times. The eventual winner of the close finish was an outsider, one not expected to win.

The name of the winning horse hovered in the producer's mind for several days (an unusual feature since, as we know, the bulk of dream material is normally rapidly forgotten). However, he attached no general significance to the dream as a whole. Yet the winning horse's name did seem somehow familiar. In the course of the next days, the producer gradually recalled that a former acquaintance of his had once had a part share in a horse of this name. He thereupon rang his former friend. This man no longer had an interest in the horse. Apparently it had never looked like doing well and he had sold his share. The friend did know, however, that the horse was due to run in a race in the near future.

The producer now searched the racing columns for some days, till he found the race in which the horse was running. All three horses named in the dream were in the race. Greatly impressed by this 'coincidence', the producer placed a very large sum of money (we are not told how much) on 'his' horse to win.

Most fortunately he told the whole story to his staff before the race and suggested they should all watch the race on television. They did so. The race ran out exactly as described in the dream. The three named horses fought out a closely-contested finish, with the producer's horse as winner. (As a gambling man, my pulse is racing just writing about this event!)

There are many fascinating and evidential features to these dreams. In each case also the format of the dream was appropriate to the life style and preoccupations of the dreamers. The accountant saw the number of the horse as it crossed the line. The school psychologist heard the names called. The television producer likewise heard the names called but, more importantly, saw the race on television, in colour.

The three dreamers in these accounts were entirely different personality types, and the two women certainly had no connection with racing whatsoever. The producer had some connection. On the other hand, he had never had any kind of previous psychic experience and was a complete sceptic about the paranormal. He had previously had no idea that it was possible to dream the winner of a race. Importantly, all three cases stem from trustworthy individuals, and are confirmed by a number of independent and trustworthy witnesses.

In the context of trustworthiness and dreams, I would like to mention again Robert Temple, the author of *The Sirius Mystery*. His book, despite its unusual content, has won the firm goodwill of the scientific and academic press. It deals with an apparent case of a visit to this planet by extra-terrestrials. Mere mention of this subject matter is of course enough to send shudders of von Däniken up anybody's spine. It is, therefore, a considerable tribute to Robert's scholarly and forthright work that he has been able to carry traditionally severe critics with him. The following is a brief comment from the book.

A lot of the people who will enthusiastically receive my researches with open arms are the sort of people one least wants to be classed with . . . Believers in flying saucers are incredulous that I am not one of them since I have written a book on extra-terrestrials . . . Those who do not entertain for one moment the notion that space-ships could ever have visited Earth naturally assume my book is about flying saucers . . . It is unfortunate that this subject has become so burdened by the oppressive enthusiasm of people whom I can only describe by the unflattering epithet of 'the lunatic fringe'.

So we have no obvious cause to doubt Robert's reports of his own dreams. It also becomes clear that it is not necessary to be 'ga-ga' to have direct experience of psychic matters. I have already mentioned that Robert's dreams often recommend courses of action to him, as when the dream suggested he volunteer to review books for *Time Out*. Frequently the suggestion is that he get in touch with a particular individual.

The results of these contacts are usually extremely favourable. However, Robert also has precognitive dreams. On one occasion he dreamt about an aircrash involving the death of a Bolivian president, before it happened.

A point well worth emphasizing is that individuals with a rich and vivid dream life are often psychic. That is, the two events usually go hand in hand. Robert Temple and myself are cases in point.

There is a phenomenon known as 'lucid dreaming'. A lucid dream is one where you are conscious that you are dreaming, while actually dreaming. Many people have an occasional flash of this experience from time to time. A rather conscious, though continuous, and certainly very intriguing form of the experience can be achieved by G. M. Glaskin's methods.[31] (See also p.93.)

My own ability to dream lucidly began quite abruptly five years ago, and has since improved steadily, though slowly. I cannot vouch for the quality of other people's lucid dreams — I can only say that the dream world which I enter for extended periods as, nevertheless, a fully-conscious individual is of a beauty and a wonder that I have no words to convey. The universe that then opens is one to which I yearn to belong ever more completely. Ordinary life seems increasingly drab and pointless by comparison.

There is, of course, a danger here which I need hardly underline — that of becoming alienated from the world of objective reality to a point where one no longer wishes at all to function within it, or even to be in it. Here, I think, we have a further meaning of the warning, found in so many fairy stories, that through involvement with the magical world one becomes changed and magicked beyond recognition. A person may be lost entirely to the real world. (But on the other hand, after seventy years or so, we are lost to the 'real' world anyway — and, as I think, for always.)

There is a great deal more to be said about dreams, and dreaming is a thread that runs through many of the following sections.

GHOSTS AND HALLUCINATIONS

There seems to me to be virtually no valid evidence for the existence of ghosts. There is, however, a good deal of evidence for hallucinations, sometimes accompanied by the paranormal acquisition of information. The two together make a 'ghost'. Without the second, paranormal element we have simply a common-or-garden hallucination, not readily distinguishable from the very many other forms of hallucination which accompany various illnesses and toxic states.

Perhaps the best point at which to begin is with strictly pathological hallucinations.

Notably in schizophrenia and other forms of psychosis, the afflicted person sees people, animals and objects which are not actually or objectively there. One patient is convinced that the Devil is sitting at the foot of his bed. Another that the kitchen is full of crocodiles. A third that a great, flaming cross is visible on the eastern horizon. The individuals we are talking about also habitually show a variety of other deviant behaviours, quite apart from the actual hallucinations, which convince us that they are indeed ill and that the visions are part of the illness. For example, such people may cut pieces off themselves with knives. They may viciously attack friends, or strangers. Or they cannot bear the sight or presence of real animals. They cannot sleep, or they cannot eat. They spend hours scribbling incoherent 'books', or they monotonously bang their heads against a wall. They may attempt suicide, and so on.

The hallucinations vanish along with these other symptoms, further evidence that all are part and parcel of disturbed mental function. We now also know of certain drugs which, when taken, produce on demand the kinds of behaviour we have been describing — and others which equally 'miraculously' suppress them in psychotic patients.

Alcohol, L.S.D., old age, fever, even tiredness and hunger can likewise all, temporarily or permanently, create the toxic conditions in the brain and nervous system which give rise to hallucinations.

Aside from such pathological and toxic states, there seem to be otherwise normal individuals who are nevertheless prone to produce spontaneous hallucinations. I stated in the previous section that psychic gifts are often accompanied by a rich and varied dream life. It also seems to be true that psychic gifts are associated with the tendency to produce spontaneous hallucinations. This is, once again, true of myself.

Outside the seance room, I do not as a rule hallucinate — though the incident with Miriam at Oxford Circus where I probably hallucinated direction signs (see pp.35–6) is a notable exception. I quite often hallucinate, however, at the point of waking — but only, it seems, when walking abruptly from *dreamless* sleep.

Invariably the experience is preceded by my sitting upright in bed having, for some reason, awakened abruptly. On one such occasion I opened my eyes to see a large snake coiled on the bed. I grabbed for it, but in the act of my reaching out the snake disappeared. Much more often my hallucinations are human figures. I am now fairly used to them — but once or twice the figure has persisted long enough for me to believe that I am, this time, fully awake and that the apparition is really *there*. To a tall 'angel' dressed in a flowing white robe I recently shouted 'What do you want?', before the figure faded. More recently still I was confronted by a shining replica of myself. I waited briefly — but the figure persisted. I shouted 'Yes!' in great excitement. But then, after all, the figure vanished.

My experiences in this area pale to insignificance beside those of Jung — who was taken on a guided tour by one of his visions. The account of that experience is given in full in a later section (pp.94–5). It has more of the quality of a dream than a waking hallucination. Certainly Jung agrees that during it he did not physically leave his bed.

Always, and especially with respect to the paranormal, we should not assume more than we must in attempting our explanations. The evidence should *force* us to widen our frame of reference and to shift our ground. We should not go running ahead of it into free-wheeling 'explanations' where 'anything goes'.

The experience of seeing (or hearing) a ghost should not (and in my opinion cannot) automatically lead to the conclusion that a person who has died is still around in some hypothetical spirit or otherwise disembodied form. We actually have to hand far less extreme explanations, which initially allow us to avoid the major assumption of life after death.

First, as I have said, we know that human beings are capable of generating hallucinations. In almost the words of the song 'psychotics do it, alcoholics do it; even young *dementia praecox* do it'.

Normal people *also* do it.

The hallucination has all the hallmarks of being a real, objective person or thing, bar one. That one is that it has no effect whatsoever on physical matter. *And vice versa.* Here, of course, we have one of the major attributes of 'ghosts' — their ability to pass through physical matter (walls, etc.) or to float clear of the floor. Bullets and buses go through ghosts. Physical objects, likewise, go through hallucinations.

What of the noises allegedly made by some ghosts? What of the alleged movement of objects by ghosts? The first, in so far as they are not noises made by a house cooling at night, or whatever, can well be *auditory* hallucinations. The mad often hear voices, bells and whatever. Normal individuals (especially mediums) also sometimes hear them, as I do myself.

As for the movement of objects, assuming such reports to be genuine in the first place — we are talking of the poltergeist ghost, in other words — there is the possibility that such movements are unconsciously generated by the real live human being involved (see the section 'Physical Phenomena, pp.142–51). Although to take the position that paranormal physical phenomena *are* genuine is a large step, this is still much less of an assumption than are those of life after death and disembodied spirits.

If the 'ghost' should give some paranormal information (as Jung's did) that, too, we can accommodate short of postulating a spirit world. For we know that human beings can paranormally acquire information both about the past and about the future. Sometimes it comes into their heads

'just like that'. Often it comes wrapped up in a little
internal drama. It is, so to speak, acted out for us by part
of our nervous system — notably by the unconscious mind
— whose normal method of communication this seems to
be. So the 'communication' habitually comes in the form
of a dream, so it comes to the entranced medium, speaking
as if with another voice, or as a picture seen in the mind's
eye; so, I suggest, it may also come as a 'ghost' which speaks
to us.

A question to reflect on here is whether a haunted house
is also haunted when there is no one there to see the
haunting. My feeling is that it is not. My strong feeling is
that psychic phenomena *only occur in the presence of a
living human being*. This proposal has very interesting
implications, which we must develop further.

It might reasonably be asked, how could we know
whether or not a house were haunted unless someone be
there to witness? One answer would perhaps be by the use
of a camera. The camera, left in position and operated
electrically at a distance, however, shows no image of any
ghost. (It also shows no image when it is operated by someone on the spot.) The alleged photographs of ghosts that
are available, incidentally, I am afraid I do consider without
exception to be fakes. I am myself certainly no kind of
expert on photography — but in this particular respect I am
willing to accept the judgment of those who are. In respect
of purely technical judgments we must bow to the expert.

Late Word

After I had completed this section, Colin Wilson's I.T.V.
programme, 'Leap in the Dark', provided further virtually
conclusive proof that ghosts really are nothing more than
hallucinations. The programme reported two research
undertakings. In the first of these a writer (Frank Smythe)
deliberately put about the completely fictitious story that
a particular place was haunted by a particular ghost,
describing the appearance of the alleged ghost in detail.
After a while reports began to flood in of people claiming
to have actually seen the said visitant.

Still more impressive, and I think really rather conclusive, was the second experiment. In this a young woman was told under hypnosis that she would in a particular place at a particular time see a ghost, which the hypnotist once again described in detail. When taken to the locality in question the woman in fact duly saw the 'ghost'.

I personally think we have every justification for treating at least the large majority of ghost sightings as hallucinations — in fact, I think we have very good grounds for making this figure one hundred per cent. But there *are* just one or two impressive reports which do tend to argue for the survival of the human personality after death (see, for instance, pp.94 and 97) and so perhaps also for some visual representation or impression of that surviving individual, if such there be. I think we cannot in all honesty slam the door *completely* on ghosts at this stage of our knowledge. But we almost can.

At the end of the last century the Society for Psychical Research conducted an investigation into what it called 'Spontaneous Hallucinations of the Sane'. Without perhaps fully realizing it, I think the Society perfectly described that which a ghost in all probability is — namely a sudden, waking hallucination, identical in point of origin with those commonly experienced by the insane, yet this time experienced by a sane individual.

In attempting to account for hallucinations, both of the sane and the insane, I am personally led to a very different understanding of the human brain than is current in academic circles. More of this in due course.

TRANCE STATES

The expression 'trance state' at once brings to mind the image of the entranced medium and perhaps also the condition induced by hypnosis. These are two examples of the usual meaning of the word trance.

I myself extend the concept of trance to cover a very wide

range of behaviours indeed. Trance becomes a central issue in my explanation of the paranormal.

Starting with the thin end of the wedge, I include, for instance, dreams and the states induced by drugs like marijuana and L.S.D. as trances. This step does not actually demand too much of a conceptual leap – and my experience has been that most people do not object strongly to considering these states as trances. But my list goes a good deal further. It includes for example being a child, being a woman, being in love, being religious and being a socialist.

I have defended these statements at length in my three earlier books on the human personality and will do so further in this book. For the moment, let us just say that one of the features common to all the 'trance' states named is that in them the chances of having a paranormal experience are increased. This is not to say that in a trance state one necessarily *will* have a paranormal experience: only that it is more likely.

This statement is obviously true in respect of mediumistic trance. Regarding dreams, Louisa Rhine, who collected instances of spontaneous psychic phenomena for twenty years, reports that sixty-five per cent of such experiences occur in the course of dreams.[18] 'Being in love', another of my trance states, refers not only to heterosexual love between man and woman but to all ties of deep emotional affection. Aside, therefore, from the greater chance of ESP occurring between husband and wife or between lovers, of which there are numerous examples, we have seen how a strong affectional relationship between owner and pet also facilitates its occurrence. (Ostrander and Schroeder note that telepathy occurs most often between members of a family, people in love and childhood friends.[73]) As for 'being a woman', more women than men are mediums. Aside from that aspect, in a large-scale survey conducted by the Society for Psychical Research, where 8372 men and 8628 women were asked if they had ever had a 'vivid, spontaneous hallucination', twelve per cent of the women replied yes, as against less than eight per cent of the men.[96]

It happens further to be the case that women dream more than men, and children more than adults. Women also hypnotize more easily than men.

So there are indeed reasonable links between all those which I term 'trance states' *and* the occurrence of (the receptivity to) paranormal phenomena.

What I especially want to do in this section is to establish the concept of the 'trance-work'. Trance-work is what goes on, internally, during trance. I have derived my term from Freud's concept of the 'dream-work', which it therefore resembles in some respects.

A central idea in the Freudian view of dreams is the distinction between what Freud calls the *manifest dream* and the *latent dream*. The manifest dream is the dream you actually have, the dream you actually recall. But, in Freud's view, this manifest dream is really only a cover-up job, designed to hide (from fearful consciousness) what the dream is really about. We find out what the dream is really about by analysing it. This analysis involves exploring the dream's multiplicity of associations and significances.

A dream, as Freud shows, is really like a diamond: a relatively small object which, when held to the light, flashes ever-new colours and fire from its suddenly-perceived, limitless depths. In another way the dream is perhaps like a kaleidoscope. Every time you shake it, the constituent parts form into another pattern.

The dream (or the layers of dream) which analysis reveals is the latent dream. This process by which the unconscious mind turns the latent dream into the dream we actually have is called the *dream-work*. Dream analysis reverses the process of the dream-work. Through dream analysis we get down once again to the original, latent dream.

One aspect of the dream-work is *condensation*. This is to say, in the manifest dream very large amounts of information have been compressed or condensed into a very brief form. How is this achieved? Well, a single symbol, for instance, may have a multiplicity of meanings. To a particular individual, a bear may symbolize childhood (he was often taken to the circus as a child and above all he was fascinated by the bears), aggression (he was also very afraid of the bears and what they might do if they escaped) and father (his father was a very aggressive man). The analyst might additionally suspect that the bear also symbolized some of the patient's unconscious wishes, which he was afraid might 'escape' and get out of his control.

Another aspect of dream-work is that of representing an object or a state of mind by its opposite. This — at first sight — strange process is in fact found in very ancient languages, where the same word is used both for a thing *and* its opposite; and in young children today, who very often confuse opposites and use the same word for both.* Therefore an item which carries a strong charge of fear (when the analyst presses the matter) may in the dream be very tiny. Perhaps one's father appears as a dwarf, for example. On a more general level, items which are peripheral or incidental to the dream, which seem to be mere footnotes or which the patient may dismiss as irrelevancies, can in fact be the truly important items. This feature is known as displacement. For example, a man has a long dream about his wife. In the dream she wears a pair of his mother's shoes. The analyst may well feel that the patient is really dreaming about his mother, but dare not face the implications involved.

It is not possible to give here a full review of Freud's account of dream-work. Nor do I think in any case that everything that is relevant to the particular subject of dreams is necessarily relevant to the broader concept of trance-work.

My own notion of trance-work is a very generalized one. It is defined as the underlying process or processes which operate when the trance condition is in evidence. Briefly, I would say that the trance-work is a process by which *information is converted into experience.*

What does this statement mean? Well, let us take dreams as an instance of a trance condition. I think that most people would agree, apart from those who rather pathologically deny that dreams have any significance whatsoever, that the dream is trying to tell us something. But it does not send us a typewritten letter. Instead we get a little 'play' or 'film' in which the message is acted

* See my book *Total Man* (Chapter 3).

out. Often the plot or structure of the play is itself so garbled that at first sight it seems quite meaningless. Symbols rather than words are always preferred. Certainly the message is not direct. It is oblique, symbolic. It is cast in a form which we can, and do, *experience*; and, moreover, experience not at second hand or one remove, as we do with a letter, but first hand by actually *living it out* for ourselves at the precise moment of dreaming.

'Living out' is another expression for 'experience', as I use the word. We could and will also speak of 'direct perception' as opposed to the 'indirect perception' of second-hand, objective observation.

Can we now see that the hypnotized subject also *experiences* (lives out, acts out) what the hypnotist is merely *telling him* (information)?

Can we also accept that the child and the woman experience the world with far greater immediacy and directness than does the adult male? Can we further accept that the objective, detached, dry scientific approach is much more the attitude of the adult than the child, and of the male rather than the female?

In religion also we have direct perception, that is, the direct experience of god. While intellectual apologists sometimes try to reason (that is, to rationalize) their way to god, the attempt fails in the sense that such an exercise does not itself produce faith. For the genuinely religious, god *is*. He is, and he is immanent in all things.

These points are further understood by a consideration of the 'anti-trance' state.

Earlier I gave a suggested list of trance conditions. There is an equally long list of 'anti-trance conditions'. This list includes insomnia, being an adult, being a male, objectivity, being a scientist, being a materialist and being a fascist.

There are, once again, many interconnections within these states and for a full defence of the position my earlier books must be consulted. But for our present purposes the important link is that in all of them the chances of having a paranormal experience are considerably *reduced*.

I said that the 'trance-work' involves converting information into experience. Conversely, the 'anti-trance-work' involves converting experience into information.

This we see variously in the 'meddling intellect' which 'murders to dissect' (Wordsworth), the breaking of the spell, 'the Medusa eye of consciousness' (R. D. Laing), the touch of Midas which turns human beings into lifeless metal, the petrifaction of sensation and warmth and love through intellectualization and objective studies such as academic psychology (in which, as with Midas, the human being becomes an *object*).

We are really running a little ahead of ourselves into matters which properly belong in later chapters of the book. What I shall be arguing there in due course is that experience (direct perception) is as valid a method of examining some phenomena, notably psychic phenomena, as information (indirect perception) is of examining certain others.

Of the aspects of Freud's dream-work that can also be found in trance-work, one is the replacement of an object or a state by its opposite. I need hardly mention the extent to which opposites play a part in magic and black magic. So in magic you move 'widdershins', that is, anticlockwise. In the Black Mass the cross is hung upside down, the Lord's prayer is said backwards, and so on. We have had one or two instances of psychic 'oppositeness' in this book. Perception buffs may already have noted that in my incorrect perception of the first of Marcel Vogel's telepathically-projected colours (blue instead of yellow), blue is the complementary colour to yellow, that is, directly opposite on the colour spectrum. And Jan Merta's striking blue eyes were *closed* in my clairvoyant picture of him.

A further possible example of the translation to opposites occurred when Jan himself was demonstrating to us his clairvoyant abilities. The procedure was that someone gave him the name of a personal friend unknown to Jan, and Jan then described him or her. Some of these descriptions were impressively accurate. One of them, however, could not have been more wrong. The character in question was an extremely forceful business man, uninterested in ethics and very tough-minded. Jan listed the opposite of all these traits. So opposite were they that some of us burst out laughing. It seemed not a question of a simply inaccurate picture, but a reversed one. Perhaps *some* of the sometimes glaring 'failures' of mediums can be appreciated in this light and seen to be genuinely paranormal.

An excellent example of trance material which contains most of the features of Freud's dream-work (puns, reversals, displacements and so on) are the *Seth* books by Jane Roberts. These I would recommend to anyone with an interest in psychoanalysis and its relation to the paranormal.[87, 88]

REINCARNATION

My own experiences of 'reincarnation' began about seven years ago, in the general context of the apparently continuing evolution of my psychic abilities.

A 'reincarnational' memory is a striking and intriguing event. Abruptly, without warning, a chance sight or sound switches one, apparently, into another time and place. These, in my case brief, transportations carry a strong conviction of reality. The other 'time and place' seems to be *really there*. The hallucination (if such it is) is perfect. The sights and sounds of another sphere of existence surround me.

I was once visiting a museum in Jerusalem. In one corner of the museum an ancient arch and part of a roadway from some archaeological dig had been reconstructed. Suddenly I was a young boy of about ten, standing under the arch and leaning against the pillar with one hand. My other hand was being clutched excitedly by my smaller sister. Past us along the road were galloping a troop of horsemen, seemingly Romans. I could feel quite clearly the clutch of my sister's hand. The noise of the hoofs and the clank of weapons filled my ears. Then I was back in the museum in Jerusalem.

Many individuals who have described such experiences attest to their *reality* — albeit a fleeting one — which fully engages most, if not all, of their normal senses. I have just used the word hallucination to describe these experiences — but it must be said that probably the majority of hallucinations as experienced in mental illness and under drugs do not have this degree of sensory integrity — nor the panoramic quality. Hallucinations are usually dream-like and almost always irrational. They involve visitations, monsters, people floating off the ground, passing through walls, and whatever. The reincarnation experience is also stronger than a dream. It is even stronger than a lucid dream (see p.71). Perhaps we should describe it as a super-lucid dream.

I have never tried to test out any of my reincarnation experiences by discovering if they are objectively accurate. I do not know, for instance, if Romans ever galloped on horses in ancient Israel. I find the experiences delightful. I am eager for more. But I am not *objectively* curious about their content, because my opinion is that 'reincarnation' memories do not actually represent incidents from some actual life that one has previously lived. Before I go on to talk about the experiences of other people, I will try to describe what I think reincarnation memories actually are.

They seem to be further examples of 'trance-work', as defined in the previous section. Specifically, they are cousins to that form of trance-work which we call dreams, and as with dreams and many other products of the unconscious mind, they contain the element of *wish-fulfilment*.

Freud considered that all dreams represent a wish-fulfilment. He believed this was true even of horrifying and unpleasant dreams. Here, he said, the wish has to be disguised to protect consciousness. Certainly in children's dreams, as Freud noted, we do often find wishes undisguised and clearly recognizable for what they are.

Dreams, then, seek to grant our wishes. Similarly, in the fairy tales and folklore from many parts of the world, the fairy, the leprechaun, the genie, the magic spell or word — all of these explicitly grant wishes when captured or uttered. These mythical entities of fairy tale and myth are, I consider, all symbols (or archetypes) representing the unconscious mind.

It is then our own unconscious which 'grants wishes' and confers 'magical powers'. For reasons not altogether easy to explain, the unconscious mind frequently presents itself to consciousness as the granter of wishes — providing, that is, that consciousness has some measure of control over the unconscious, or at least maintains a friendly rapport with it.*

As I said, my own 'reincarnation' experiences come only in the form of brief flashes. They are triggered by events around me. Visiting an old castle and looking up at the outside walls I 'knew' that I had been there before. Abruptly, and momentarily, I was in the thick of a siege. Arrows were pouring against the walls, shouting figures lined the battlements.

On another occasion, I even had the memory of having been an Eskimo, during a film about Eskimoes.

With some individuals the flashes are of a longer duration. As in my case they may be triggered off by a sight or sound, or they may come out of the blue in moments of tranquillity. Importantly, for many they come under hypnosis (see Jeffrey Iverson's *More Lives Than One?*). This last circumstance establishes a clear link between 'reincarnation memories' and trance conditions. Especially under hypnosis, then, but also without it, some individuals have so many memories, and of so structured a nature, that they feel able to piece together a whole previous lifetime. We shall come to these shortly.

Still considering the occasional flash experience, some of these do create an extraordinarily impressive effect, even at second hand. The impressiveness derives from the fact that in the 'memory' is embedded a chunk of the genuinely paranormal. Nils Jacobson has collected a number of these together in his book, *Life Without Death*. Here is one.

---

* If consciousness does not obtain control but conversely *is controlled* by the unconscious, then consciousness becomes enslaved and perhaps destroyed altogether. We see this variously in the case of Rip Van Winkel, who slept for a hundred years and lost family and friends, the sailors of Odysseus who were turned into swine by Circe, and Tannhäuser ensnared by Venus.

We are touching on some very fundamental issues here. Ultimately, I feel at least some of the origins of the wish-granting position lie in the fact that among primates — monkeys, apes and man — and in mammals generally it is the female who displays in the sexual encounter and the male who is attracted by the display. The male is ensnared by the female.

A spring day, before I had learned to talk properly, I found cracks in the drying earth in front of my parents' home. A memory surfaced that I had seen things like that before — and that the cracks had widened — and I knew that they were the first indications of an earthquake. I couldn't say 'earthquake' so I screamed 'the trembling, the trembling', but no one understood me.

A second example takes us nearer to the coherent, continuous 'story'.

As a child I used eagerly to tell my brother, who was some years younger than I, what it was like 'when I was big before in the world'. I had a lot to tell, especially about America, among other things about when I was around when living people were thrown into a well (something which as far as I know I had never heard about). Later I read about the Aztecs and recognized my story exactly. The name Arras also existed for me even when I was very little; I kept repeating it to myself but didn't know what it meant. Later it disappeared, but the awareness that it was something special returned in the forties, when I heard the name for the first time.

The two incidents occurred to very young children. Assuming they are genuine, we have hints of a paranormal acquisition of information. I am quite sure paranormal information is sometimes included in the reincarnational memory — but that this is evidence only for the paranormal, not for reincarnation as such.

As we saw in the previous section, a notable function of the trance-work is to cast information in the form of little plays and stories. This seems to be the style or manner of the unconscious. It is not surprising if we find it here again in connection with 'reincarnation' memories.*

---

* I believe the strong tendency of the unconscious to produce stories is connected with a desire of the unconscious — the 'female principle' — to divert and entertain. Again the basic situation seems to derive from the circumstance that the female seeks to attract and hold the attention

Recent examples of individuals piecing together flashes of 'former lives' to a point where a coherent and continuous picture is built up are contained in books like Arthur Guirdham's *Cathars and Reincarnation* and E. W. Ryall's *Second Time Around*. What is presented here closely resembles a historical novel. In fact the two types of product — the reincarnation account and the historical novel — differ really only in so far as the reincarnationist claims the story to be a true memory of past life.

I first made the acquaintance of full-length reincarnation material in Joan Grant's novels (*Winged Pharaoh*, *The Eye of Horus* and others). She claims incidents in them are her 'far memory' of previous lives. Some of her books she apparently writes in actual trance.

I have a good many objections to treating Guirdham's, Ryall's and Joan Grant's books as fact, and not fiction — though that is not at all to say that I do not admire them *as* fiction. Let us first consider Mary Renault. More than any of the writers mentioned she has a gift for capturing and evoking the spirit of the past. Written in the first person, and set usually in Ancient Greece, her stories — *The Last of the Wine*, *The Bull from the Sea* and many others — are quite spell-binding. Yet Mary Renault claims no past lives as the basis of her work.

I think all the ground we have covered so far has to do only with the relationship of the unconscious mind to consciousness, and in particular to their working together in the creative process. In a previous section I described how I have on occasion dreamt the plots of short stories and other literary items. To do so is not an uncommon event for individuals working in the creative arts. The

---

of the male in, and after, the sexual encounter. The sex *act*, after all, is very quickly done with and the male's attention then notoriously starts to wander to other activities of the male's world. In legend, Scheherazade — who was due, like all the other girls of the harem, to be put to death after spending a night with the Sultan of India — invented a continuous story which for a thousand and one nights so beguiled the Sultan that he spared her life. I believe this tale describes in symbolic form one aspect of the enduring pair-bonding of the human male and female in the course of evolution.

choreographer, Lindsay Kemp, has said that he gets most of his ideas for costumes from dreams. Robert Louis Stevenson stated that the inspiration for most of his novels and stories came from dreams, including the famous *Dr Jekyll and Mr Hyde*. Coleridge dreamt his famous poem *Kubla Khan* — but woke up before it was finished. And we have seen already the important part that dreams can play in scientific creativity — p.65.

However, perhaps because of a relationship with the unconscious that is more of an ensnaring or trapping of consciousness than a free partnership, it seems that some individuals cannot make a firm distinction between inspirational products of their own minds and events in the real world. Instead of creating an imaginative novel or play and realizing that that is what they are doing, they believe they are remembering a past life (also that they are being spoken to from the 'other side', or whatever). These apparently 'separate' pictures and thoughts and voices I suggest actually arise *within* us, as do dreams. Thank heavens for dreams. *They* seem to show us the true nature of all the other material we are discussing.

By reason of the many interrelations between dreams and, especially, literary creativity, I have no hesitation in presenting the diagram in Figure 1 as an accurate account of what is involved in so-called reincarnation experiences. Of course, we must not forget to add a dash of genuinely paranormal information throughout.

Considering the diagram, the closer one is to dreams and the unconscious mind proper, the greater the chance of the appearance of genuinely paranormal and clairvoyant material. However, a clear link between 'ordinary' creativity and the paranormal is contained in the following instance. A novel, *The Titan* by Morgan Robertson, was published in 1898, long before a ship called the *Titanic* was even thought of. The novel deals with the sinking of the *Titan* on its maiden voyage. A great many details contained in the novel — the length of the ship, the weight, number of propellers, engine power, top speed, numbers of life-boats and passengers, time of sailing, and place and nature of disaster — are almost identical with the actual statistics of the *Titanic*, which

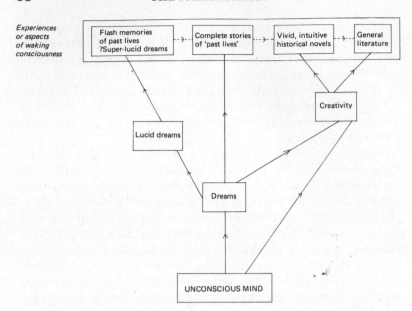

Incidentally, it would be perfectly possible to re-write the top line of the diagram putting 'trance medium-ship' in the top left-hand box and 'acting' in the top right-hand one. In the intervening boxes would perhaps come 'auto-suggestion' and 'method-acting'.

The kind of processes which take place under 'creativity' are aesthetic in the Schillerian sense (see F. Schiller's *On The Aesthetic Education of Man*). They include 'distancing' oneself from the material in order to give it genuinely independent artistic form. This distancing is, I believe, imperfectly achieved by Guirdham and others.

FIGURE 1 Some aspects of the relation between unconscious processes, the conscious mind and creativity

fourteen years later sailed on its fateful maiden voyage. (We note, of course, that the paranormal influence here is in respect of the future, not of the past.)[50]

Objections to memories apparently from past lives being anything of the sort run along many lines. I notice, for example, that nobody seems to have memories of being someone distasteful — of being a child molester or a pervert, a torturer or a psychopathic murderer. It seems on the contrary that everyone was basically a solid, rather decent chap — possibly someone lowly such as a shopkeeper or nurseryman (though suspiciously often someone rather glamorous) — but still, an upright citizen, a devout person, a friend to the poor and defender of the weak. (I am reminded of the circumstance that every Frenchman was a member of the Resistance and no German was a member of the Nazi Party.) Often this individual suffered at the hands of others — was tortured, or died in battle, or gave his life not to betray a trust or a comrade.

This whitewashed and morally sanitized picture of a personal past seems on the one hand to be part and parcel of the general 'niceness' and convenience of all superstructures built on and around the paranormal. So, as we saw, the name of the medium's guide is always readily pronounceable in English and has no unfortunate associations with any English word. This same tendency is further instanced in the sugariness of general mediumistic commuinication.

An incisive point has to do with the 'search for significance' which so notably characterizes the human race. I am talking here about *personal* significance. The large majority of human beings seem to be preoccupied with 'making something of their lives', of achieving something, getting somewhere, becoming somebody, realizing their potential, obtaining qualifications, getting on, earning other people's respect, showing them what you can do, and so on. (Not all of these concepts should be interpreted in 'rat-race' terms, though the rat race is a particular manifestation of what I am talking about.) The mirror that reflects the truth of my emphasis is the great ceremonial with which we *bestow* that which has been won. Prize day, the graduation ceremony, the Oscar awards, the Nobel awards, the giving of medals, conferring of knighthoods, presentation of certificates — all these award ceremonies in their pageantry and pomp underline the importance of the exercise of 'winning'. Achieving significance is certainly one of the prime, if not the prime, motivator of human behaviour.

Yet, of course, most people are not really in a position to achieve very much in the way of awards. The blocked impulse can then turn towards joining or identifying with a group which has achieved or is likely to achieve significance. So one supports a particular football club, becomes a registered fan of a film star or pop star, or becomes extremely nationalistic. This way some of the glamour of achievement rubs off on oneself — and one wears a particular uniform or a symbol to make sure the connection is noticed. (It is relevant how rapidly the number of 'supporters' of a team diminishes when the team begins losing consistently.)

Astrology is one of these arrangements which confers membership, reflected glory and also a high degree of exclusivity. Let us say you are a Libran. About eleven-twelfths of the population are not: roughly ninety-two per cent. So Librans form really quite an exclusive club. By definition, you are automatically held to be good at anything Librans are supposed to be good at. Of course, you will never be asked to prove it.

Perhaps an even better way to achieve distinction is to have had past lives — where additionally you performed romantic or worthwhile deeds. (It is also a distinction for a railway worker or a laundry woman to have spirit guides.) The unconscious knows how miserable and limited life is for most of us most of the time. So it grants our wish for glamour and interest in the best way it knows how.

The impetus of religious views generally can also be understood in these terms. But especially in reincarnation theory, the idea of past lives and the present one constituting a path of continuing development can obviously help one to bear the nonsense and pain of existence on this planet. Meaningless parts can be claimed to be meaningful in the larger context, tribulation now the price for happiness later, and so on.

There are further points.

It turns out that the large majority of cases of alleged reincarnation occur in remote parts of the world among primitive peoples (see for instance I. Stevenson's *Twenty Cases Suggestive of Reincarnation*). I am afraid my heart sinks a little when I hear such news — usually with good reason. (Compare, for example, the report on the Philippine healers, p.111 of this book.) It is not simply that the individuals concerned may be inventing the material in a consciously fraudulent way — it seems that even when speaking in all sincerity they are not very good at separating fact from fiction. They are what we call unreliable witnesses. Their very strong will to believe functions as an active distorter of objective reality.

However, I have a more positive explanation of my own why 'reincarnation' experiences — perhaps with a genuinely-high paranormal content — should be more common among the peoples of India, South America and elsewhere in the third world. This is based on my own view of man's evolution.

I consider that modern man is the result of a hybrid crossing of two forms of early man, Neanderthal and Cro-Magnon. Neanderthal was by nature far closer to the mystical and the paranormal than Cro-Magnon. The mixing of the two basic types is uneven in different parts of the world. There is a stronger Neanderthal inheritance among the peoples of Asia and Africa — hence the closer association of these peoples with the paranormal, with superstition and religion generally.

I believe also that dreams and all trance states, as well as actual paranormal abilities, are closely connected with that part of the brain we call the cerebellum (see Chapter 5). Asians and Africans have larger cerebella than Europeans, and Neanderthal man had a larger cerebellum than modern man as a whole. Populations (as well as individuals) with larger cerebella will, I suggest, exhibit stronger traces of all forms of trance-work in their general, conscious culture — in addition to being more prone to paranormal experiences.

On this general reasoning we would expect more, and stronger reincarnation stories among so-called primitive peoples.

It is commonplace for mediums and other psychics to obtain paranormally information known only to a now-deceased individual. This point is excellently illustrated when a psychic correctly pin-points where something has been hidden, in a hiding place known only to a dead person. Swedenborg is credited with such a discovery. A widow was being asked to pay a considerable debt, which she knew had already been paid by her late husband. However, she could not find the receipt. She asked for Swedenborg's help. A few days later he told her of the whereabouts of a secret panel in her husband's study, of which the woman herself had no knowledge. Behind it was the receipt.[57]

But in these cases, for obvious reasons, there is no suggestion that the medium is a reincarnation of the dead person —

although he does have access to the dead person's memories. So access to the memory of a deceased individual is by itself not sufficient proof of reincarnation. Instead we take the lesser — although no less miraculous! — interpretation that a living person is somehow able to reach the mind (?) of a dead person. And what, in any case, of the situation where a medium obtains paranormal information about the future? Are we willing here to talk about future, that is, *pre-*incarnational lives? This seems an even more unlikely assumption.

I think that the great bulk of the 'memories of past lives' that reincarnational stories contain is most likely material acquired in childhood and perhaps in a subliminal way in later life also. In this age of compulsory schooling, of books, radio, films, theatre and, most recently, television, it is quite impossible to avoid acquiring some knowledge of virtually every period in history. Consciously, a great deal of this material is genuinely forgotten. But it is available to the unconscious mind, that inveterate writer of plays and weaver of tales. Significantly, during psychoanalysis and under hypnosis large quantities of such 'forgotten' material is dredged up from the depths of the mind.

Very instructive is the case of the experimenter who read a Greek poem aloud to his fifteen-month-old son, once every day for three months. Many years later — the boy had studied no Greek in the meantime — the youngster was set the task of learning by heart two Greek poems. One was the poem read to him at age fifteen months. He learned that one thirty per cent more quickly than the other.[9]

In *More Lives Than One?* Jeffrey Iverson discusses a woman who had, under hypnosis, a memory of a previous incarnation as a Jewess in medieval York in England — and she described among other things the 'great copper gate' of that city. She claimed to have no knowledge of York in her present life. Nevertheless there *is* a street in present-day York called Coppergate. However, this originally Viking name means 'the *street* of the *coopers*' or carpenters. So there never ever was a gate, let alone one made of copper. The probability therefore is that the woman had once seen a picture or a film, or heard a play or read a book about

York, in which the name Coppergate occurred.

It is a source of constant disappointment (as well as suspicion) to me that all the many accounts of previous lives tell us so very little about the past that is not common knowledge already. I only know of one *possible* case where a real discovery was made. I believe that Joan Grant claims that she said certain small ancient Egyptian bottles were used by women for keeping tears in *before* archaeologists found evidence that this was indeed the case. I do not know whether Joan Grant's claim of priority has been authenticated. This incredibly low rate of discoveries per mile of reincarnational novel inclines me to think that the vast bulk of the material is not paranormally acquired at all, let alone is evidence of a past life. It is just everyday trance-work, with a very occasional dash of telepathy or clairvoyance.

G. M. Glaskin's method of inducing what others would call astral travelling to far-away parts (though I think it is a form of lucid dreaming, involving no travel at all) is also claimed to be a method of investigating past lives.[31] I do not believe that either. I do not believe there are any 'out-of-the-body' experiences at all – only, so to speak, 'into-the-body' experiences. The point really is that nobody ever sees anything verifiable on any of these 'trips'. They never see a gang of Egyptians robbing an Egyptian bank, or a man strangling his wife, or the torturing of prisoners in Russia or Chile. How strange to go on a trip to these countries and never see anything that actually goes on there! The 'past life' experience likewise yields no solid information. It is, I believe, only the play of the imagination.

I once asked a leading figure in the British psychic world why, if we have all gone through so many previous lives and experiences, the large majority of us on this planet are still so unbelievably foolish. 'Foolish' was the kindest word I could think of. Ah, he said. That is because only a part of us, the foolish part, remains on Earth. The wiser parts of oneself are on the higher astral planes.

A typical response, I am afraid. The rule is: always use a more outrageous idea still to defend an idea that is being questioned. Never *give* ground. Always take more.

In gambling there is a saying 'double up to catch up' or

'double up to beat the house'. It is advice gaming promoters give to green gamblers. In reality, doubling one's bets is the quickest way to go bankrupt.

The doubling up of extravagance likewise leads to the certain bankruptcy of the paranormal.

SURVIVAL AFTER DEATH

C. G. Jung's autobiography, *Memories, Dreams, Reflections*, contains the following account.

One night I lay awake thinking of the sudden death of a friend whose funeral had taken place the day before. I was deeply concerned. Suddenly I felt that he was in the room. It seemed to me that he stood at the foot of my bed and was asking me to go with him. I did not have the feeling of an apparition; rather, it was an inner visual image of him, which I explained to myself as a fantasy. But in all honesty I had to ask myself: 'Do I have any proof that this is a fantasy? Suppose it is not a fantasy, suppose my friend is really here and I decided he was only a fantasy — would that not be abominable of me?' Yet I had equally little proof that he stood before me as an apparition. Then I said to myself: 'Proof is neither here nor there! Instead of explaining him away as a fantasy, I might just as well give him the benefit of the doubt and for experiment's sake credit him with reality.' The moment I had that thought he went to the door and beckoned me to follow him. So I was going to have to play along with him! That was something I hadn't bargained for. I had to repeat my argument to myself once more. Only then did I follow him in my imagination.

He led me out of the house, into the garden, out to the road, and finally to his house. (In reality it was several hundred yards away from mine.) I went in, and he conducted me to his study. He climbed on a stool

and showed me the second of five books with red
bindings which stood on the second shelf from the top.
    This experience seemed to me so curious that next
morning I went to his widow and asked whether I could
look up something in my friend's library. Sure enough,
there was a stool standing under the bookcase I had seen
in my vision, and even before I came closer I could see
the five books with red bindings. I stepped up on the
stool so as to be able to read the titles. They were trans-
lations of the novels of Émile Zola. The title of the
second volume read: *The Legacy of the Dead.* The
contents seemed to me of no interest. Only the title
was extremely significant in connection with this
experience.

Many people would take this account — and far weaker ones
than that also — as conclusive proof of the survival of the
personality after death. Jung's friend, they would say, had
paused on his journey into the hereafter to assure his sorrow-
ing comrade that there really is a life after death.
    I cannot myself accept either this story or the multitude
of others equally strong as *conclusive* evidence of survival of
death. These *are* certainly paranormal experiences, and
certainly at first sight they are suggestive of survival.
    Yet we have to remember that we do have conclusive
indications that the living, here-and-now human mind can
obtain, paranormally, information both about the past and
the future. Our minds seem, in principle, capable of knowing
anything that has been known by some other person in the
not-too-distant past or will be known in the not-too-distant
future. (The phrase 'not too distant' is an important one to
which I will return.) It seems also, as I have said, that that
part of our mind which is able to acquire this information is
a great actor and a dramatist. It is not interested in bald,
objective facts. That is not its style or nature. Instead it
loves situations and action. It delights to perform a play or
masque, or to paint a picture, for our diversion and its own.
So everything that comes through that part of the mind
comes laden with pageantry, symbolism, relationships, interactions — all the very stuff of life and romance, of literature

and art.

This is really the trance-work, of which I have already spoken in detail (pp.78–82).

So the paranormal plus a play ('The play's the thing, wherein I'll catch the spirit of the king' as Hamlet observed) may look like life after death. But it may after all be only the paranormal, plus a play.

Let us not overlook that most of us *hope* for a life after death, and a better life, than this. It does seem not unnatural that a sentient, self-aware creature faced with inevitable old age and death should nurse that hope — with or without justification.

The unconscious mind, which likes to help when it can, perhaps obligingly fulfils our hope. We may not overlook Freud's demonstration that all dreams are wish-fulfilments. We must not overlook that the creatures of the magical world always offer to grant our wishes. In the barren times of my life my own dreams, as I related earlier, have freely granted me the colour and adventure I craved for. In something of the same spirit, perhaps, the unconscious mind grants our wish for a life after death. But possibly the palace of the after-life is built with fairy gold which will stand neither the light of day nor the harsh glare of honest inquiry.

I am hard put to state what I personally would regard as conclusive evidence of survival after death. The sensed presence of a loved one who has departed from us? The voice or the mannerisms of that loved one issuing from the mouth of a medium? No, I think not. Trance-work can account for all of these — plus a dash of the paranormal. Perhaps we only discover the truth about it all at our own death (the ultimate subjective confirmation).

Ingenious proposals have been put forward by psychic researchers to test the hypothesis that we live after death. These consist of imparting back, through mediums, information of a rather special kind known only to the deceased. R. H. Thouless and T. E. Wood have, for example, both published ciphers, the key to which is a word or phrase known only to them and not written down anywhere. The idea of such ciphers is to communicate this key word through a medium after death.[103, 114]

The idea for these experiments probably comes from the famous case of F. W. H. Myers, a renowned psychic research- er and classical scholar. After his death a medium, Mrs Verral, attempted through automatic writing to give Myers the chance to communicate if he so wished. Not only did Myers apparently communicate with her, but also with a number of other automatists in England, India and the United States. It seemed very much as if Myers's personality were attempting to communicate fragments of a classical puzzle to these various psychics, incomprehensible to any of them in isolation. These communications continued growing in complexity for the next few years. Then eventually one of the mediums involved, Mrs Willett, died in 1956. Since then a communicant calling herself Mrs Willett, and giving much detail about her own private life, has put in an appear- ance. With long gaps, the affair has been continued some sixty years.[14]

The final verdict cannot be given, for the case is still continuing.

In principle, however, the kind of arrangement we see in the Myers affair is preferable to one where the would-be communicator lets on before his death (a) that he is going to communicate and (b) more or less what he is going to try to communicate. The out-of-the-blue communicatory incident, especially when as complicated as in Myers's case, does carry rather more conviction of a surviving, coherent, directing *personality*.

Yet is even this enough? I am not sure.

In trying to think what, for me, would constitute proof of life after death, I once set up the following unlikely condi- tions. The dead communicant would have to transmit something that had not only never been known to a living person, but was not even known to the dead person at the time of his death. The psychic communication would reveal the truth for the very first time.

The following case, cited by Nils Jacobson,[52] comes close to meeting these criteria, but not quite; for the hospital surgeon involved knew the true facts.

My uncle was run over by a truck in 1928 when it drove up on a sidewalk and slammed him against a wall. He was unconscious for three days and nights and then died, as we all thought he would finally, of a concussion in the back of his head.

During a seance in England in 1934, my father was put in contact with someone said to be his dead brother. He told of his death, and stated that he did not die of his skull injury but that 'it came from the bones'. This was considered strange by his relatives, for they all believed he had died of the skull injury; they had accepted that as a fact and had never discussed any other cause for his death.

It struck me first in 1956 that I could check the facts through the hospital records. They indicated that he had received a concussion at the back of his head at the time of the accident and he was then operated on. But his unconscious state did not alter and so then he died three days later. During the post-mortem the cause of his death was found to be not the skull fracture but a brain embolism caused by a lower bone thrombosis (a clot from the bone which causes a blood stoppage in the brain). So verification of the 1934 communication came about twenty-two years later.

On his deathbed, Goethe is alleged to have cried out, 'Licht, mehr Licht!' His phrase, translated into English, is 'Light, more light!' The question, which has divided interpretations of this last remark of the famous scholar and visionary, is whether Goethe was saying, 'I see light, more light,' or, 'I need more light.' The question, for me at least, remains unanswered.

RAUDIVE VOICES

This particular side-show of the psychic circus set up in business in 1959. In that year Friedrich Jürgenson, a

Swedish artist, thought he detected human voices on tapes he had used to record bird song. Subsequently he became convinced that these voices were speaking personally to him and did not come from Earth. He worked further on this phenomenon for several years and then published his book, *The Voices from Space*, in 1964. A follower of Jürgenson's ideas, Konstantin Raudive, took up the work and in 1968 published his book *Breakthrough*. The phenomena nowadays are usually called after Raudive.

The claim of those who have occupied themselves with this material is that the voices on the tapes are from outer space, or from the 'other side', the world of the dead.

The following considerations, however, are those that carry weight with me.

A friend of mine taped an interview with a medium in a quiet house in London. When she played the tape back to herself at home she found superimposed on the tape parts of a conversation between a mini-cab driver and his office. (Was it a dead taxi driver carrying on his work in the beyond?)

I have a still better example of my own. A male acquaintance had purchased some very expensive hi-fi equipment and he invited me round to hear its miraculous qualities. He played me one record, and I was duly impressed. Then, while he was sorting out which record to play next, to our amazement we suddenly heard from the speakers the sound-track of the film showing at the cinema 200 yards down the road!

I think we can safely rule out discarnate film sound-tracks.

It seems to me significant that in recent decades tape-recorders, tapes, hi-fi equipment and whatever have become dramatically more sensitive. We have had a developmental explosion in this whole field of communication and recording. Aside from this point — though I think it is the crucial one — we have also seen year by year a significant growth in the amount of broadcast material, both television and radio, put out on this planet, as well as the development of the Telstar and other satellites which effectively blanket the whole Earth surface with transmissions. The volume and range of broadcast material is quite phenomenal. What we now seem to be witnessing is an increasing contamination (radio pollution, if you will) affecting all kinds of electronic devices in unlooked-for ways.

What, nevertheless, of the claims by the Raudivists that the voices address them personally and answer their questions? And that it is possible even to have a running conversation with a tape-recorder? As far as I understand this procedure, you ask your question, and then allow the tape to run 'blank' for a while. When it is played back it apparently has an answer on it.

We best approach the problem from a slightly different point of view. We put the question: what happens when people are given a burst of fairly faint 'nonsense' noise to listen to? The answer is: they hear words spoken.

As we have long known, when an individual is shown a *picture* of random splodges or shapes, and asked to say what is in the 'picture', or what the 'picture' represents, he or she is not stuck for an answer. Our nervous system and our personal psychology work together to produce a picture from the non-picture. The Rorschach inkblot tests are one well-known application of this principle. Psychologists use such tests to gain information about the unconscious mind. It seems that a basically similar process occurs when a person is presented with random *noise*.

D. J. Ellis has conducted a detailed study of, and written a wholly excellent paper on, the Raudive phenomenon. In this study he actually worked in direct collaboration with Dr Raudive himself, and used some of Raudive's actual recordings.[20]

To read the paper itself is a must for anyone who imagines there is anything of substance in the Raudive phenomenon. Here I can give only a glimpse of the results of the study. Briefly, there were two main test conditions, the first where subjects listened to the 'voices' on the tapes in the presence of the experimenter (Test 1) and the second where the subjects listened to the tapes on their own equipment at home (Test 2).

Here are the differing interpretations of one 'voice' obtained from different subjects.

Test 1	Test 2
sē mulendrēnas	Seeman Brenz
c'est mon venir	come on then
say mumblings	sa mun den
sey man ben	zu mand Wein
semānthen	deman dring
ze alarm things	samanda/the/sa man drinks
demanding (American accent)	der Mann ringst
command/come on then	der Mann bringst
	ze man rings
	de man brings/the Mandarin's
	de mandrins
	demand Denis
	demmon minus
	zay-munn-drainus
	sa mann veenis
	Imam Rene

Raudive's own interpretation of this fragment was Tja Mambrin.

A further instance:

Test 1	Test 2
die kesthavagen	de fegavagon
dee skavigum	dies um anagon
ee bufamigun	easy cavya
die be/ge farrigen	in Italia
eelen hamegan	die Italigon
die pfālligen	gestadigen/getadigen
ze Italians	dez e tadio
	die Decabilung
	sea de kay tarragon
	de harrigot
	dees argen
	die Habin
	die Kabin
	dee cabin
	die?

Raudive's own interpretation here was: diese Farbigen.

These examples are already sufficient for our purposes. But I cannot resist adding the following hilarious interpretations of a further fragment: make beans my lovely/ late sleep I'm serviette ong/lately mikye bien/late leave Mike shairries/let's leave Michael here Kevin/nimst die Michael as yet/make me quite clear gemmell/methylene Mike is here.

Raudive's own version here was: may dream, my dear yes!

So appallingly wide is the range of interpretations of the 'voices' (some of which, incidentally, were reported by subjects as being just 'background noise' or 'recording noise') that one could almost suspect that the experimenter was perpetrating a hoax. Perhaps I should therefore add my own experience in this area.

At one time I was hired by another writer to transcribe and type out tape-recordings he had made in India with various holy men. I mistakenly thought this would be easy money. In some cases there was a good deal of background noise, which did not help at all. But even where the voice was uninterrupted, the task was a nightmare. One could play a remark over and over again and still hear: 'The spirit of God two one and ninepennies in the balcony'; or 'Jelly and cream are nicer than chakras in Bombay'. Sometimes persistence, and the general drift of the conversation, enabled one to decipher what must have been said, while other items remained obstinate nonsense — and, moreover, *different nonsense to different people*.

Finally, confirmatory evidence of the non-event of Raudive voices comes also from one other direction. It appears that when a recording of the same baby's prattling is played to mothers of different nationalities, Chinese mothers detect Chinese words, Italian mothers snips of Italian, English mothers traces of English, and so on.

Before summing up the evidence of this section, I would say there is just the *faintest* possible chance that a few rare individuals — such as Marcel Vogel — might be able to impress occasional thoughts on to sensitive tape (perhaps in the way Ted Serios alleges he can impress his thoughts on to film). This is a *very* remote possibility, and if genuine would come under the head of physical phenomena.

As far as any other aspect of the Raudive effect is concerned (spirit or space voices, and whatever) we can sum the whole matter up in one word.

Rubbish.

KIRLIAN AURA

The phenomenon is so named by reason of the extensive research conducted by Semyon and Valentina Kirlian in Russia during this century. They were not the first to note or study it, however.

Briefly, the alleged Kirlian effect is produced when an electric spark is passed through an arrangement of electrode plates, photo-sensitive paper and the object which is to be photographed. What appears on the photograph is a dark outline of the object in question (which may be a leaf, an insect, a human finger or whatever) surrounded by a luminous corona or halo.

The corona or halo is the so-called 'Kirlian aura'.

A great many claims have been made concerning this aura, based on its relative brightness or dullness, its colours, its distribution and patterning, and so on. It is said to be a reliable indicator of health or ill-health. It is said to show differences between psychics and non-psychics, and between a psychic at rest and a psychic at work. It is claimed that a Kirlian photograph of an unopened bud shows the outlines of the leaves or flowers which are not yet actually there, of the flowers-to-be. Some have claimed that in the Kirlian aura we are viewing the aura that psychics have always claimed to discern around people and organisms. Some others claim it as evidence for the 'subtle anatomy' and 'etheric blueprints' talked of in connection with acupuncture and esoteric physiology.

There is really no need for us to pursue any of these points in detail. Not only is it the case (one feels like saying 'as usual') that the claims made by some experimenters have not been reliably duplicated by others, but it would seem that an article in *Psychic* (of all places) stops the whole Kirlian road-show in its tracks.

This article, 'Kirlian Photography Revealed?', written by Carolyn Dobervich, reports the work of William Tiller, a Professor in Stanford University's Department of Materials Science, and his assistant, David Boyers, a doctoral graduate in electrical engineering.

These two scientists, having observed many Kirlian researchers at work, realized that there were many possible sources of error (uncontrolled variables) in the equipment researchers were using.   Accordingly, Tiller and Boyers designed equipment of their own in which they could precisely control such matters as the gap between the object photographed and the electrode, object moisture, the timing of the electrical pulses and so on.

Tiller and Boyers found that using just *one* object, and varying the parameters mentioned, they could reproduce to order any of the various kinds of Kirlian aura required. They showed that results are purely a function of variables under the control of the experimenter.

Further, they worked with a well-known psychic, request-ing him to place himself in the various states of his calling. During this time the experimenters held all other variables constant.   The result was that the 'Kirlian aura' of the psychic remained unchanged in any way in a series of thirty-six photographs.

Other workers had reported marked differences in the 'auras' of psychotics and non-psychotics (of the mentally ill and the normal). Tiller and Boyers duplicated this work — as ever, holding all other variables constant — and found no differences between the 'auras' of these two types of individual.

The researchers conclude (as, of course, the evidence clearly demonstrates): 'From our studies, the use of Kirlian photography as a physiological state monitoring device has not been found to be effective.'

If we are talking in the context of scientific research — and we *are* talking in that context — at this point the Kirlian band-wagon has to be brought to a halt. It may *only* be started again *if* and when other workers, using the Tiller and

Boyers apparatus, can once more produce their own earlier results. Pending that day, all previous results, and still more so all the theories based on them, must be held in suspension. In blunter terms, they must be scrapped.

What a hope! Since the publication of the Carolyn Dobervich article at the end of 1974, articles and books on the Kirlian phenomenon have continued to flood out. Once again we see it confirmed that a majority of people would rather hear lies which are in line with what they want to hear than the truth which is not.

Some of the more intelligent writers in the field have since referred to the Tiller—Boyers findings. But even so we see what, really, is even more depressing than ignoring that work outright — namely, the continued refusal to accept its implications, and a persistent unwillingness to kill off that which has no value.

Thus Nicholas Regush writes in his *Exploring the Human Aura*: 'William Tiller . . . *argues that* all the halos peculiar to the Kirlian process remain quite constant when voltage, finger moisture, photographic timing . . . are carefully controlled. Tiller *believes that* . . . differences in the halo can be attributed to the many ways that this light is influenced by physical factors.' [my italics]

Tiller does not 'argue that' or 'believe that'. He has *scientifically demonstrated that*. His demonstrations stand as the last word on the subject, until someone is able to produce a counter-demonstration, using his conditions.

I am sorry about everybody else's fine hopes, but that is the position and there is no way round it with words.

Jeffrey Mishlove is worse. He spends six pages in his *Roots of Consciousness* describing the findings of Kirlian photography, with a great many pre-Tiller colour photographs. In the middle of his text he accurately describes the Tiller—Boyers work and findings; and adds moreover that their findings (their *non*-findings, that is) have now been duplicated by other researchers. These other researchers have also shown that the 'phantom leaf' effect, for instance, can be produced by a buckled film.

None of this, however, persuades Mishlove that he cannot write 'positively' about Kirlian photography and the Kirlian aura. It does not prevent him publishing a great many very pretty and, in the circumstances, phoney pictures of pre-Tiller auras. Mishlove ends by saying:

> I am sure that most readers will agree that the astounding reports of some Kirlian photography researchers do point towards an understanding of these priceless experiences which we all sometimes enjoy — and which conventional science has sometimes thrown on the rubbish pile. Most of us can assume that the stairway to the heavenly city exists and that scientists are now also walking on that golden pathway. Thus, with a certain warm wonder at the excitement of our age and culture, we go about our business.[66]

Others may feel it is Mishlove's chapter which deserves the rubbish pile.

There is, of course, nothing like having your cake and eating it. But I find this catering for the gullible by the back door — which I think is what Regush, Mishlove and others are doing — far worse than catering for them by the front door. We will make no progress with an all-that-glitters-is-gold approach.

The current and summarizing word on Kirlian auras is therefore: kaput.

Note

I myself very much believe that there *is* an energy body (or bodies) surrounding the living organism (see Chapter 5). The point made here is that the Kirlian aura is *not* this energy body. There is, currently, no such thing as the Kirlian aura. We must never let our hopes of discovering proof of what we believe run ahead of, let alone fly in the face of, the actual evidence.

PSYCHIC HEALING

The case for psychic healing, apart from a vigorous word-of-mouth reputation, rests on some rather strong experimental evidence, which I am inclined to take as conclusive. What we are talking about is mainly the procedure known as 'laying-on of hands'. This has no connection with what is called faith-healing, since results are obtained whether or not the *patient* has any belief in the procedure. Some remarks are made later about faith-healing in connection with the so-called Philippine healers, and acupuncture is dealt with in Chapter 7.

In the laying-on of hands the healer clasps or strokes the affected area, and accelerated healing and remission of pain is said to take place as a result. This is all that the psychic healer does.

The lynch-pin of the experimental evidence mentioned is Oskar Estebany, a psychic healer in private practice in America. However, he is not the only healer involved. The fact that the experimental evidence rests heavily (though not exclusively) on one man's performance does not at all mean that there are very few healers about or that they are necessarily less able than Estebany. It means only that most psychic healers are unwilling to submit to tests under the control of experimenters. I do not especially blame them for this, in view particularly of the punitive attitude of many scientific researchers. However, Bernard Grad, Justa Smith, Norman Shealy (see pp.125—8) and others show us that it *is* possible for a scientist to establish sympathetic rapport with a psychic, and to have the imagination (and courtesy) to let the psychic work as he wants. The experiment must accommodate the psychic, and not vice versa.

Dr Bernard Grad, a research biochemist at McGill University, has mounted two very extensive experimental investigations involving Estebany.

In the first of these, a small area of skin was removed from the backs of a large number of carefully screened mice. Details were noted of the precise area, depth, condition and so on of the wound. In other words, full standard medical observation procedures were employed (by medical personnel) before and during the experiment.

The wounded mice were then divided into three groups. The first group were, individually, held by Estebany between his two hands in small cages for twenty minutes each day for fifteen days. The second group of mice were similarly and individually held by volunteer medical students claiming no psychic powers, who merely copied what Estebany did. The third group of mice received no treatment of any kind.

At the end of fifteen days the mice treated by Estebany had made significantly more recovery than either of the other two groups. No difference in healing was observed between the mice 'treated' by the students and the mice which were untreated.

Some years later Grad mounted another experiment with Estebany, this time using plants.

Mild salt solutions of water in beakers were treated by Estebany, by his holding them between his hands for fifteen minutes (one hand above, and one below the solution). Other identical beakers of solution were not so treated. All the beakers of solution were then randomly poured into standardized pots containing seeds. All the pots were subsequently dried in an oven for forty-eight hours. After drying they were placed in a small, windowless room and all watered identically with ordinary tap water.

The plants that grew in the pots which had received the solution treated by Estebany showed many significant gains over those in the control pots. Estebany's pots had significantly more plants per pot, produced the highest individual plants and had greater average height of plants per pot.

As a further control, the experiment was re-run, *not* using Estebany. This time no significant differences were found between any of the plants in any of the pots.[39, 40]

Estebany has also worked with Dr Justa Smith, another biochemist. She had him treat, over a period, solutions of trypsin (a pancreatic enzyme involved in digestion). There were four equal amounts of trypsin in beakers. One beaker was held by Estebany between his hands. A second was immersed in warm water of the same temperature as the healer's hands. A third was placed in a magnetic field. And a fourth was first 'de-natured' by irradiation with ultraviolet light, and then subsequently treated by Estebany.

The results of the experiment showed that Estebany raised the activity level of the normal sample he treated by a statistically significant amount, as compared with the control sample. Further, that he significantly improved or 'cured' the de-natured sample.[94]

In terms both of elegance and repeatability, I do not think any scientist can dispute these results. The range of the experiments, using animals, plants and enzymes, is also quite remarkable and in itself impressive.

Other studies, involving another (unnamed) psychic healer, are reported from the University of Chile. Mice were inoculated subcutaneously with a tumoural suspension, as a result of which actual tumours developed. Then the mice were divided into three groups. The first group was treated on a daily basis by the healer. The second group was not treated at all. And in the case of the third group, the healer was requested to try to make the tumours *worse*.[72]

A significant retardation of tumour growth was found in the mice positively healed. No difference was found between the negatively treated group and the control group. Either the task of inducing tumour growth was inherently distasteful to the healer — or healers cannot in fact produce negative effects. If the second statement is true, interesting implications are raised.

A final experiment was performed in America at the Institute for Parapsychology. A number of mice were bred from one parental couple. The offspring were assigned to pairs — each pair consisting of two litter-mates of the same sex. All the mice were rendered unconscious by a dose of ether. The dose of ether given was regulated by its effect on the animal.

One of each pair of anaesthetized mice was taken to one of two rooms. There *either* a known healer or psychic *or* a non-psychic volunteer attempted to rouse the mouse from sleep. In some of the trials the human beings involved sat in the room with the mouse, but were not allowed to touch it. In other trials the reviver (psychic or non-psychic) sat beyond a two-way mirror, and so could see the mouse but not affect it in any normal way.

The psychics roused their mice from sleep significantly

more quickly than the non-psychics. Importantly, the experimenters comment: 'There is no evidence that the average person is capable of achieving better than chance results in such experiments.'[106] The same was true, of course, of the non-psychic individuals involved in the Estebany experiment.

These various results seem to me to place the reality of psychic healing beyond any doubt. For once science has been met on its own terms and has been vanquished. It seems, in fact, that psychic healing is a topic highly amenable to scientific investigation. For this very reason, I am myself inclined to think that psychic healing is *not* actually paranormal! For me, it is merely, like acupuncture in Western countries, rather unusual. These are matters to return to. If, however, psychic healing is amenable to objective study, there is for me even more reason here than in the exercise of the paranormal generally that the rigmarole of spirit surgeons and doctors operating from beyond the grave be discounted, in objective terms, altogether.

One notable course of action, which this time need in no way affect the susceptibilities of the religious, seems clearly dictated. If the capacities of a psychic healer can, under favourable conditions, be demonstrated on animals and plants, the National Federation of Spiritual Healers should now incorporate such demonstration in an examination of the alleged or would-be healer, prior to issuing a certificate of professional competence. I am not suggesting that such an examination be in any way punitive, or that it could not be taken as often as the applicant wished in the event of initial failure. Nor should (or could) any healer be forced to take such a test.

But if psychic healers are eager to see their work more widely accepted, such a test of proficiency, leading to a professional qualification, is a way to go about it. Only good could come of this step. The psychic healer could then take his or her place as an able and valuable member of society, instead of existing on its fringe as something of a freak. The public for its part would be reassured about the whole procedure. Indirect pressure would be placed on those refusing to take the (as I say, non-punitive) examination, ultimately flushing out the charlatans who contemptibly trade on the afflictions of others.

Further points arise here also. I have visited the homes of professional healers, seen them taking pills prescribed by a normal doctor, heard them complaining of headaches, constipation, back-pains. There is nothing absolutely wrong with this situation as such. Psychic healing does not have to be a miraculous cure-all. What does disturb me in the situation is that in their lectures these healers never mention their own dependence on orthodox medicine and their own illnesses. Instead they excite the audience with wild tales of cures at the snap of the fingers. This, I am afraid, is flieing again.

Rick Carlson at least had the good grace to tell at the May Lectures how he once went to address an audience of American surgeons on the shortcomings and evils of orthodox medicine. Shortly before that lecture Rick was taken seriously ill with appendicitis and had to undergo emergency surgery. He told us that the irony of the situation was not lost on him. But I see that he has left this incident out of his book.[11] We shall never make real progress in this way.

The Philippine Healers

The Philippine healers are a group of alleged psychic healers, who practise chiefly in the neighbourhood of Manila in the Philippine Islands. These men (and only one or two women) do not merely practise the laying-on of hands. They allegedly actually operate on their patients, using not the techniques of modern surgery, however, but very powerful psychic forces flowing through them from the 'other side'. On the 'other side' are, allegedly, numbers of former surgeons and doctors, now dead and co-operating in spirit with the healer.

Taking first the most extreme claims of the Philippine healers, it is alleged that using only their bare hands (plus psychic power) they literally split open the bodies of their patients (who are fully conscious throughout) and 'remove the illness'. During this operation, a certain amount of blood, or at any rate a red liquid, flows over the patient's body and the hands of the healer — as if the body really were open. The psychic operation, incidentally, takes place in a simple peasant hut, in full view of many onlookers and without hygiene precautions of any kind. The illness which the patient brings to the psychic healer may vary from just 'pains' to actual malignant tumours, thromboses and diseased bones, which have been fully diagnosed and confirmed as existing by orthodox surgeons and doctors.

The Philippine healer, during his operations, may remove a tumour from a patient suffering from a tumour. Or, equally, he may remove a tumour from someone who is not. Tumours, pieces of liver or stomach lining are not the only objects removed. The healer may take out a six-inch nail, a leaf, a stick, a bird's nest or any of a wide variety of such objects.

These objects, it is claimed, 'symbolize' the illness or affliction. The actual illness is said to have simply gone or been transformed during the operation into the object which appears in the healer's hands. The 'evil' has been materialized into a physical object.

'Materialized' is the correct word. Apologists for the healers consider that the objects are at least apports: para-normal physical phenomena, either materialized out of thin air or psychically transported (apported) from some actual physical location on this planet, where they originally existed.

This description of the procedures of the Philippine healers will suffice. We would, naturally, be much more interested in the details if something genuine, specifically something genuinely paranormal, were going on. I am afraid it seems absolutely clear that neither anything genuine nor anything paranormal is involved.

I heard the first reports of the work of the Philippine healers with great interest. One is, naturally, always hoping for some major breakthrough. I also saw a few hundred feet of jerky and not altogether well-lit film. Though this did not arouse my active scepticism, it also did not create in me any sense of conviction. I was willing still to retain an open mind on the subject.

My first misgivings were actually aroused by Ronald Rose's excellent book, *Living Magic*. Here he has written about his investigations of psychic powers among the Australian aborigines. He confirms, for example, that many aborigines are capable of sensing the distant death of a fellow-member of their own totem group — who, incidentally, is always a blood relative on their mother's side.

He writes at length, too, on the medical practices of the aborigine. Without any intention on his part of so doing, he planted the seeds of real doubt in my mind regarding the Philippine healers.

The Australian witch doctor or 'clever man' is, for example, alleged to possess a magic snake or 'magic cord' which aids him in working his miracles. Here is one aborigine's account concerning a magic snake.

> The clever man looked closely at the boys and they could see fires burning in his eyes. 'Watch me,' he said. He lay on his back. His body gave a shiver and his mouth opened. From his mouth the boys saw a thing come forth, a live thing that was not a snake, nor was it a cord. But it looked like a cord and moved like a snake. Slowly it issued from the gaping, quivering jaws, the length of a man's finger but not so thick. It moved about on the man's face and became longer, almost as long as a man's arm. It left his mouth and crawled in the grass. Then it returned to the man's body.

Rose's research has revealed that the 'magic snake' is a fresh-water worm, a matter of inches long only, which the clever man secretes in his mouth. He produces it on appropriate occasions and even trains it to enter and leave his mouth of its own accord.

The worms are themselves 'magical' in one sense. Because they pass their infancy in the body of another water animal, they emerge into the water as full-grown adults. Thus they appear overnight in a water-hole and are never observed to grow.

The water worm/snake, known by the aborigine to have its own 'magic', is seen to be a willing ally of the clever man. He is therefore magic too. Such demonstration of magical powers by the clever man is an important and potent factor in the process of auto-suggestion, which caused the

boys to see a snake 'as long as a man's arm'. In reality, the
'snake' is only a couple of inches long. The water snake is
the Australian magical equivalent of the 'spirit doctors' of
the Philippine healers. A convincing link with the supernatural is probably an indispensable prop to the work of
both kinds of healers.

The 'clever men' of Australia also perform psychic
operations. They also 'remove' stones, bones, twigs,
porcupine quills and whatever from the bodies of their
patients. The patients themselves are absolutely convinced
that these objects have been drawn from their bodies. Rose,
however, put the question bluntly to a clever man that all
that was involved was skilful conjuring. 'Smiling, he agreed,
but immediately stressed the psychological point of view:
"They bin get better all the same." '

Unhappily, the sufferers from the West who visit the
Philippine healers do not get better all the same. A follow-
up study in connection with Mike Scott's second documentary (Granada T.V., February 1975) of a large group of
Britons who visited the Philippines for treatment of medical-
ly-confirmed illnesses conclusively demonstrated that none
of those involved improved in any way as a result, in the
sense, that is, that none of their own medical doctors were
able to detect any change, let alone any improvement.

Long before Mike Scott's documentary, ominous cracks
were appearing in the legend of the healers. Actual tumours
and other organic material allegedly removed from patients,
when examined, were found to be animal tissue. The
healers and their apologists then retracted the statement
that these were the patients' tumours. These were, after
all, also apports or materializations. It was at no time easy
for researchers to obtain specimens of allegedly removed
organic material. Apparently samples of these disappeared
magically from sealed containers (perhaps in the same way as
Puharich's tapes from outer space disappeared). It had been
observed that healers almost always operated on the stomach
and other soft areas of the body, regardless of where the
actual complaint was. It was suggested, by sceptics, that it
was far easier in such areas to give the impression of one's
fingers being actually inside the patient, which is what the

healers claimed was happening.

Mike Scott's programme has now effectively demolished the Philippine healers once and for all. Apart from the follow-up study of patients, some of the close-up camera stills show a healer with his fingers doubled, digging only his knuckles into the patient, but allegedly burying his fingers in her. During the shooting of this documentary, the agents for the healers apparently realized that they had shown too much, for they abruptly withdrew facilities and hustled the camera team out.*

Most damaging of all, perhaps, was the exposure of the myth of poverty put around by the healers and their sym-pathizers. The story was that healers took no money, or very little money indeed, from their patients. Their work was done for the love of god. They were themselves simple peasants living simple peasants' lives. They had no wish for wealth or fame.

The documentary showed the real home of one noted healer: a palatial affair, outside which were parked the healer's two new, large American cars. Both the publicity given in this documentary to the very high 'booking fees' paid by patients to agents and hotels, and the style of life that the healers enjoy, suggest overwhelmingly that the whole operation is based on the profit motive. Watching this exposure, I was reminded of the wise words of Mr Benno Schneider of the Tzabar restaurant in London: 'Where is cash money, is fiddle.' It is something always to be remembered in connection with psychical research and the paranormal.

What, however, of all the eye-witness accounts by priests, doctors and researchers (perhaps notably by Lyall Watson)

---

* A different film has also been shown on television, this time of Arigo, the Brazilian psychic healer, at work. There we saw Arigo extracting a patient's eye — without anaesthetic and without the patient experiencing any pain — which then lay on the patient's cheek at the end of the optic nerve. Later Arigo reinserted the eye. How-ever, a Western doctor, interviewed in the studio after the film, stated that the eye in his opinion could only have been a rubber demonstra-tion model — for when the real eye is removed, the optic nerve is completely floppy. In this film the nerve of the eye was stiff.

who have witnessed operations performed by the Philippine psychic healers and pronounced them genuine? I am afraid that these sometimes well-qualified and always well-intentioned people were deceived, just as a professional conjuror so readily fools us in spite of all our precautions. We see what the conjuror wants us to see. Lyall Watson and others claim to have thoroughly searched the room in which the healer worked, looking for hidden objects, and the healer, wearing only shorts, has been frisked on entering the operating room. Whether all the healer's assistants, official and unofficial, were frisked is perhaps another matter. But the Australian clever man in any case goes one better. He works completely naked.

There is one final aspect that merits comment. Many Philippine healers, like their counterparts in Brazil (notably Arigo, 'surgeon of the rusty knife') make genuine cuts in the flesh of their patients using unsterilized knives, and no anaesthetic. They perform such operations to remove cysts and other growths. The healer undoubtedly does make a genuinely deep cut, that ought to cause the patient a good deal of pain and, at least in a majority of cases, severe septic poisoning. None the less, the patients seem to feel little or no pain, and sepsis following the operation is extremely rare (though it seems doubtful that this is one hundred per cent absent in all cases).

Here, I think, we fall back on that known ability of the human body to resist injury and pain in appropriate circumstances. Nowadays not a few Westerners (for example, Jack Schwarz, whom I shall be talking of later) have mastered the knack, long known in the Middle and Far East (among the Whirling Dervishes, for instance), of inserting needles and knives into one's body, but without causing bleeding, or anything but the smallest of marks. Jan Merta can also stub cigarettes out on his tongue and hold irons red hot from the fire in his hand. Primitive peoples generally — such as the indigenous populations of the Philippines and Brazil — have these abilities to a higher degree than the majority of Westerners. I believe myself that it is not just a question of training or of received belief, but a difference in the precise structure of the nervous system. For this same reason, it appears that acupuncture works less well in the West than it obviously does in the East. Of course faith does come into the question also. It is without doubt easier for these reactions to come into play when you believe in them — but, in my opinion, 'faith' is *itself* also in part a product of the structure and nature of the nervous system.

So much for pain, and partly also for infection. But in respect of infection there is a further factor. In primitive communities, almost totally lacking the standards of care and hygiene which we have enjoyed in the West for many generations, the general population is largely immune from local infection for the simple reason that those who are not die in infancy. The Darwinian phrase 'survival of the fittest' means, in primitive communities, the survival of those with a high natural resistance to infection.

Significantly, there are very few reports indeed of Europeans and North Americans undergoing rusty-knife surgery — for all of the reasons we have been discussing.

Arigo in Brazil, like the Philippine healers, claimed to be under the influence of psychic doctors from the beyond. In his trance state he would, apparently, write hundreds of prescriptions for a stream of patients, without examining the patients first. It is claimed that his prescriptions were nevertheless always appropriate for the respective illnesses of those receiving the prescriptions.

But it seems that the prescriptions written by Arigo were indecipherable, except by his assistant, who wrote them out properly. I must confess this circumstance worries me very considerably. I am sorry once again to play the sceptic here, but it occurs to me that Arigo and his assistant could have had some simple code, whereby a particular mark on the prescription cued the assistant what drugs to prescribe on the fair copy. Alternatively, the assistant, or Arigo together with the assistant, could have had ample opportunity to observe the patients prior to the prescription session. Many, though not all, of the patients' complaints would be obvious to the eye, especially that of a trained observer. The prescriptions of Arigo might even have been quite meaningless. His assistant may have been doing the prescribing entirely off his own bat.

I know that many people will feel I am being unreasonable. After all, I was not there. How can I possibly know
what went on? Surely I am just fabricating objections, as
any sceptic can if he puts his mind to it?

Well, possibly. But two quite separate points stick in my
mind: that at the time of his death Arigo was wanted on
fraud charges; and that by far the strongest champion of his
cause in the West is Andrija Puharich.

ASTROLOGY, PALMISTRY, GRAPHOLOGY

At around the age of twelve I was taken one Christmas time
to a large West End department store in London. Among the
other attractions, the store had a machine that for one penny
issued a card describing your character, as based on your
birth sign.

This printed card — no doubt identical ones were issued to
all with this birth sign — impressed me enormously. It
seemed to me exactly to describe my state of mind and the
course of my life at that time. I carried the card around with
me in my wallet for several years. This was the only brush I
had with astrology in about the first twenty-five years of
my life. I felt no urge at all to pursue the subject further.
Perhaps that shows how satisfying and final was the magical
card.

Astrology enthusiasts who are familiar with my earlier
books and my theory of human personality, which divides
the psyche into two macro-units of Self and Ego, will no
doubt be further delighted to learn that my birth sign is
Gemini (the twins). As most people know, Gemini individuals are alleged to possess a double or dual personality.

Despite this promising opening to this section (promising
for astrologers, that is), my considered opinion is that the
objective value of astrology and palmistry — which I then
further divorce from graphology — is not great.

I have over the last decade and more talked to and consulted practitioners both of astrology and palmistry. I have also

sampled leading books on these subjects. Apart from other considerations, I have been, I am afraid, very unimpressed with the character-analyses and predictions obtained in respect of myself and of people well known to me. Both the books and the actual practitioners, in my own experience, go in extensively either for vague generalizations which can be twisted to fit almost anyone or any situation — or for precise statements which turn out to be wrong.

My 1977 *Prediction* diary, given to me by a friend, and compiled by leading astrologer Mary Anderson, tells me that of we Geminians some will marry this year or have success in exams. No doubt of the roughly four million Geminians in this country some will marry or have success in exams. However, I am a bit puzzled about the one-year-old babies. They are a bit young for marriage or exams, after all. The point here is — to whom exactly do these predictions apply? At what age do we begin or cease to be affected by them? One has the suspicion that astrological predictions are deliberately couched in terms appropriate only to the age-groups of people who actually take any notice of them — and so are irrelevant to young children, to the bedridden and to old people, for example.

In Alan Leo's *Practical Astrology* we learn that the eyes of Sagittarians are 'usually dark brown, though sometimes clear sky-blue'. The hair of Aries individuals is 'black or sandy'. The eyes of Librans are only 'generally blue' (so they might not be). How do these physical characteristics apply to Negroes? The key-note of Capricorns is understanding. That of Sagittarians is insight. Of Librans, it is intuition. I wonder exactly how these qualities differ? Now, admittedly, I have singled out here some of the vaguer and more overlapping descriptions. But *always* in this field there is a lack of precision. In the range of psychological characteristics given for each sign there are sure to be one or two that fit you (or that you imagine fit you!).

The best test really, which you can make for yourself, is to find another with the same birth sign, and see just how far you and that person resemble each other — or either of you a third such individual. Try guessing the birth sign of strangers — and see whether in the long run you score more

than one in twelve. Naturally, there is always the excuse
(or reason) for individual differences of the particular planets
that were in ascendance on any particular day of the month
of birth. So try guessing those too.

I once asked a well-known astrologer this question:
Suppose she were allowed to spend a month with a given
individual, during which time she could ask him or her any
question whatever, *except* his actual date of birth, would she
then at the end of the month be able to tell me that individual's birth sign? She said no, she would not.

For me, such an admission is the death-knell of astrology
as an objective or logical study — *which is what it claims to
be*. For if you cannot argue *back* from detailed outcomes to
the premises which have produced them, then the alleged
predictive value of such premises must be regarded as zero.

What astrology claims in general terms is that the juxta-
positions of the heavenly bodies (the planets and the stars)
at the precise moment of a person's birth fix and determine
the overall course of that person's life, and give rise to many
detailed character traits, predispositions, susceptibility to
certain illnesses, and general physical characteristics. That
basic proposition of the astrologer — no matter how guarded-
ly it is expressed or how much hedged around with qualifiers
and provisos — is none the less *a statement of objective fact*,
or of alleged objective fact. Therefore, although perhaps
complex, the claims of astrology must in principle be
objectively testable. Moreover, the claims then stand or fall
by the outcome of the tests.

In this connection I am very impressed with two sets of
results, though for quite different reasons in each case.

Michel Gauquelin, in France, claims to have established a
statistically significant relationship between the position of
certain planets at the time of an individual's birth and his
choice of profession in later life. We shall come to these
results in more detail shortly. It is the second set of results
obtained by Chris Evans and his research team when making
the television series 'Into the Unknown' which we consider
here. Setting out to test Gauquelin's claims, the team contacted a large sample of leading sportsmen and another large
sample of leading actors. According to Gauquelin, Mars

should have been dominant at the time of birth of a significant proportion of the sportsmen, and Jupiter similarly
dominant at the birth of the actors. Of the ninety sportsmen
who replied only twenty-six had Mars in ascendance — a
result *below* chance level. Of the eighty-nine actors who
replied only twenty-nine had Jupiter in ascendance, a result
identical with chance expectation.

It is true that Evans's samples were what we call self-
selected — that is, only those people who responded to the
initial inquiry were involved. This was not a truly random
sample therefore, and such a non-random factor can have a
material influence on an outcome. It is also true that the
samples Chris Evans used were far smaller than those of
Gauquelin. Nevertheless, when a hypothesis is strong, its
workings do tend to show up in small-scale investigations
and even in biased samples.

Despite such reasonable objections we can make to the
Evans investigation, its findings do nevertheless tend to
weigh against the Gauquelin results. This is because in
science (and we *are* talking about astrology as science) when
one survey or experiment indicates a positive result and
another a negative, we have to take the second in preference
to the first. For in science one positive result by itself does
not constitute proof — the result must first be independently
verified many times by other workers. But one negative
result does, provisionally at least, constitute a disproof,
because scientific laws admit of no exceptions. It is always
up to those who produce positive findings to explain and
accommodate negative findings — not the other way about.
This is the way of science. The ruling may seem hard — but
we must remember that science has only made progress
because of its harsh laws, sternly applied.

The objections to astrology do not rest on statistical
grounds alone.

The stars were grouped by the ancients into constellations.
These were given names according to how the rough (very
rough!) outline of the group of stars in question suggested a
figure — Capricorn, Libra, Virgo, Aquarius and so on. The
ascendancy in the sky of a particular constellation at the time
of your birth is held to be the major astrological factor

predetermining the course of your life.

Now, first there is the problem of slippage. In employing the signs of the zodiac the astrologer takes the position of the constellations as they were at the time of the Babylonians, that is, around two to three thousand years BC. But due to a gradual movement of the Earth's poles of which the ancients were not aware, the constellations are continuously slipping back. The constellations are now in the 'house' (the zodiacal sign) *before* the one to which they were originally assigned! The sign Aries, for example, almost completely corresponds to the constellation Pisces. Quite what havoc this creates in our lives the ancients, alas, are not here to tell us.

Slippage aside, the constellations are in any case meaningless groupings. Apart from the question of forcing them into outlined figures which they do not very closely resemble — the ancients in fact mis-drew the early star-maps to make the figures seem more probable — the stars in any given constellation bear no genuine relation to each other at all. I will explain what I mean. Let us look at the constellation Orion and in particular at its four brightest stars. These, in order of brightness, are known by the Greek letters Alpha, Beta, Gamma and Delta. (The first two actually have names of their own, Betelgeux and Riga, but we will stick with the Greek letters.)

First, a light year is the distance which light travels in one *year* at a rate of 186,000 miles per *second*.

The brightest star of Orion, Alpha, is 520 light years away from Earth. The second brightest star of Orion, Beta, is 900 light years away; the third, Gamma, 470 light years; and the fourth, Delta, is 1500 light years distant.

So Delta is *further away* from Alpha and Gamma than either of them is from us! That is, a greater distance separates individual stars of the alleged constellation of Orion than separates us from the nearest of those stars. In other words, if we stood on Delta looking back towards Earth, we would have more justification for assuming Earth, Alpha and Gamma to form a unit than we on Earth have justification for considering Alpha, Gamma and Delta to form a unit!! Delta is almost four times further away from us than Gamma.

Consider this already ridiculous situation from just one more point of view. Suppose we (on Earth) are standing on the rim of an enormous circle. Let us walk one quarter of the way round the circle, and then look at the constellation of Orion again. It has disappeared! It no longer exists. (*It never did.*) Its component stars are now scattered untraceably all over the star-map above us. We have now no reason at all, not even a very bad one, for linking these stars to each other in any way.

Let us now come closer to home. The effect of the ascendant constellations on us at birth is apparently modified and refined by the particular planets of the solar system which happen to be in ascendance at the time. In 1930, however, a new planet was discovered, Pluto. And Neptune was only discovered in 1846. (There is talk now of yet another planet lying beyond Pluto — one, moreover, whose orbit goes in the opposite direction to all the others.)

So the calculations of the ancients did not include the influence of Neptune and Pluto (let alone that of the putative new planet). And what *is* that influence — since the ancients are not here to tell us about it?

One last error on the part of ancient astrologers should be mentioned. They did, of course, think the sun was a planet. Actually it is a star.

From this very brief review of the 'science' of astrology we have seen that it is saturated with the ignorance and misconceptions of a pre-scientific age and with the notion of an Earch-centred universe, that is, of how the heavens look to us. The Earth is in fact nowhere near the centre of this galaxy and our particular galaxy is nowhere near the centre of the known universe. But some astrologers' views are, as we saw, more parochial still. They are Europe-centred.

On the positive side, the impressive findings of the French psychologist Michel Gauquelin have already been mentioned.* Incidentally, I met Gauquelin about a year ago and was forcibly impressed both with his integrity and modesty, and with his firm grasp of his subject matter. I do not hesitate

* *Cosmic Influences on Human Behaviour*, (Garnstone Press, London, 1974).

to take him very seriously indeed.

Gauquelin, as already stated, examined the position of various planets at the time of birth of very large numbers of famous sportsmen, actors, scientists, doctors and so on. In France and some other countries (but not in England) the time of birth is automatically recorded on the birth certificate. Gauquelin's research findings seem to show that certain professions contain significantly more individuals whose birth coincided with either the rising or the zenith of a given planet. These findings were rigorously and independently examined, and subsequently confirmed, by a committee of Belgian scientists. Professor Hans Eysenck in Britain has likewise approved the statistical model used and the results Gauquelin obtained.

Should these results stand the further tests of time, what seems a possible explanation is that the planet in question, at a certain point in relation to the horizon or the zenith, somehow triggers the moment of birth. This notion is not an unacceptable one in principle. We already know that both the moon and the sun can release pre-set behaviours in both land and sea animals. We also know that star patterns are among the items that influence the migration of birds. The difficult part to conceive is how a tiny object like a planet could come to have a direct relation with ourselves at this late stage in our evolution. Here indeed is a most formidable mystery.

Michel Gauquelin, we should note, is emphatic that his work has nothing to do with constellations of stars; while Professor Eysenck is on record as *still* saying: 'There is no doubt that much that goes on under the flag of astrology is nonsense.' Both these statements however tend to be ignored by ga-gaists, who then go on to claim triumphantly that 'astrology has been proved'. All that the findings in fact appear to show is that *rather more* of certain kinds or professions of people are associated with certain astronomical (not astrological) events at birth, involving only one or two planets, than one would expect by chance. *Many other individuals born at these same moments do not show these same tendencies*; while, equally, many others born at quite different times nevertheless *do* show them.

But still, is it not possible, now that Gauquelin has apparently come up with some hard evidence supportive of one aspect of astrological belief, that other scientists will at some point come up with further support for other aspects? The answer here has to be yes, this is indeed a possibility. However, we must not take possibilities for probabilities, and absolutely not for certainties.*

The kinds of general criticisms I have made of astrology as an objective science can still more be made of palmistry. I do not intend to undertake a detailed review of palmistry as such, but the investigative study we now look at is revealing in this respect. My own firm conviction is that astrology and palmistry do not work in the objective terms claimed for them — and on the occasions they do appear to work in those terms they are actually serving as a vehicle for clairvoyance and telepathy. Nevertheless, I think the underlying *psychic* processes in fact work better without the vehicle. So that such 'disciplines' as astrology and palmistry are not a help to paranormal processes, but a hindrance.

Norman Shealy is a neurosurgeon and Director of the Rehabilitation Centre in La Crosse in America. He decided to test the abilities of a number of psychics of various kinds in diagnosing physical illness. The phrase 'physical illness' is an important one. The La Crosse clinic specializes in the treatment of chronically ill patients with severe organic defects. All patients have a long history of illness and all have had multiple surgery, and suffer chronic pain. There is no question simply of 'psychological' or psychosomatic illness and allergies which might in some sense be open to

---

* In this present book I am, obviously, trying both to limit specula-tion to acceptable levels and to examine (for instance) astrology as it is currently purveyed and understood in twentieth-century society. But I am now working also on a further book, *Bearers of the Message*, in which I attempt to examine matters such as astrology and alchemy back in farthest time and at their point of origin. Here I follow initially the trail blazed by such recent books as Robert Temple's *The Sirius Mystery* and Geoffrey Ashe's *The Ancient Wisdom*, but then carry matters, I hope, significantly further. It is not just probable, but I think absolutely certain that mankind once had a far clearer understanding of facets of the 'alternative universe' than we find in the often garbled remnants that come down to us in present time.

doubt or to wide interpretation.

Norman Shealy chose as his psychics individuals with a firm reputation in their field of paranormal activity. These consisted of three clairvoyants, one palmist, one graphologist, one numerologist and one astrologer.

The three clairvoyants received a photograph of the patient, with his or her name and date of birth on the back, in someone else's handwriting. The astrologer and the numerologist received only the patient's name and birth date. The palmist had a palm print, with the patient's name and the date when the print was taken. The graphologist received most information of all — he had a one-page letter from the patient saying anything the patient wished, though of course giving no direct data on the illness. Two control conditions were also employed, of which more in a moment.

Each patient had, of course, actually and objectively been thoroughly diagnosed by doctors and surgeons, using every modern technique of diagnosis. Aside from these profession-al verdicts, standardized medical/psychological questionnaires were also completed in respect of each patient. The result was a detailed, reliable and also standardized medical descrip-tion of the patient's condition. This was the base-line against which the diagnoses of the psychics were to be checked.

The two control tests mentioned were as follows. A Professor of Psychology, claiming no clairvoyant abilities, was given a photograph and the name and date of birth of every patient. He then wrote down what he imagined each patient might be suffering from. As a further control, a random selection by computer of patients' names was matched against a selection of random diagnoses. Such procedure yielded results purely dependent on chance.

In giving their diagnosis of each patient, the various clair-voyants (and the Professor) completed a standardized questionnaire. It was established that the chance level of scoring on this questionnaire — the extent to which one could be correct by accident — was twenty-five per cent.

The results of this study are striking. The Professor of Psychology scored at slightly *below* chance level, proving his claim that he had no psychic abilities. The *average* score of all the psychics was sixty per cent correct replies

— a result more than twice as good as chance expectation. The highest scores were achieved by the three clairvoyants: eighty per cent correct answers. This result is more than three times better than chance and very highly significant in statistical terms.

The graphologist did least well of all the psychics. His low scores are important — because he had most information about the patient and *because he was working under his normal conditions.* All that a graphologist usually ever sees is a sample of his client's handwriting. Certainly palmists and as a rule other types of clairvoyant also see their clients face to face and, deliberately or otherwise, can gain a great deal of information about them from their appearance and demeanour. In this study the other psychics apart from the graphologist were therefore working at some disadvantage.

To summarize: of all, the three clairvoyants had the best scores, the graphologist the worst, with the astrologer, palmist and numerologist falling between. For me, the fact that the astrologer, palmist and numerologist did less well than the three clairvoyants is significant. For the first three are supposed to be dealing in hard 'fact'. The palmist had a palm print: on the palm is supposed to be 'written' your past and future. The astrologer knew the time of birth: at that time your fate is supposed to be 'written' in the heavens. The values of the letters of your name predetermine your fate in numerology. The clairvoyants, working on thin air so to speak, nevertheless produced the best results. And, of course, the trained specialist in human affairs, the psychologist, got nowhere at all.

I see these results first as a vindication of the existence of psychic abilities. I also see them as a criticism of the 'factually' front-loaded professions of astrology and palmistry. These have most 'information' up-front, the allegedly most solid basis on which to build, and yet they were bested by the free-floating clairvoyants. Finally, I myself see in this study evidence that graphology in particular is not really a paranormal or psychic activity.

We ought to add a word here in praise of Norman Shealy. He applied the scientific method to his psychics, without seriously limiting them and without imposing any conditions on their method of working. They were allowed to complete the questionnaires at their own speed when they felt inclined to do so. Nobody watched over them while they worked. The design of the experiment was such that cheating was extremely difficult (the clinic patients were not from the psychics' locality) although perhaps not impossible.

My firm conviction is that the charts and diagrams of astrology and palmistry (these coloured beads for gullible natives) are not only nonsensical in themselves, but that they act as a barrier to the exercise of the psychic faculty. The paraphernalia of such 'disciplines' are pseudo-scientific props for those not brave enough to accept the paranormal on its own a-scientific and objectively baffling terms.

SYNCHRONICITY AND COINCIDENCE

In a recent pilot television programme designed to test the limits of intelligence, the names of the three contestants were Hartston, Burton and Walkington. All three end in -ton, and all three are names of towns — except for one letter (Harston *is* a town.) The contestants were not of course chosen because of their names but because each of them had done extremely well in similar competitions on previous occasions.

The press recently carried a story of two men driving their cars in an out-of-the-way part of the countryside. Theirs were the only two cars in the area, yet they contrived to crash into each other. The two men were also complete strangers to each other, but each had the same surname and Christian name.

Once in the Middle East I was asked by a hippie with whom I got into conversation if I would ring his family when I got back to England and tell them he was all right. The telephone number he gave me was the same as my own, and the telephone exchange the one immediately adjacent to mine.

These items are three examples of what we call coincidence.

They do not signify anything. In respect of such happenings we often prefix the word coincidence with the word 'meaningless' — we say 'a meaningless coincidence'.

It is perhaps not generally appreciated that before ever we approach the paranormal as such, we find Freud using the opposite expression, 'a meaning*ful* coincidence', in respect both of normal and neurotic individuals. The Freudian 'meaningful coincidence' is also known as the Freudian slip or motivated error. Examples are, briefly, as follows.

A man arranges a non-urgent business trip for a particular day. Later he realizes that the day he has arranged to be away is the anniversary of his wedding. A wife telephones her husband — but discovers she has dialled the number of a former boyfriend instead. A father, sending his absent son a cheque as a Christmas present, omits to sign it.

In Freud's view these are not genuine errors or accidents. They are motivated by unconscious desires and resentments, consciously denied expression but nevertheless finding it. The Freudian 'motivated error' is, as we shall see, possibly not entirely unconnected with the meaningful coincidences of the paranormal.

It is with Jung that the notion of the meaningful coincidence is applied to the paranormal and raised to the status of a general theory of the paranormal. He calls his general theory 'synchronicity'.

Jung believed that we require three levels of explanation for the clustering or coming-together of events. First we have meaningless coincidences. These are fortuitous or chance hits. Inevitably, two or more people coming together in chance circumstances will occasionally be found to have the same name. If that were to be otherwise, there would have to exist some natural force that kept people of the same name from crossing each other's paths. There is, of course, no such force. For similar reasons a seven occasionally meets another seven. Or a factory produces, say, ten thousand dresses of a particular design. It therefore happens that once in a while two young ladies, quite independently, turn up at a party wearing identical dresses.

Depending on the precise circumstances, coincidence can sometimes be a very striking or astonishing business. In fact we have the phrase 'the long arm of coincidence' in recognition of that truth. Jung, who I believe never studied the behaviour of the roulette wheel, would perhaps have been surprised to learn that chance events with odds against them of 95,000,000,000 to 1 do observably take place there (see 'How to Get Rid of Statistics', pp.151–67). At any rate, it can be generally agreed that accidental coincidences and correspondences of quite a high statistical improbability do nevertheless occur and that we require no special explanation for them.

At the other end of the scale from coincidence, so to speak, we have causality. Causality is the principle deriving from or underlying the sequence of cause and effect. It is causality that underpins the endless chains of events and the consequences of events that in totality make up the visible universe. So a pulled trigger causes a gun to fire; as a result a bullet emerges and enters the chest of a man; as a consequence of its doing so the man dies. Here we see a simple chain of cause and effect.

Scientists (physicists, chemists, biologists, mathematicians) through careful study of the events of the physical universe, understand a large number of the causes which lead to a large number of the effects. By carefully controlling these causes, they can produce given events to order. 'To order' means *one hundred per cent of the time*, with *one hundred per cent accuracy* and reliability. At least as far as such localized or non-Einsteinian fields of events are concerned, say, the events on this planet, nature *never* cheats on the laws of cause and effect. Cause(s) ABC *always* produce effect(s) DEF.

It seemed to Jung, however, as it seemed to some others before him, that there was a third class of groupings of events which were not mere coincidence, and yet were not causally linked either. He states: 'The connection of events may in certain circumstances be other than causal and require another principle of explanation.'

Following Jung, I myself, along with other serious thinkers on the paranormal today (Arthur Koestler, for example), accept the idea of three principles of explanation for the connecting of events, namely, coincidence, synchronicity and causality. The main body of modern science, it must be emphasized, still recognizes only the first and last of these.

The normal word *'synchronous'* when applied to two events means that both events take place at the same time. Hence the command given in novels to individuals about to embark together on a hazardous mission where timing is important — 'synchronize your watches'.

With the paranormal we find that meaningfully-related events are not necessarily *synchronous.* Jung, for example, quotes a case known to him personally where it was established that the death of a friend at 1 a.m. was experienced, in a detailed dream, by another friend at 2 a.m. The vision here occurred after the event. However, what to us is still more impressive are the occasions when an event is seen or experienced *before* it happens (as with the dreams of the horses winning their races — see pp.66–9). As Jung puts it, we experience this coming event 'as though it already existed'. It is however not *synchronous* with our experience of it, because its actuality and ours are, in fact, at different points on the normal time scale. Yet, clearly, the two *are* in some way meaningfully linked — are, in a sense, the same event. Jung says in such cases that the events are *synchronistic* with each other. Synchronistic events are events which can be seen logically and meaningfully to belong together; yet they are separated in serial time as well, of course, as by space.

To understand how events separated by time might nevertheless touch each other, we first make an analogy with a strictly spatial situation. Subsequently we will take the further step of considering time as a dimension — a fourth dimension additional to the three dimensions of normal space.

If I take a piece of paper and write the letter 'a' in the top right-hand corner and the letter 'b' in the bottom right-hand corner, these two 'events' (the two letters) are separated by the length of the paper. But if I now fold the paper in two from bottom to top, the two originally separate letters touch each other. They are fully adjacent.

Turning to time, if we think of it as a further extension of space, then two events separated in time can be brought together by folding time just as I folded the paper.

The analogy is an attractive one, not least by its neat way of presenting simply a difficult concept. But I think we cannot without further ado take time to be simply a further extension of space (more of this in Chapters 4 onwards). While still retaining the idea of folding time as a very useful one, I myself am inclined to look at the position through a different analogy.

A theoretical, and at the same time eminently practical, movement in psychology was one known as Gestalt psychology. 'Gestalt' is the German word for a figure or pattern. Gestalt psychology argued (argues, in fact — for it still has its active supporters) that we tend to see phenomena not as isolated events, but always in terms of meaningful patterns. A picture therefore is not just several square inches of red and several square inches of blue. Still less is it a series of marks on a piece of paper — it is a *picture*. It presents itself to us as an organized, three-dimensional whole, in its totality, at once and at first sight. (Yet it *is* only marks on a piece of paper!)

It probably seems a truism to say that a picture looks like a picture. But in fact we also tend almost equally to see meaningful pictures where, in actuality, there are none at all. The 'shapeless shapes' of the Rorschach inkblot test are good examples. Everyone sees pictures in them — and everyone sees different pictures. But in fact the inkblots really are just that — random blobs. Our strong tendency to 'organize' all incoming information is a built-in property of our nervous system. We are 'meaning-seeking' creatures, so to speak.

The general proposition of Gestalt psychology can be admirably demonstrated in respect of visual signals. It is reasonably demonstrable also in respect of some other senses like hearing and touch. It is not quite so easily demonstrated in respect of our abstract conceptual behaviour, although there is no doubt that here too a similar predisposition to organization, and moreover to certain kinds of organization, likewise exists. Some of our organizing tendencies are built in, while others we learn from our environment and culture in the course of growing up.

It is the basic notion of the *Gestalt* that I am concerned with — and I am going to use the word in a slightly broader sense even than would a Gestalt psychologist. I am concerned with 'meaningful wholes'. These might equally be patterns of shapes, or they might be sequences of events, or a series of numbers.

If, for example, I told you that the square of numbers in Figure 2 is a meaningful or logical one, and asked you to supply the missing element, you would have little difficulty in producing 6.

2	4	
8	10	12
14	16	18

FIGURE 2

Similarly, you could readily supply the missing element in the equation $3 \times 3 \times ? \times 3 = 81$.

These are very simple and straightforward examples. But the power we possess to 'examine', instantaneously, also very large and even very-hard-to-define groups of events is rather surprising. Some individuals are better at it than others, of course. But all of us have had the personal experience to know, without necessarily being able to put our finger on quite why, that some particular situation is 'wrong', 'not quite right', 'fishy' and so on. Pressed for our reasons we may say: 'Tom wouldn't have said that'; 'She would have telephoned'; 'Not at that time of night', and so on. Somehow we are able to review several years of a relationship, and a whole complex of variables (at least some of which are completely new to us, in respect of the situation with which we have just been presented), and say, 'No, this isn't right.' Of course, our hunches or intuitive judgments on these occasions are not always correct. *But they are correct far more often than chance alone allows.*

Looking at *part* of a macro-Gestalt of this kind, as well as at *part* of the mini-Gestalts of a simple equation, we are able to fill in the gaps — to see what is not actually present. We are able to generate the wholes from a knowledge of some of the parts. This ability is, I suggest, more an attribute of the unconscious than of the conscious mind.

It is perhaps not too hard to understand the ability to grasp Gestalts when we confine ourselves to the three conventional dimensions of normal space and the normal events of everyday life. But suppose our ability, at the unconscious level, extends *also* into time. Or suppose, putting it another way, that we can generate 'fourth-dimensional' (= time) aspects of a multi-dimensional Gestalt (= space) purely by reference to aspects of it existing in three dimensions. Suppose, as a further possibility, that quite apart from the Gestalts we generate in and through our nervous system there *really are* Gestalts in the universe. Organisms, after all, have Gestalt-forming tendencies — and *they* are both a part of the universe and a product of it. So perhaps Gestalt-generation is somehow a general property in or of all events of many kinds.

I must say that I would still be very hesitant to put forward this last suggestion — were it not for one thing. That is the existence of the Chinese *I Ching*, the Book of Changes.

It would seem very much that the authors of this altogether remarkable book somehow succeeded in identifying the 'Gestalts' of the macro-universe of events. And it seems, equally, that these Gestalts do extend into what we call the future; for I have myself for many years used the *I Ching* to chart the future, with an astonishing degree of accuracy in detail, and will report this a little later.

There are two separate points I would like to make in concluding this section.

One is that the attempts of Jung and others to produce statistical odds against chance (in respect of paranormal events) that will dumbfound the sceptic — and described in Jung's essay on *Synchronicity*[55] — are mainly failures. Observation of the roulette wheel (for details see again the section 'How to Get Rid of Statistics') shows that chance events of the order of 37^6 (that is, around 95,000,000,000) are perfectly possible.

(However, when we concentrate on the *meaning* of events

as opposed simply to the incidence of events, we do break through what I shall refer to as the chance-barrier completely. A simple example suffices to demonstrate the point. The odds against any eight letters on this printed page occurring in the sequence that they do is well in excess of 26^8 — well in excess, because the chances of individual letters occurring in the English language are not in fact equal. This figure is in turn in excess of 37^6, which, as I will later demonstrate, looks like approaching the highest level of 'significance' produceable *by chance*. In fact, the odds against the letters just of the sentence I am writing at this moment occurring in the order they do by chance is a simply-frightful 26^{120}. This number written in full would itself occupy many lines of this page.)

My second point is by way of being two footnotes for the interest of the statistician.

A good many years of watching many kinds of games of chance has left me with the strong suspicion that the types and extent of coincidental runs of consecutive numbers, or suites, or colours, are to an extent dependent on the circumstances they arise in. To take a simple case, the notches in a roulette wheel alternate red and black around the edge of the wheel. There are eighteen black notches and eighteen red notches (ignoring the zero). Therefore the chances of either a red or black being produced on any one spin of the wheel are even — a straight fifty—fifty. The chances of a coin spun in the air landing either heads or tails are also exactly fifty—fifty. Yet my suspicion is that the chances of a *consecutive* run of, say, reds differs from the chances of a *consecutive* run of, say, tails. There are no grounds in statistical theory for such an assumption. But my feelings in this matter are, I know, shared by a large number of gamblers. Perhaps it is only our superstition — but perhaps not.

The second footnote is a completely valid one. What statisticians cannot forecast — and statistics makes no provision for this — is the point (or points) at which consecutive runs of a particular event, although still *theoretically* possible, *will never ever be observed to occur in actual practice.* This important issue is dealt with in the later section on statistics.

It seems possible, then, that the statistician does not yet even fully understand the principles of chance — much less the principles of paranormality and of meaning.

ESP IN ANIMALS

The question of whether animals are influenced by and/or generate psychic phenomena is important for several reasons. First, perhaps, the animals themselves have no interest in perpetrating fraud (although, of course, an owner might have).   In general they do not have any concept of fraud (though in this case see Appendix II) nor any at all of the miraculous.   In this sense at least we can trust their reactions.

Second, and still more significantly, the demonstration that animals receive and emit psychic influences is of considerable importance in considering the physiology and evolution of ESP. Not only is ESP not something that man alone has evolved, and no other creature, but *we can therefore be fairly sure that the main seat of ESP is not in any part of man's more recently-evolved nervous system.* Probably, therefore, it is *not* located in the cerebral cortex.

I think, too, that the demonstration of ESP in an animal context creates a problem for the more conventionally religious person who thinks that psychic phenomena are evidence of man's special relation with god.   If psychic phenomena indicate 'soul' (or spirituality), especially a soul which survives the death of the body, then animals, including insects, have souls and spirituality too. For they have ESP.

We saw instances in Chapter 2 of animals reacting at considerable distances to the unexpected homecoming of their owners. The literature is actually stacked with authenticated cases.   These already demonstrate that animals *are* involved in paranormal activities. There are many further cases on record of pets (principally dogs and cats) reacting to the distant death of an owner, not known to anyone else locally at the time.

Mention must also be made of numerous and extensively authenticated cases of pets, who are accidentally or deliberately left behind when owners move, finding their way, unaided, sometimes across thousands of miles of territory, to the new home. An especially well-known case is that of Prince, an Irish terrier, who found his way from London across the Channel to his master in the trenches in France during the First World War. Equally famous, by reason of the endorsed details of the route taken by the dog, and her apparent sense of purpose, is the story of a young collie bitch, Bobbie, who found her way over several thousand miles from Indiana to Oregon, practically from one side of America to the other.[30, 85]

A further form of this behaviour (technically known as psi-trailing) involves similar journeys, but here the animal is returning to a *former* distant home in order to give birth to a litter. These cases effectively establish the total independence of animal ESP from human ESP — for the animal is currently living with its owners in the new home, and goes away from them back to where the owners once lived, but now no longer live.

One or two writers give instances where an animal removes its young from one place to another (distant) place — and the first place is then destroyed by fire or natural disaster.[8]

Though there are only a few stories of such spontaneous *precognition* in animals, they are, rather surprisingly, supported by a fair amount of experimental evidence. I am no kind of enthusiast for the application of the experimental method to the paranormal. (With respect to the truly paranormal you may get positive results by an experimental approach on the first or second occasion. But you do not get them repeatedly.) Nevertheless, in the case of experiments involving animals placed in danger, the results are rather interesting.

Pierre Duval and Evelyn Montredon placed single mice in a situation where they were randomly electrically shocked in one half of their cage or the other; the cage was divided by a climbable partition. There is of course no way of 'solving' a random pattern of events of this kind. You are shocked *exactly* as often if you stay in one place as if you move

around — namely, fifty per cent of the time. The experimenters considered only those moves of the animal where
it moved, without having last been shocked in its present
position, back into the side where it *had* last been shocked.
One would not ordinarily expect an animal to move back
into the area of its last bad experience. But even given that
it does so, then it should, as a result, still get shocked fifty
per cent of the time — neither more nor less often than
chance demands. *For no normal evasive action can avoid
the consequences of a random pattern.*

In fact, however, in 612 of such trials the mice avoided
shock on fifty-three more occasions than chance demands.
This result is highly significant statistically. The experimenters conclude that the mice had some paranormal
knowledge of where the next shock would occur.[19]

Robert Morris has conducted other experiments.[70]

Rats are known to become less active when threatened. A
number of experimental rats were rated on their degree of
activity. *Then* only, a random sampling process determined
which of the rats were to be killed. The rats that were subsequently randomly chosen for sacrifice were those with the
lowest activity ratings.

Unlike rats, goldfish become *more* active when threatened.
Three goldfish in a tank were observed for a one-minute
period and rated on their degree of activity. Then a randomi-
zation procedure arbitrarily selected one of the fish to be
briefly lifted out of the water — a traumatic experience for a
goldfish. Over a large number of trials, the most active
individual of the three at any one time proved significantly
often to be the fish that was next to be extracted.

In general animals can be shown, experimentally, to have
little concept of the 'future'. They live very much in the
immediate present. Nevertheless, field observation and actual
experiment both suggest that, in addition to paranormal
communication at a distance in the present, animals occasionally have paranormal anticipation of danger, that is, paranormal knowledge of the future.

An interesting question which does not seem to get asked
very often is whether animals can create or experience
physical phenomena (see pp.142—51). Some psychic

researchers have, nevertheless, asked it and attempted to test the proposition experimentally. Evidence has been obtained in a number of experiments that cats, lizards, cockroaches and other organisms can apparently influence the action of a random number generator. They apparently cause an increase or decrease in the number of 'on' or 'off' positions of the generator. When tested both before and after the experiments, the machine produces exactly the same number of 'ons' as 'offs', which is precisely what it is designed to do. These results being as they are — there are nevertheless no reports at all of 'poltergeist' phenomena occurring in connection with animals.

Affinities with Animals

Brenda Marshall believes that psychic individuals have a greater than usual affinity with animals — including insects! A good many people, and I myself, agree with her. Mrs Marshall's insect story concerns a cockroach, whose life she and her husband spared. Thereafter it would come from the bathroom, down a long corridor into the room, and up her husband's chair, to sit by him on the arm of the chair. Mrs Marshall writes: 'During the remainder of our stay in the flat the cockroach would often join us on quiet evenings, a somewhat embarrassing third.'

One experience of my own concerned a female orangutan. I was visiting the zoo in Jersey in the Channel Islands. The orang got up from her place in the middle of the cage, took a handful of straw, and reached out as far as she could through the bars across the little ditch to give it to me. (Perhaps she knew that in the third part of my *Total Man* trilogy I was announcing that man is more closely related to the gibbon and the orang than to the chimpanzee and the gorilla!) There were, incidentally, a number of other people around at the time of this event and it was actually witnessed by Mrs Lort Philips. Brenda Marshall's husband had a very similar experience to mine. When he visited a monkey reserve in Brazil, a large female monkey darted to the back of the cage and returned with a handful of rice, which she offered him through the bars.

Two especially impressive stories, one of them very moving, offer further evidence of close affinity between man and animal. In these stories we *need* not invoke the paranormal in explanation, in the sense that they do not violate the laws of time and space. But the account that follows these, at the end of the section, as well as yet other accounts, argues strongly that the paranormal is in fact involved throughout.

An already full-grown dog, a half-breed retriever, was given as a present to an old farmer living near Maidstone, in England. In the next three years the farmer and the dog became inseparable companions.

One morning the farmer did not get up and the farmer's son came upstairs to find out why. The farmer said he did not think he would be getting up any more and asked for his dog to be brought up to see him for a last time. The son thought the old man was just being foolish and argued with him. But in the end the dog was brought. It first jumped on the bed and nuzzled the old man affectionately. Then it retreated into the corner of the room and began to howl. It was taken away, petted and comforted, but it would not cease its howling. It then went away to its kennel, and died there at 9.30 that evening. The farmer himself died half an hour later.[24]

A woman twenty years of age had a young brother of only two years old. The family also had a young dog, which was the constant companion of the woman and the young brother she looked after. One day the boy, playing in the living room as usual, fell over the carpet. He was picked up, comforted, and the fuss was as usual soon over. Later during the evening meal the family noticed that the boy was using his left hand to eat instead of his right. They massaged the child's right arm with alcohol. The boy, however, made no complaint about the arm, so the family still assumed that nothing serious was amiss. The baby was set back at the table to finish his meal.

Now, however, the dog approached the boy's chair and began howling in an odd, plaintive manner. It was then shut in the next room, where it continued to howl. Then they put the dog out in the garden. Now he took up his position under the window of the baby's bedroom and continued as ever with the noise. The howling went on all evening, despite the dog's being chastized and attempts made to shoo him away from the house. The baby died at 1 a.m. The dog abruptly ceased the behaviour he never showed before or after.[7]

There are a great many stories of this kind on record, both from the past and from reliable sources in the present. In trying to explain them we need not absolutely assume the working of the paranormal. On the contrary, if these stories stood alone, we would be justified in looking for some normal, though unusual, explanation. But the stories we have considered already in Chapter 2 argue conclusively for a paranormal factor here.

The general 'affinity' (whatever that means) of at least some psychics with animals in general is scarcely to be doubted. My own experience of visiting homes with a particularly surly dog or a notoriously shy cat is that the animal will often immediately come and jump on my lap. 'He *never* does that,' says the astonished owner. This minor gift of my own pales beside the well-documented powers of many mystics. Renée Haynes has drawn attention to the many historical figures (such as St Francis of Assissi and King Solomon) who apparently possessed marked abilities in attracting the friendship of *wild* animals. She cites especially the case of St Hugh of Lincoln.

Unlike some of the individuals who display the gift of establishing rapport with wild animals, St Hugh was not a hermit or a recluse, living a solitary life away from the haunts of men. He was a busy individual, actively involved in the affairs of the world. Frequently he took long journeys away from his residence. But whenever he was on his way back (and often no one otherwise knew this) the 'fierce, wild swan' flew around the gates of the palace at Lincoln, announcing his coming. The ungentle swan not only waited excitedly at the gates for St Hugh, 'but would not be parted from him when he came, plunging its head into his wide sleeves, as if it were drinking cool water'.[48]

This case of the wild swan that, like the kennelled dogs of Dr Tarver, knew that its human companion was once more on his way home, and had no possible normal way of knowing this, places all the instances of affinity between man and animal we have discussed rather firmly in the realm of the paranormal.

PHYSICAL PHENOMENA

I have to go on record as *not* being completely persuaded that so-called 'physical phenomena' exist — certainly not as far as the materialization of objects out of thin air, apports and levitation are concerned.

As I have said in earlier chapters, frequent, reliable testimony from others concerning particular phenomena can and should carry us forward to a state of open-mindedness, a state of being willing to concede that a particular phenomenon might be genuine. Yet, in the final analysis, we must always fall back on our own personal experience of a type of event as the only reliable touchstone. Even then, we still have to be careful, because it is possible for us to deceive ourselves or, through ignorance, to misinterpret an event. With that proviso, personal experience always remains the only sound basis for the acceptance or rejection of phenomena.

My own experience of physical phenomena, I regret to say, has been inconclusive.

First I had better attempt a definition of what constitutes a physical event, in the paranormal sense. Perhaps the simplest definition is that the occurrence of a truly paranormal physical event — such as a materialization — demands the violation of one of the most basic laws of physics, the Law of Conservation of Matter (more usually called, since Einstein, the Law of Conservation of Mass—Energy). This law states that matter can neither be created nor destroyed *except* in the presence of the loss, or creation, of very large amounts of *energy*. A small amount of matter is actually 'destroyed' when an atom bomb explodes, releasing an enormous quantity of energy. In a conventional explosion matter is simply converted into other forms of matter. In the nuclear explosion some matter absolutely ceases to exist and is converted into energy. The amount of energy produced exactly corresponds to the amount of matter 'lost' and a very *small* quantity of destroyed matter produces a very *large* quantity of energy. The reverse of this statement is equally true. A colossal amount of energy is involved in the creation of matter, at the heart of the sun, for instance.

The claims of paranormalists in respect of most paranormal physical events cheerfully violate the Law of Conservation of Mass—Energy in a number of ways. However, not all need do so, as we shall see. It is claimed, for example, that objects — quite large and heavy objects — can move or be moved without anyone physically touching them, and without any known force (such as gravity or electricity) acting upon them. A similar claim states that objects — chiefly metal, but not necessarily — can bend or warp, also without the forces being applied that are normally required for such effects. More extremely still, it is also maintained that physical substances can materialize out of thin air in the presence of certain mediumistic individuals. These are what the Spiritualist terms 'apports'.

Digressing just for a moment, the question of apports opens up a very interesting line of inquiry. If the alleged apport is, say, a saucepan — well, one saucepan is much like another, and there is no way really of establishing whether there is now one more saucepan in the world than before; or whether, conversely, the saucepan has been 'brought' paranormally (the French word *apporter* means to bring) from some spot many miles or hundreds of miles away; or whether the medium's assistant merely brought it in under his coat earlier in the evening. However, when the apport is, say, a bank-note or a revolver, the object carries on it a serial number. In theory at least, it is therefore possible to establish whether there are now two bank-notes, or two revolvers in existence bearing the same serial number; or whether, conversely, some distant stranger is now inexplicably minus one of his bank-notes or his gun. It is an interesting statistic that the very, very large majority of allegedly apported objects do *not* carry a serial number. Uri Geller and Andrija Puharich once allegedly apported a bank-note. That was perhaps not very fortunate for them, and we come to this particular event later (pp.148—50).

Turning to my own personal experience of the possibly physical paranormal, it is as follows.

In the days of my stay in Coventry (see Chapter 1) Peter had often talked to me about physical phenomena. The first time we discussed the subject we were sitting on a settee in the drawing room of his parents' house. During the conversation, a solitary book that had been on the centre table fell to the floor. (As chance would have it, the book was Joan Grant's *Time Out of Mind*.) 'There you are!' said Peter. He had just been telling me that objects frequently moved around the house. I, however, was not too impressed. The book had been near the edge of the table. And although this was a quiet road, with no cars passing at the time, there is such a thing as vibration. (My flat in Hampstead, for example, vibrates very slightly in response to the traffic in the Finchley Road, two or three hundred yards away. It is said that devices linked to a particle accelerator in Switzerland can detect waves breaking on the shores of the Bay of Biscay.) On another occasion, seated again in Peter's drawing room, and again discussing physical phenomena, a number of coats slid off the back of the drawing room door. Well, coats do slide off doors sometimes. Peter laughed uproariously at my disbelief.

What of the tingling sensations I experienced at the seances in Coventry? These were real enough, but I could certainly accept that they were possibly only a physiological by-product of my own psychological state. However, there is some slightly stronger back-up evidence on this score.

Many years later I met Jan Merta, as described in Chapter 3. He is said to be a powerful physical medium. I was not aware of this fact at the time I met him. It will be remembered that prior to his arrival at Simmona de Serdici's house that afternoon, I had succeeded in giving paranormally a description of some aspects of his appearance and current life style.

Now he actually arrived, and a few of us sat discussing various paranormal events. One of those present (Brendan O'Reagan) had been part of the team that investigated Geller at Stanford University in America. He was telling us that the tests on Geller had been dramatically successful, but that the team was having trouble getting the results published in respectable journals. But almost immediately Jan and I instead began an argument about the nature of physics. It is clear (looking back on it) that each of us, although we were total strangers, regarded the other as some kind of challenge. The argument soon developed into a shouting match. None of this is too important in itself. What is of interest is that the whole time we were arguing, and before the argument even began, I was aware of my muscles literally twitching and jumping all over my body. This was an experience I have never had before or since.

There is one other incident concerning Jan. On a later visit to Simmona's, he stayed two nights as house-guest. On the morning following the first night Simmona rang me in some agitation. She asked if I would be willing to come over and stay the second night. She said that during the previous night books had been falling off shelves and all kinds of bangs and noises been going on. She was sure this was due to Jan's paranormal powers, and she was worried lest things should get worse the second night.

I must say that I assumed Simmona's anxieties were those of a young lady who has a personable and forceful young man staying as house-guest, whom she does not know very well. At any rate, I agreed to come over. That night I slept downstairs in what is normally the lounge, while Jan slept upstairs in the guest room as before. During the night (which from everyone else's point of view was totally uneventful) I was wakened from dreamless sleep by an almighty crash on the door of the lounge. I sat bolt upright, thoughts racing, straining my ears for the slightest further sound. Was it Jan playing a joke (though he knew nothing of Simmona's fears, incidentally)? Had some late-night reveller banged the *front* door of the house in passing, only a yard or two away from the lounge door? There was, however, total silence in the house and outside in the street.

Or had I in fact had an *auditory* hallucination, similar to the visual hallucinations I frequently have, as described earlier (p.73)? If so, this was the only auditory 'night-vision' I have ever had — although I do sometimes hear 'voices' and other psychic sounds under normal waking conditions. The paranormal production of sounds *audible to others* and not just to oneself is, incidentally, considered to be a physical phenomenon also.

I have already described Marcel Vogel's astonishing demonstration of mental mediumship at the May Lectures. Subsequently, I was invited to attend a select seminar of two or three dozen people, where Marcel Vogel (among others) addressed us. I was now sitting some ten or twenty feet from him, as opposed to thirty or forty yards on the previous occasion. Now, as I looked at him, it was as if someone was placing the heel of his hand on my forehead and forcing my head down to one side. This condition persisted intermittently through most of Vogel's talk. It is tempting to think of a 'beam' of energy passing from him to myself — roughly from 'third eye' to 'third eye'. Like myself, incidentally, Vogel attaches very considerable importance to the third eye (the pineal gland), which though sited internally is said to 'see' through the forehead. Vogel actually believes that he projects his psychic energy out through this 'eye'.

One final event. I had at one point been given a pendulum by Simmona (a piece of natural crystalline stone suspended from a thread). Some psychics claim to be able, variously, to diagnose illness, to locate water, to obtain accurate yes/no answers to questions, simply by observing the movement of the pendulum as it hangs freely from their hand.

This particular evening I was at home watching an interview on television with the well-known psychic healer, Bruce Macmanaway. I had not been aware that he also made use of a pendulum. However, during the interview the interviewer asked Macmanaway whether he would be willing to attempt to respond to six questions, to which he could not know the answers by normal means, using the pendulum. The psychic agreed. In the event, Macmanaway got five out of the six questions right, but to his credit said that as far as he was concerned less than one hundred per cent was failure.

Now, having my own pendulum handy, it occurred to me that it would be interesting to attempt to answer the questions myself. On the first question my pendulum swung

about aimlessly. Then suddenly it 'took off'. It began
circling rapidly and in a second or two was spinning at great
speed in a full circle, parallel to the floor. The sensation was
as if the stone were trying to tear itself out of my hand.
Since I was holding tightly to the other end of the thread,
the best the stone could manage was a flat circle. I caught
the stone with my other hand and brought it once more to
the perpendicular rest position. Again it took off at once
into the flat circle. I put the stone down, and then tried
again. The performance was repeated, as it was every time
I picked the stone up. This state of affairs persisted through
the remaining twenty minutes of the broadcast. As far as I
could observe I was in no way consciously contributing to
the action of the pendulum.

Nevertheless, despite their apparently physical nature, I
am still of the opinion that all the events I have described,
barring possibly the movement of objects at Peter's house,
can adequately be described and understood as psychological
events, as much as physical ones. They might, of course, be
paranormal physical events, but I feel no compulsion to argue
that they must be. We should always accept the lesser
explanation, if it is equally good. So far, for me, my own
experiences of the physically paranormal have been only
suggestive.

We come then to the question of the evidence offered by
others.

I am greatly impressed by the fact that Jan Merta has
apparently produced paranormal physical effects to order
and under controlled conditions. Full accounts of these
matters are given in Nicholas Regush's book *Exploring the
Human Aura* and elsewhere. Briefly, Jan is said to be able
to cause a feather sealed in an airtight jar to move at will
and, of course, from a distance.

I have not seen this demonstration, nor any other of Jan's
physical demonstrations — though he has convincingly
demonstrated his mental mediumship to me (see p.81). My
willingness to entertain the idea that Jan's physical mediumship is genuine rests mainly on the fact that he tells me it is.
Naturally, this does not itself constitute final proof, neither
to me nor to anyone else. But I consider, having got to know

Jan better, that he would be *unlikely* to lie on these or other matters. I cannot say the same, I am afraid, for many other psychics of my acquaintance.

The question of the character of the individual claiming to be able to produce paranormal phenomena is a very important one. In all our doings with our fellow-men we take past record and general performance into account. This is why we ask for testimonials, character references, curricula vitae, and so on. In our affairs we soon cease to lend money to people who do not pay it back, and soon refuse to believe at all people who habitually tell lies.

In no way must we lower these general standards with respect to the paranormal.

Conversely, just as we trust someone in a particular matter who has proved trustworthy in general — so the good character of a person in areas outside the paranormal can, cautiously, be taken into account when assessing any paranormal claims he makes. Nevertheless, human leopards *do* sometimes change their spots, for the strangest of reasons — and previous good character can be no kind of final proof of the validity of paranormal claims.

In the case of Uri Geller, who above all others at this time is treated as the master exponent of paranormal physical phenomena, we have every reason to doubt his alleged abilities. He was for many years a stage illusionist in Israel. He left Israel after his psychic claims had been exposed by other illusionists and by some of his assistants, at which point Israeli audiences lost interest in him. A full account of these events is given by H. C. Behrendt, Chairman of the Israeli Parapsychology Society.[2, 3]

An alleged paranormal physical event reported by Geller/ Puharich in 1973 deserves special mention. This event attracted the notice of G. L. Playfair, who wrote up his connection with the matter in a letter to the *New Scientist*. It involves a bank-note.

Playfair was initially struck by a remark made by Geller in an interview given to *Psychic* magazine in June 1973. These are Geller's words.

One experiment I did with Andrija Puharich was when
he asked me to go to Brazil out of the body. I got to
this city and asked a person where I was and he told me
it was Rio de Janeiro. Then someone came up to me
and pressed a brand new one-thousand cruzeiro note in
my hand on the couch by Andrija — to prove I was
there.

Mr Playfair (who lives in Sâo Paulo) was impressed by this
story, but not for reasons that would flatter Geller — one of
them being that 1000-cruzeiro notes were no longer in
circulation in 1973; they were withdrawn or overprinted with
larger values in 1967. Mr Playfair also remarks that people in
Rio do not give money to strangers, though they often
relieve them of it. Still, we could perhaps accept this aspect
as a part of the trance-work (see pp.78—82) — we do not need
to consider that all the events of the experience Geller
reports objectively happened.

Replying to a letter from Mr Playfair, published in
Psychic, Puharich obligingly gave the serial number of the
note. Mr Playfair checked on this and found that the note in
question had probably gone into circulation in 1963 — the
note was shipped to Brazil from the printers in April 1963.

Notes in circulation do not of course remain new and
unhandled for very long.

Playfair wrote to Puharich, asking if he could have the
note in question for finger-print testing. New notes retain
finger impressions. The finger prints of all Brazilians, as it
happens, are on file. Therefore, if the note was genuinely
given to Geller by a real person, it might prove possible to
discover who this person actually was.

Playfair received no reply to this or subsequent letters,
either from Puharich or from *Psychic*.

Again as it happens, Puharich himself had visited Brazil
in 1963. A 1000-cruzeiro note was then worth about fifty
American cents. The kind of item, perhaps, one might well
keep as a souvenir.

The incident of the cruzeiro note is not mentioned in
Puharich's book on Geller. Playfair leaves us to form our
own conclusions. It is not difficult to draw them.[75]

As I suggested earlier, my opinion is that the only sensible thing to do is to strike every single one of Geller's and Puharich's claims from the record. In saying this I am not saying categorically that no single incident involving either of these men was genuinely paranormal — how could I presume to do that? What I am saying is that we have no way of knowing which events, if any, those might be.

Fortunately, we do have a good deal of reliable material from other sources on most aspects of the paranormal — although, unfortunately, very little that is reliable in respect of the more surprising forms of physical phenomena.

There is, as most people know, the case of D. D. Home, a medium who died in 1886. He is alleged, among many other startling things, to have levitated himself paranormally off the ground on numbers of occasions in the presence of numerous witnesses. What bothers me terribly, however, is that we apparently have no one living today who can perform this feat. I think the best thing we can do is to treat levitation purely as a speculation for the time being. To ignore cases that allegedly once occurred in favour only of those which occur today does not weaken the argument for the paranormal. On the contrary, it strengthens it. And if paranormal levitation is a fact, then we will discover it again one day on the path to the truth. It will not get lost.

Associated with many physical mediums are so-called poltergeist phenomena. Jan Merta is perhaps a case in point. Matthew Manning certainly is.[60] I have not personally met or seen Manning, so I have formed no opinion of him. He has a strong reputation and seems sincere. Perhaps he is a genuine case.

Poltergeist phenomena — such as allegedly occurred in Manning's house during his youth — are apparently inexplicable movements and breakages of furniture and other objects, sometimes accompanied by noises and electrical side effects, usually all of a rather violent nature. The old 'explanation' for these events was that some malevolent or unhappy spirit was haunting the premises and producing the effects.

This is not an explanation to which I personally subscribe. There are, however, interesting features to these cases that suggest they are not altogether to be attributed to earth tremors, practical jokers or any of a variety of other normal explanations. The events often seem to occur in the presence of one particular individual, and not to occur when the individual is absent. This person is usually an adolescent youngster, and often a girl. In both sexes the emphasis seems to remain on the young. For me these observations have considerable interest in connection with comments I shall be making on the physiology of ESP in later chapters. Once again, possibly, non-paranormal and reasonable elements in the total equation may lend independent support to aspects that are paranormal, and at first sight unreasonable.

Meanwhile, let us remember that an apport is always an object small enough to be concealed under your coat.

HOW TO GET RID OF STATISTICS

Suppose there were a man who throughout his whole life told the truth, except that on one single occasion he told a lie.

The occasion of that lie would be of the greatest interest to us. We would be very curious to know what combination of conditions and circumstances could have forced, or tempted, this unswerving lover of the truth from his otherwise straight path — at this one point only, in a whole life of predictability. Interest, and especially the human interest, centres on the lie.

Yet in purely statistical terms the lie is not of the slightest importance. In the midst of such a vast number of non-deviations, so tiny a deviation does not even show up in our calculations. It is not worth considering. It would be rather like asking the Meteorological Office to consider the effect of a single drop of rain on the flow of the River Thames.

Sometimes, as we saw in Chapter 2, an individual, in the course of a lifetime of non-paranormal dreaming, has one dream containing a single flash of the paranormal. Statistically this is a non-event. Should the person concerned attempt to claim the dream as genuinely paranormal, the academic psychologist can (and does) simply point to all the thousands and thousands of other dreams the same individual has had, which were not. The case is dismissed before it ever comes to court. For the scientist, the academic psychologist, the statistician, there *is* no case.

We need to be very clear on this. Science is not saying that it is not or would not be interested in paranormal dreams. It says there is no such thing.

In terms of credentials, science would ideally like paranormal dreams to be produced to order. Failing this, it wants enough paranormal dreams to occur to show up in a statistical analysis as a statistical drift.

The attitude of science, however, is not wholly reasonable here. To deny the validity of the one paranormal dream of a lifetime is rather like denying that anyone has ever jumped twenty-nine feet (a) because one man has only ever done it once (Bob Beamon in the 1968 Olympics) and (b) because he himself is quite unable to do it again. It is true that he performed this feat before witnesses — but there have been plenty of occasions where a precognitive dream has been 'witnessed' by being announced to others before the predicted event occurred.

In fact the difficulties which confront the attempt to study the paranormal statistically are colossal. I personally believe that these difficulties are insoluble for two quite different main reasons. The first is an eminently practical one and it boils down to this. How exactly do you study statistically an event which occurs only once (which only *may* occur only once!) over an almost indefinite span of time? The second reason, however, is the real stopper. I believe that certain aspects of the total constellation of events which make up a paranormal incident *do not exist in the material universe at all.* They themselves have no physical *objective* existence and are therefore, unlike normal events, not subject to the otherwise universal laws of cause and effect — the various limitations of the normal space—time continuum. It is for this reason, I think, that many paranormal events are trivial and inconsequential. They have no 'weight', either literal or metaphorical, in the physical universe. They arise in another frame of reference entirely.

This point will be developed in Parts III and IV.

It remains true, however, that paranormal events must somehow affect or show up in the normal universe — otherwise, by definition, we would not know that they existed. If they were not in some sense here, so to speak, we could not know that they were there. The fact that paranormal events do, obviously, have some kind of existence has led many paranormalists (I think unwisely) into the endless swampland of attempting to prove that existence statistically.

For among other things, although the paranormal exists in, that is, has an effect on, the here-and-now world, it does *not* repeat itself as non-paranormal events do when the conditions are duplicated that led to the first occurrence. So the efforts of J. B. Rhine and many other parapsychologists to obtain repeatable telepathy results between individuals, using Zener cards (see p.162) and other standardized guessing material, have in the long run proved futile. The occasional high-scoring runs (which possibly sometimes involve paranormal effects) are followed by an indefinite series of chance scores, which *statistically* finally cancel out the high scores. The compulsive drive for repeatability (scientific respectability) has been and continues to be the ruin of the parapsychologist. For example, in 1974 it drove Dr W. J Levy of the Institute of Parapsychology to falsify in later experiments his originally promising results in an initial experimental series. The fraud came to light, and Dr Levy's career was at an end.[83]

So sure am I that repeatability in the narrow sense is not achievable in respect of the paranormal (has indeed nothing to do with the true nature of the paranormal) that I myself tend to take evidence of repeatability as an indicator of fraud! It is one of the reasons why I mistrust Geller, who produces not only to order but, in public at any rate, always the same limited range of effects. (However, in Geller's defence here, my own theoretical thinking has led me to a point where I consider *physical* phenomena, including psychic healing as practised by Estebany, not to be paranormal at all. Possibly therefore the 'Geller effect', if genuine, may prove to belong to a repeatable type of phenomenon, as the scientist understands repeatability. See Chapter 4 and after.)

My deep conviction, then, is that the statistical approach to psychic phenomena must be abandoned. I have already indicated some of the reasons for my conviction. Further of my reasons look suspiciously like common sense (not that there is anything wrong with that) but I will try to express them in a more structured way later on. The argument here involves a mouse and an elephant.

If you were to ask a statistician to state the size of the largest mouse that could be produced under normal conditions, he would not give you an immediate answer. Instead he would take and measure a large sample of mice from all over the country (or perhaps from all over the world). Then, using well-known formulae, he would perform certain calculations. These calculations tell the statistician what is the likelihood of a mouse of any given size being produced. It does not matter whether or not there was actually any mouse of that particular size in the original sample — the statistical calculations make provision for hypothetical mice also.

Now we repeat our question. What is the largest mouse that could be produced under normal conditions? The statistician, again instead of answering directly, counters with a question of his own. What degree of probability are you talking about, he asks? He tells us that the chances (the probability) of a mouse size X, for example, are a hundred to one. Of size Y, a thousand to one. Of size Z, a million to one, and so on.

The larger sizes become more and more unlikely, more and more improbable, as one proceeds further up the scale. The chances of especially large mice become always increasingly more remote. *But*, although the chances of a given large size become millions and millions to one against, in statistical terms these *never reach impossibility*. There is no absolute cut-off point whatsoever, in theoretical terms.

In other words, the statistician never says 'never'. He only says 'more and more unlikely'. Statistically speaking, therefore, there is no final answer to the question, what is the largest size of mouse that could ever be produced under normal conditions?

We would get a similarly dusty response from the statistician if we asked the question, what is the *smallest elephant* that could be produced under normal conditions? Statistically speaking, there are no absolute limits to the possible smallness — only an ever-increasing degree of improbability.

Yet it is — I hope — quite clear to all of us that the largest mouse ever produced under normal conditions will *never* be as large as the smallest elephant produced under normal conditions. *Never.* *

The kinds of paranormal events which the laboratory parapsychologist produces under his controlled conditions are 'mice' (as are the 'mere coincidences' which they resemble). This is not to say that the parapsychologist's results are not sometimes genuinely paranormal. But they are of an order which the statistician can argue about. The kinds of events we see in spontaneous paranormal phenomena, however — and such as we looked at in the first chapters of the book — are all 'elephants'. They cannot be confused with mice. They are unmistakably larger. They are unmistakably of an entirely different order.

What I am saying here parallels and reinforces the remarks I made in the chapter 'Footprints in the Sand'. Robinson Crusoe needed no statistician or scientist to tell him that there was another human being on the island. The matter was proven beyond any doubt and argument by the simple existence of the footprint. Similarly, in the present case, we do not need a statistician to tell us the difference (in size or in any other respect) between a mouse and an elephant. We are all equipped to make judgments of this kind without any specialist help — and I insist that we must not allow the specialist to tell us otherwise.

I will now, nevertheless, try to explain my position in terms more acceptable to the professional statistician.

---

* The phrase 'normal conditions' as I am using it here excludes the possibility of mutations and other evolutionary change.

A Statistical Defence and a Proposition

In the game of roulette, the wheel mainpulated by the croupier has on it thirty-seven divisions, marked zero to thirty-six, into one of which the ball falls randomly every time the wheel is spun.

The chances of any particular number occurring as the result of any given spin are one in thirty-seven. The odds against the same number occurring twice in succession are thirty-seven squared, minus one, that is $(37^2) - 1$. The odds against the number occurring *three* times in succession are thirty-seven cubed, minus one, and so on. The highest number of times in which a number has been observed to repeat in succession on a properly balanced wheel is believed to be six. The odds involved here are $(37^6) - 1$, or 94,931,877,132 to 1.

The thirty-seven divisions of the roulette wheel, apart from being numbered zero to thirty-six, are alternately coloured red and black (with the exception of the zero). The chances of a red or black occurring as a result of any given spin are equal, a straight fifty—fifty. The chances of any two successive spins producing two consecutive reds (or two consecutive blacks) are one in two. The chances of three consecutive reds (or blacks) are 2^3, of four reds 2^4, of five reds 2^5, and so on. The longest successive run of one colour observed on a correctly balanced wheel is believed to be thirty-two (though I have heard unconfirmed reports of longer runs). The odds against this event occurring are $(2^{32}) - 1$, or 8,589,934,591 to 1.

The odds-against produced by a run of the same number six times and a run of thirty-two reds are not too dissimilar. (A run of thirty-six reds would make up the difference in the two results.) I suggest therefore that somewhere around 37^6 are the actual and *final* upper limits of chance. I had better explain exactly what I mean by this statement.

It is my convinced belief that chance *does* have firm upper limits. I am now suggesting that in a tightly-structured situation of known parameters such as the roulette wheel, where events occur by chance and for no other reason, we actually observe the actual upper limits of chance. These

are both *real* and *universal* limits. They are not confined to
the roulette wheel, but apply to all games of true chance and
all other situations where only chance operates. These limits,
I suggest, are not confined to artificially-structured situations
— where we are in a position to actually observe and calculate
them — but to the operation of chance throughout the
universe.

When I say 'firm upper limits' I do not mean we can precisely draw a line at a given point. But we *can* indicate a
fairly narrow band of probability beyond which chance does
not operate (in fact, cannot operate). Why should we want
to do this? Because events lying beyond the band would
then by definition be other than chance — they would be
meaningful events.

There have been two observed runs of the same number
occurring six times in succession in roulette. May there one
day occur a run of seven consecutive repeats? Perhaps.
Eight repeats? Well, perhaps. Fifty repeats? *No.* Never.
Not ever, ever, ever, ever in the life of this universe, even if it
endures for time infinite. *Somewhere* between six and
fifty repeats is the uncrossable barrier. Fifty is of course a
completely arbitrary choice. Twenty will do as well. In my
own opinion, twelve will do as well — that is, I consider
there will never be a run of the same number repeating
even twelve times on a properly balanced roulette wheel.

My proposal is shown in diagram form in Figure 3.

What is needed by way of further verification of this
claim, that there is a fixed upper limit to the operation of
chance *in actual practice*, is extensive observation (such as we
already have for the roulette wheel, because players have
been keeping a written record of its behaviour for almost two
hundred years) of the behaviour of thrown dice, of
randomly-dealt playing cards, randomly-sampled numbers,
and whatever. Statistical theory cannot help us here — for
we need to know what chance achieves *in actual practice*.
Statistics is silent on this point. If the suggested upper limit
of chance is in fact found to be similar in several observed
practical situations, we would have good grounds for confirming a general, practical upper limit to the operation of
chance in *all* random situations.

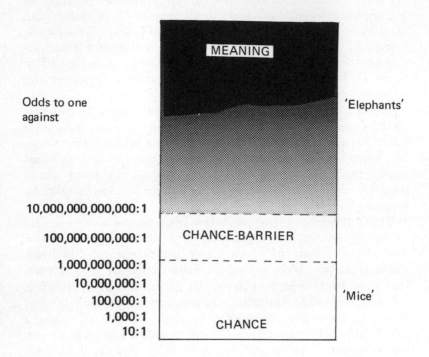

Odds to one
against

10,000,000,000,000:1
100,000,000,000:1
1,000,000,000:1
10,000,000:1
100,000:1
1,000:1
10:1

FIGURE 3 The Chance-barrier

Monkeys and Typewriters

We can take the discussion into another area, with which everyone is familiar, and which is of greater general interest.

It is often said that if an army of monkeys were to bang aimlessly away on typewriters for the rest of eternity, they would sooner or later type out the whole of Shakespeare's works. This in some ways intriguing idea is, I am afraid, complete nonsense.

Let us suppose for the sake of argument that these hypothetical typewriters had only twenty-six keys, one for each letter of the alphabet. Let us forget about the need for spaces between words — although that space in fact makes an astronomical difference in statistical terms.

The chances of any particular letter being typed by any particular hit are one in twenty-six. The chances of a particular second letter following it are a further one in twenty-six, giving us 26^2. A third stipulated letter raises the odds to 26^3, and so on.

We can readily see now that the first, say, eight letters required involve us in odds against chance of 26^8. This is a number of the order of our earlier 37^6, which, I have suggested, itself nudges the upper limits of chance. According to the behaviour of the roulette wheel, that is, according to the play of chance not in theoretical terms *but in actual observed practice over a very long period of time* (as I say, for about two hundred years) the monkeys would *never* get eight letters correct in a row, much less a whole sentence.*

The scenario of the monkeys and the typewriters producing the works of Shakespeare falls apart also for another and even more fundamental reason. The odds of any particular letter being hit by the monkey are one in twenty-six. But the incidence of particular letters in written English is nothing like one in twenty-six. The letters e, s and n occur enormously more often than letters like q, z or x. A glance over this printed page will prove that point. But any *large* sample of the monkey's output will *necessarily* contain *all* the letters of the alphabet *in equal numbers*. The repeated random sampling of one letter from twenty-six available letters averages out in a large sample to exactly the same number of choices for every single letter. Therefore no matter how much we randomly shuffle any large sample of the monkey's output, we will always have far too many letters of one kind and far too few of another.

---

* This makes even Bill Duffy's cartoon madly over-optimistic. One scientist is saying to another, against a background of a sea of monkeys chained to typewriters: 'The best we got today was "To be or not to be, that is the @@*£??%&".'

I think that here we perhaps have a statistical definition of meaning. Meaning can be said to be present in any context where the statistical against-chance value of any sequence exceeds, say, 100,000,000,000 to 1 (or whatever the chance-barrier value actually proves to be); *or where items randomly available for choice are chosen in non-random quantities and ratios.* Written language is then meaningful simply and precisely because the letters in it do not occur either in random order or in random quantities.

The last statement, however, will not do as it stands. For example, supposing we have an electric typewriter typing in response to a computer programme; and suppose the typewriter develops a fault, so that it types 'z' not only when instructed to type 'z', but also when instructed to type 'm' and 't': and types 'p' for every other letter. Now we have a non-random output that is nevertheless quite meaningless in the normal sense.

So let us rephrase the earlier statement. We state: in a situation where events display a non-random patterning, that is, where sequences exceed the known values of sequences obtainable by chance, *there is always a logical, causative, non-random effect at work.* In respect of language, the non-random production of letters is what human beings call meaning. In the case of the dud typewriter, the cause of the non-random (though to us meaningless) sequences is an ascertainable, mechanical fault.

I have a suspicion that some statisticians reading this will by now be impatiently feeling that what I am saying, in a very clumsy and roundabout way at that, is what statisticians and statistical formulae already say in an extremely elegant way. Perhaps I can change any such impression in spelling out what now follows.

What Statistics Does Not Do

The science of statistics tells us what the odds are against a particular event occurring. That is *all* that statistics does. It makes no prescriptions about what is and is not possible. It never says 'never'.

So that had we asked a statistician, before the invention of the roulette wheel, what would *in practice* prove to be the highest number of repeats of a single number, or the longest run of reds, he not only would not, but *could not* have given any answer. As far as the statistician is concerned, fifty consecutive repeats of the same individual number are perfectly *possible*, although extremely unlikely. Similarly, to statistics, a run of two hundred consecutive reds is perfectly *possible*, although extremely unlikely.

I myself am saying that a run of fifty repeats of the same number is *impossible*. I am saying that a run of two hundred consecutive reds is *impossible*. I am saying that if every atom of matter in the universe were converted into indestructible roulette wheels, and these were spun for the rest of eternity, the events I have just described would never occur. Not ever.

How can I know this — especially when theoretical statistics makes no prescriptions at all in the matter? My answer rests, as I have said, on the observed behaviour of the roulette wheel. Thousands of such wheels have been closely (very closely!) observed in many different parts of the world, to say this once again, for almost two hundred years. We have the distilled results of many thousands of millions, and in all likelihood of millions of millions, of spins of the wheel. *And we have not the slightest reason for supposing that these millions of spins are in any way untypical of the spins that will occur in the real, or would occur in any hypothetical, future.*

For the fact is that samples of a statistical population tend to be typical of the whole statistical population. So true is this statement that the commonest formula employed by statisticians is the one that allows you to describe the characteristics of a whole population of events on the basis of a small random sample.

One word here on a common and widespread fallacy. Lay people (that is, non-statisticians) often imagine that if you say a particular event is likely to occur once in a thousand occasions, you have to work through a thousand occasions, or very nearly, before you come across that event. This belief is totally incorrect. The event in question can occur anywhere in the series. It could even be the very first event. When a statistician says that an event occurs once in a thousand occasions, he means that if you examined many, many thousands of such occasions, you would find *on average* one of these special events occurred for every thousand non-special events.

So the hypothetical run of two hundred consecutive reds (if it were possible) could just as easily have occurred the very first two hundred times the very first roulette wheel was spun, as at any subsequent time. The run of two hundred does not in any sense have to be earned. Just as the person who buys one premium bond today has exactly the same chance of winning next time as someone who has held one premium bond for the last fifteen years; or just as the man who today sends in his first football coupon has the same chance of winning as the man who has sent one every week of his adult life.

To summarize, in respect of the roulette wheel *we have very good grounds for believing that we have seen everything we are going to see.* The so-far highest run of six repeats of one number may one day become a run of seven. Perhaps even of eight. But a run of fifty? Never.

Zener Cards

Zener cards were devised by J. B. Rhine during the 1930s in an attempt to create a structured framework within which telepathy and clairvoyance could be studied statistically. The cards resemble playing cards. The pack consists of five of each of five symbols (a cross, a square, a circle, three wavy lines and a star), each symbol printed individually on its own card. In all, then, there are twenty-five cards in a full pack.

I have personally a great many objections to Zener cards and their rationale. I consider them inhuman and unemotional (in fact, downright boring). They have none of the stuff of life about them — whereas we know on the contrary that the paranormal is always full of the stuff of life and always close to it. The Zener cards are arid, intellectual abstractions.

Even statistically they leave a great deal to be desired. When a subject is guessing his way through a pack of unseen cards, he or she is often aware of having already chosen, say, four stars — so that the person may well be influenced by the fact that he has only one star 'left'. In fact, of course, all the stars may still, in reality, be among the cards that remain to be guessed. It would, in my opinion, be a far better arrangement if the subject were drawing on an infinite (that is, statistically infinite) pool of symbols — where long runs or a high incidence of a particular symbol are theoretically, and practically, possible. The subject need then have no reservations about having 'used up' some of his guesses. This arrangement could be easily managed by the construction of a Zener roulette wheel, divided into twenty-five sections, bearing five sequences of the five symbols. Over to you, J. B. Rhine.

These criticisms are not the points I especially want to highlight here. Instead I want to compare two results attained with Zener cards with the observed behaviour of the standard roulette wheel. I can only make this one direct comparison, for the following reason. The runs of events I discussed in respect of the roulette wheel and the alphabet were *continuous* events. In the Zener-card operation, it is considered to be of no significance whether the correct guesses appear in consecutive runs or as isolated events; a subject might get two right, then one wrong, then one right, then four wrong, and so on. This irregular pattern does not matter. The only criterion is how many correct guesses the subject makes in all, the chance score being five correct out of every twenty-five.

On two occasions, however, two subjects have achieved on one run the astonishing score of twenty-five correct out of twenty-five (one was a man, one a woman). Because there were no intervening errors, we know that the run of correct guesses was in fact a consecutive run.

Jung gives the odds against chance of this remarkable score of twenty-five out of twenty-five as 298,023,223,876,953,125. I consider this figure stands a very strong chance indeed of lying beyond the chance-barrier.

(Incidentally, odds against of 5^{25} approximate to 2^{58}. Compare this with the 2^{32} observed on the roulette wheel. Also, by the way, we do not know how much *higher* these successful guessers might have gone if the Zener pack had not ended at twenty-five — a further undesirable weakness of this system statistically.)

None the less, I do not want to make too much of this apparent 'victory', for the following reason. We do not know what kinds of runs arise by chance when 'hands' of Zener cards are dealt out randomly. It will be remembered that the statistician can in no way forecast what limits of consecutive or sequential runs occur *in practice* when a roulette wheel is in actual operation. All the statistician can tell us is the probability or improbability of a set of events occurring. Statistics performs this same theoretical exercise in respect of the sequences of the Zener cards, and informs us of the theoretical odds involved. But a statistician cannot tell us the practical limits of what the cards will actually produce in the way of runs and sequences when in use. I would myself like to see the kinds of results and runs that actually arise when a machine shuffles and deals out the Zener pack a few thousand million times — this being the order of observation we have made in respect of the roulette wheel — and what agreements would be obtained if the output of two such machines were then matched, as if one were 'guessing' the other. Two points in conclusion, one for and one against. First, it should be a sobering thought for those working with Zener cards that simple, sequential events with odds against of around 100,000,000,000 to 1 *can* occur by chance, as we know from roulette. Second, a majority of those who have been tested with Zener cards over the last forty years have tended to score successfully in the initial period of testing, but much less well later. This itself *cannot* be a chance effect, given that so many individuals are involved. Chance would require that as many people did well *later* (after doing badly at first) as did well *initially*. Though the demonstration of a clearly paranormal effect here is not without value in itself, the main outcome of the experiments is to underline the essentially non-repeating and uncapturable nature of paranormal influence.

The Statistical Evaluation of Spontaneous Phenomena

Many attempts have been made to express statistically the against-chance odds of paranormal events that occur spontaneously in everyday, unstructured situations. Jung himself made such attempts. The idea of evaluating such events statistically is attractive, because one does have the intuitive feeling that the odds which the paranormal event flies in the face of are so astronomical, that if they could be stated objectively the sceptic would be forced to capitulate. This idea would become still more attractive if the chance-barrier I proposed earlier really proves to exist.

Yet I think this hope is both a forlorn and ultimately an unnecessary one. The principal pitfall is that in unstructured situations the statistical calculation performed rests always on a number of arbitrary assumptions. An objector can always dispute the preliminary assumptions and either make others of his own or dismiss the attempt out of hand as unfeasible. It is the influence of initial assumptions on the outcome which, not unjustifiably, gives rise to the popular saying that with statistics you can prove (or disprove) anything.

Suppose, for example, we were asked to estimate the chances of any leaf in London flying in at the open window of any bus in London. Actually, the only sane response to such a request is to raise your hat, politely say goodnight and go home. But still, let us take a look at the problems involved in calculating this likelihood.

One might be able to get a reasonable guesstimate of the number of leaves on trees in London at a particular moment. The actual number of trees in each locality is probably known to the various local authorities. No doubt, too, estimates (or even actual counts) have already been made by biologists and horticulturalists concerning the number of leaves a type of tree will tend to produce. However, the type, as well as the age, of tree is an important variable, so we would also need to know the relative incidence of different types of tree and have some estimate of their age. All one hell of a task — but, still, just about a possible one. Then we could obtain from London Transport the total number of buses in service in the London area.

Now the real problems begin. As far as the leaves are concerned, the chances of our event are obviously much higher in the autumn than in the summer. But as far as open windows on buses are concerned, the chances are highest in summer. Furthermore, some trees are near bus routes, or actually on bus routes, while others are in the middle of parks. Some again are in front gardens, some are in back gardens. Then, how far does the average leaf travel, before it finally disintegrates or is swept up and burned? How long is its 'life' away from the tree? How often does the wind pick it up from the ground during that life and what is the average height attained by the average leaf? (Of course, when it first falls from the tree it starts a good deal higher.) These last factors also vary enormously in dry and in wet conditions, and with strong winds.

The project in fact grinds gradually to a halt. There are too many imponderables, too many unknowns. The statistician can form no reasonable estimate.

In terms of events, the complexity of human life already far exceeds the complexities of leaves and buses. But that aside, the example of leaves and buses contains no element of meaning or coherence, and no idea of intention. The entry of a leaf into a bus does not *mean* anything; and the leaf does not *intend* to go into the bus.

But as we saw for example in the paranormal dreams of Chapter 2 and elsewhere, the paranormal dream is coherent in terms of the individual's life structure and life style — and it conveys a meaning, a message. (Far from giving a message, *chance* cannot even spell a word of eight letters!) I do not think there is any way at all whereby we could assign statistical values to these aspects of the paranormal.

Professor Darlington has stated that that which cannot be measured 'is intolerable to many otherwise rational scientists'.* I agree with his implied criticism of science. Surely that which is measured exists before it is measured, and continues to exist even if it is not measured. Measurement does not confer existence. It is the other way about.

* *The Times*, November 23rd, 1976.

Statistics is of no help to us in the study of the paranormal. It is a lower-order phenomenon, which is superseded by meaning. Establishing the existence of the chance-barrier might, however, be of good use in persuading 'otherwise rational scientists' of this position.

The psychic does not pluck just any leaf from the incalculable complexity of human affairs. He plucks the appropriate leaf for the appropriate occasion (the appropriate bus). Chance cannot do that. We must not allow anyone to claim that it can.

BYE-BYE SCIENCE

Despite the farewell title of this section, it nevertheless opens with a statement 'In Praise of Science'.

The debt which we all owe science can scarcely be overstated. Directly because of the application of the objective or scientific method — and *only* because of this — the children of the advanced nations (and, increasingly, of the underdeveloped nations) no longer die in hordes. The remaining adults no longer bear the terrible scars of the diseases of childhood and of later life. The horrors of syphilis, smallpox, tuberculosis are very largely behind us now. Apart from actual death from and disfigurement by many diseases, science has with very rare exceptions also abolished the agonies of unremitting pain. Can we really imagine today what it must have been like to have teeth removed and legs amputated without benefit of anaesthetic? Even assuming one became unconscious during the process, what of the waking up afterwards?

A bad harvest no longer inevitably signals the lingering deaths of hundreds of thousands of individuals — because thanks to science we can store up the surplus of previous harvests. These harvests are themselves in any case far more abundant. As an added luxury we can now eat any *kind* of food at any season of the year.

The entertainment which is offered to all, even to the

poorest members of our society, in terms of television and films, exceeds anything available to the most self-indulgent Roman emperor. We have gone unimaginably beyond anything formerly devised to fill the leisure time and pander to the tastes of the wealthiest individual of former times.

These comments are not to suggest that present-day life is anywhere near perfect. Far from it. But, thanks to science, life is incomparably better than ever before.

I would personally emphasize in the strongest possible terms that none of these advances — in sanitation, in the curing of disease, in the feeding of the hungry — owes anything to prayer or to the holding of religious beliefs. There was, I would say, far more prayer in the Middle Ages than ever we have now — and simultaneously incomparably more human degradation and pointless misery. Certainly many scientists themselves have also held religious beliefs — but that is a different point, and a tangential one, to the question of the *actual contributions* of religion.

The immediate point for us here is that mysticism and occultism of whatever varieties have contributed nothing to our understanding and control of the material, physical universe. In all the exhortations and raging of prophets, in all the solemn communications of priests and popes, from all the endless ramblings of the seance room, there emerges not one single *fact* about the moon, or Mars, or Venus, or the circulation of the blood, or the life cycle of bacteria, or the speed of light.

If we now know, as we do, that Mars is an inhospitable desert whose surface temperature can drop to minus 160° Fahrenheit at night, with winds of 300 miles per hour, and that the surface of Venus is by contrast at plus 980° Fahrenheit, beaten by rains of sulphuric acid, we know this solely thanks to the almost incredible ingenuity of the scientist.

There is no point in taking up time here in further considering what, for instance, astrologers thought of the nature of the planets (see pp.118–23) or what the Aetherius society currently thinks of them   (see Chris Evans's excellent book *Cults of Unreason*). It is not even true to say that modern astronomy developed out of astrology. Modern astronomy developed in spite of astrology, with the leaden weight of those misconceptions tied around its ankles. Need I mention, in passing, the role of the Catholic Church as a relentless, active repressor of astronomy in particular, and science in general? The story of Galileo's fate at the hands of Pope Paul V is a notorious instance (see, for example, Arthur Koestler's *The Sleepwalkers*). Nor is it true to claim, as some do, that modern chemistry developed from ancient alchemy. The main body of alchemy *as chemistry* was (and is) a blind alley of wild beliefs and bad ideas. It was from the footnotes of alchemy, so to speak, that true chemistry began to develop, by-passing and abandoning as it did so the main mass of the alchemist's dubious and fantastic speculation.* Let me emphasize once again that I am here criticizing alchemy as chemistry. There is no doubt that alchemy carries important messages to us concerning the human psyche — as of course Jung well emphasized.†

With the foregoing charges levelled and admitted to, we must now, however, turn about and change the direction of our comments. For science today is behaving no differently and no better than religion did before it. Science has itself become a god. The religion of this god is measurement.

It is quite beyond me to grasp how science is going to measure, for example, the fact that I know I exist. My conscious existence *is* a fact, even if only to me. Even if I were the only person on Earth I would still exist and still know that I existed. My experience of other events — my conscious experience of other events, that is — is then an extension of my existence, and that is also itself a fact. As R. D. Laing puts it: 'The experience of oneself . . . is primary and self-validating. It exists prior to the scientific or philosophical difficulties about how such existence is possible or

* I am myself no enemy, and in fact a veritable addict, of fantastic speculation in fairy story and in science fiction. (See especially my chapters in *The Significance of Science Fiction*, ed. Richard Kirby.) But at the same time I am not among those who confuse science fiction with practical science.
† As I suggested earlier (p.125) we very much need to reconsider these forms of ancient wisdom at their point of origin and in their original form.

how it is to be explained.' Still more succinctly he says: 'A person is the me, or you, whereby an object is experienced.' Existential matters, then, precede science. They do not follow from science. On the contrary, science follows from them.

Our own existence remains absolutely the prime factor in all things. When we as it were apply or extend our existence, we have experiences. Science studies some aspects of our experience — more precisely, it studies the objects and phenomena external to us which give rise (but only in second place) to many of our experiences. This is 'objectivity'. What I am arguing in this book is that there are some events in a sense 'external' to us which science nevertheless cannot study — which cannot be studied *objectively*.

I consider that the physical universe goes on being 'there' even when human beings are not — that is, even after our death. These *other* events of which I am now speaking also have an existence of their own — that is, they are in some sense discontinuous with us. Yet nevertheless, despite their being discontinuous with us, these special events are only found *in association with human beings*, or with other organisms. Somehow organisms cause these events to manifest themselves in the physical space—time universe (even though the events *themselves*, I suggest, are not of the physical space—time universe). We somehow bring them in on our boots, as we might bring snow into a house.

As long as *we* are here in the physical universe, these special events — and obviously I am referring to paranormal events — will occasionally be observed. I do not believe that paranormal events would in any sense continue to exist in this universe if all organisms were to die. By contrast, the stars and the planets and physical matter generally *would* continue to exist. These exist before we appear and after we are gone.

Where do paranormal events, then, come from — where is their real home, their point of origin? I suggest in all seriousness that *paranormal events reach us from another or alternative universe*. Or better, from another Dimension, as I will define that term in Chapter 4. Organisms somehow provide a bridge between the two (or possibly multiple) universes or Dimensions.

The methods of science, which work so very well in respect of the material, physical universe, are in my opinion completely inappropriate for the study of paranormal phenomena.

So what is to be done? Since paranormal events come to us not only primarily but solely as subjective experiences, I think the first and, for the time being, only step is for us to try to broaden our experience of them. In the course of that experience we may begin to attempt some tentative definitions or descriptions — and I shall be making some later. We must then see what the next best step might be.

In the previous section I suggested that statistics cannot be of any help to us in the study of meaning. Rather similarly, I am now saying that science cannot be of any real use to us in the study of the paranormal. I believe, on the contrary, that it can only hinder us. We must put science and the scientific method firmly aside.

In my — certainly at this stage — stumbling attempts to describe an 'alternative universe' I hope to be able, at least to some extent, to make up to occultists and mystics for the severe bruisings I have given them (and other bruisings yet to come) in my rejection of astrology, alchemy and religion. I think we can do better for ourselves than any of these.

PART III

FOUR
Dimensions

Conventional mathematics — more precisely, conventional geometry — deals in three dimensions. A straight line extends in one dimension only. It is considered to have only length, no width. A second line, crossing the first line at right angles to it in the same plane, gives us the second dimension. A third line passing *vertically* through the junction of the first two lines, and at right angles to both of them, gives the third dimension. These three directions, all at right angles to each other, exhaust all the directions possible in the normal physical universe.

To human beings events, as well as moving in the three dimensions of physical space, seem also to move through time. Nevertheless, is 'time' just a figment of the human imagination, or does it *really* exist? Is it, in other words, a purely subjective phenomenon or does it have an objective existence? Or, again, is it partly subjective and partly objective?

At first sight, the concept of time as an objective fact seems reasonable enough. Our observation and memory tell us that things change, that situations once existed that no longer exist. Our reason, or imagination, tells us that there are future events to come — tomorrow's sunrise, our own death, and so forth. The passage of time, as shown by change and our own life-experience, appears to us to be a journey *through* something, from somewhere to somewhere — a directional movement that is, nevertheless, different from and other than the three movements of normal space — side to side, forward and back, up and down.

Time seems to us different from the movements of normal

space and is special certainly in that it seems to go only one way. We call that way 'forward' (although the term is itself an assumption). Whatever we choose to call this movement, time at any rate never seems to go the other way. It never seems to go backwards.

I personally find all these conventional ways of considering the so-called dimensions of space and time extremely unsatisfactory. The conventional notations do not help us, for example, to connect space and normal time with the *paranormal* in particular or with the nature of life in general. For instance, though normal time itself never seems to go backwards, we know that human consciousness can go back in time paranormally, to produce information not known to any living person.

Especially, I am entirely against the idea of space being granted three whole dimensions. To me space is one-dimensional, or uni-dimensional. It seems, that is, to be a *unit*, self-contained and ruled by laws which it does not break. All physical directions in it are equally possible.

I am, naturally, aware that the normal concept of three space-dimensions, each at right angles to the other, is extremely useful at a certain level. This conceptual framework enables us to handle our physical environment very well. It makes possible engineering and the construction of three-dimensional objects, buildings, bridges, aeroplanes and whatever. The interactions and relationships of the three space-dimensions are the basis of Euclidean geometry, even the basis of Newtonian physics. These three dimensions of conventional space actually serve us very well as far as handling the environment of this planet is concerned.

However, as is now known, these sturdy concepts prove to be of not too much use, and are even a hindrance, when we come to consider the larger aspects and pieces of the visible universe. Once we get into the relationships of star with star, or galaxy with galaxy, we have to broaden the basis of what *I* none the less still think of as the 'conventional' position. We have to introduce the concept of time, and that even into geometry.

At this point Newtonian physics gives way to Einsteinian physics. Among other things, what now emerges is that there is no such thing after all as a straight line. All lines, every-where, are curved. Even the path of light is curved. The reason for the general curvature of everything seems to be that the entire material universe, space as a whole, by its very construction, is curved.

It is not difficult to demonstrate to a reasonable person that a straight line he draws on a piece of paper must be curved, even though it looks perfectly straight. For the whole surface of our planet is curved and every object on that surface ever so slightly accommodates the same forces that made the planet round. But what if we draw a straight line between two planets — surely that is not curved? According to Einsteinian physics, however, this line too is bent, now in response to the general curvature of the material universe as a whole.

Time is heavily involved in the Einsteinian view. While to the business man time is money, for Einstein time, in a sense, is space. One well-publicized effect of the position described by Einstein, that is, of the falling together of at least some aspects of time and space, is that an organism travelling near the speed of light would age very slowly. The faster the organism travels, the slower it ages. If a man travelled away from his home planet in a space ship at very high speeds, returning in what seemed to him to be only a few years, he would find those he had left behind him far older than himself, perhaps even long dead.

I do not question — how could I? — Einstein's demonstra-tion of the relative interaction of time, as he describes it, and space. Instead I want to say that the time Einstein is speak-ing of *is* just an aspect of space. It is a 'new' aspect of space that man has just recently got around to discovering. There are no doubt still other aspects or 'dimensions' and laws of normal space that are not yet known about — the nature and behaviour of matter in the region of the 'black holes' for instance.

My insistence, however, is that there are aspects of time which have nothing to do with space — nothing to do, that is, with physical matter.

Before further outlining and defending my position here, I need to make a general distinction between my own basic model of the universe and one towards which many progressive thinkers, including many paranormalists, are today striving — in my opinion, quite wrongly.

The Ground Plan of the Universe?

For reasons I have already attempted to explain and defend in earlier books, but which remain nevertheless intuitive rather than demonstrable in any scientific sense, I believe that the universe as we know it (and life itself also) arises by reason of the interaction of two macro-forces or conditions. I refer to these two conditions as 'spirit' and 'space'. These forces or conditions, I consider, originally existed as quite separate events, each in its own right.   As to what these events were originally like, each in its own separate right, we can only speculate in the most indirect way.   At some point, however, they begin to interact.   I believe the interaction took (and takes) the form of 'spirit' moving *into* 'space'.   The consequence, or rather consequences, of this coming-together — we ourselves being part of the consequences — give us the condition of 'spirit-in-space'.   The total equation of 'spirit-in-space' contains all events and aspects of the universe we know — including not only all physical matter, but life, consciousness, understanding and so on, and so on — everything that we can ever in any sense be aware of.

All aspects of the present universe — perhaps I should write Universe here with a capital letter — bear the mark of the hybrid origin I have described.   Every event contains an element of the original, once separate 'spirit' and an element of the original, once separate 'space'.   Moreover, the position is not a static, but a dynamic and ever-changing one.   As 'spirit' progressively continues to enter 'space', a different balance is struck — a more complex balance.

Let me try to give a clear picture of my position.   The picture is probably too simple, but no matter.

Suppose a being is going about its purposes in the environment which has given rise to it.   Then at some point it comes upon a region which bars its progress.   There is some actual barrier between the being and what lies 'ahead'.   The laws of the being's nature are such, however, that it must continue its progress. It has no choice in this matter. So the being now breaches the barrier ahead of it by force. It then begins to transfer itself into the previously sealed, and perhaps original-ly entirely static, area. Two things now happen. One, the original stasis or balance of the sealed area is lost and it becomes active. Possibly activity arises simply in the sense that the sealed area — 'space' — resists the further passage of the being or 'spirit'. And two, the nature of 'spirit' is altered.

('Space' is probably nevertheless best thought of as an *inanimate* set of conditions, a complex of forces. 'Spirit' is best thought of as in some sense *animate*, as we understand that term.)

There is no need for us to imagine, either, that 'spirit' breaches the barrier of 'space' at one point only, or that 'spirit' is necessarily uniform throughout its whole being. Just like organisms as we know them (and as we ourselves are) 'spirit' may be both complex and differentiated in terms of its many attributes and functions.

No doubt the 'religious' flavour of my model will already be obvious to all. In case this is not clear, I will say quite categorically that it does indeed reflect the dualistic core-message found at the heart of all the great religions — in the 'word made flesh' of Christianity, or the void made manifest of Buddhism, for example. In Gnosticism we find the following interesting and relevant account of ourselves and our universe. In this account it is matter (i.e. 'space') which devours light (i.e. 'spirit'), but the notion of an interaction and union of two opposed conditions or macro-forces is clear.

> [Darkness] came by chance upon the boundary bet-ween the kingdom of darkness and light — saw, desired and invaded the realm of light. At this point light was swallowed by matter [i.e. darkness] and light lost awareness of its own nature. Matter for its part now grew dependent on the swallowed light and sought to retain it.

This passage is interesting in its insistence that the interaction of the two forces produces a state that differs from either in isolation, which parallels my own proposal of 'spirit-in-space'.

We shall see, however, that my account does not conform with the views of religion in all respects. Also, and importantly, that my view does no essential violence to scientific descriptions of the nature and origins of the universe.

In the wake of data from the latest radio-telescopes, the following outline seems to be agreed by scientists. The present universe began with an explosion, thirteen billion years ago, which essentially lasted 100 seconds. The material that emerged from this explosion was 25 per cent helium and 75 per cent hydrogen.

In my own terms, this explosion was the result of, and is a description of, 'spirit' making its entry into 'space'.

There is obviously a good deal more to say on these points, but for the moment the essential purpose of my remarks here is to show how my own basic model differs from the model increasingly urged by paranormalists today.

I said earlier that the whole of the present universe reflects the hybrid or two-fold nature of its origin. Subjectivity and objectivity are respectively, I suggest, the 'spirit' and 'space' aspects of our own conscious life. (Further examples in human affairs of the pervasive 'spirit' and 'space' dualism inherent in spirit-in-space are: word—number; organic—inorganic; female—male; as well as less immediately obvious pairs like past—future.)

I said also that 'spirit' transfers or *moves into* 'space', in a continuous sense. We can think of this as a 'forward' motion, or at any rate a movement from simplicity towards complexity. When we ourselves *look back* in any sense we more nearly approach the 'spirit' which gave birth to us (one of the reasons, I think, why objects and events from past ages affect us 'romantically'). When we *look forward* in any sense we see what 'spirit' — that is, spirit-in-space — is to become (whence, for example, the intense excitement generated by science fiction, exploration and visions of the future generally).

Diagrammatically this gives us something like Figure 4. Perhaps the main point about this rough model is the idea that *development* is continuous and *uni-directional*. It never turns back. It always moves 'forward'.

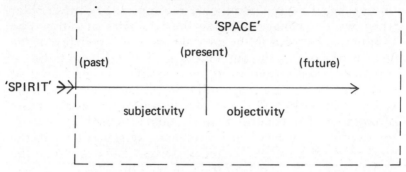

FIGURE 4

The suggestion the diagram makes about subjectivity and objectivity does not at all reflect how most paranormalists conceive the universe today. Their idea seems to be that 'subjectivity' (religion, intuition, and so on) and 'objectivity' (science, logic, mathematics, and so on) are two paths to the same goal (two sides of one coin), in fact two *convergent* paths which are about to meet and join forces. This view is diagrammed in Figure 5.

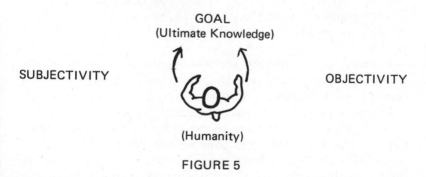

FIGURE 5

I do not entirely disagree with this position, at one level. I have in fact written at length in previous books on the need for man to acknowledge both sides of his nature and, more importantly, to bring the two together within himself — the subjective with the objective, the spiritual with the material. Following Friedrich Schiller (whose *On the Aesthetic Education of Man* I cannot too highly recommend) I consider that when we do manage to bring the two sides of our nature together, as happens in the creation and the experience of the great works of art, the outcome is an 'aesthetic' and releasing experience, conferring on us momentarily a higher level of integrated being. But, again like Schiller, I believe that some of our daily tasks will inevitably and always involve far more of *one* side of our nature than another. The making of steel, for example, involves our objective powers, and only in the most minimal sense our subjective selves. The exercise of the paranormal faculty, by contrast, heavily involves our subjective side. Though we are always, and in everything we do, spirit-in-space, the spirit side of the equation is more important when dealing with aspects of 'spirit', and the space side more important when dealing with aspects of 'space'. In terms of day-to-day living, it is both reasonable and desirable to render unto Caesar that which basically *is* Caesar's, and to God that which is God's. (*But* in so doing we must not deny that the other side exists, much less attempt to destroy it — which is what most people do at present.)

Beyond these levels, I disagree emphatically and fundamentally with the view that 'spirit' and 'space' are the same or ever could be: that Caesar *is* God, or God Caesar. Neither of the two macro-forces can be reduced — or elevated — to the other.

I believe we intuitively and unconsciously understand this position. That is why so often in common speech we insist that oil and water do not mix, that East and West never meet, that man does not live by bread alone.

So I consider that otherwise excellent books like Fritjof Capra's *The Tao of Physics* and Robert Pirsig's *Zen and the Art of Motor Cycle Maintenance* are misconceived, and, in the last analysis, misleading in their attempts to make the two one. My detailed reasons for the stand I take here will, I hope, become clearer as we proceed.

I want now to propose a framework of Dimensions within which we can meaningfully group all the complex phenomena of our spirit-in-space universe (matter, life, consciousness and so on) — for unquestionably this universe of ours operates on many different levels. No *one* set of terms will do for it — not even the terms of advanced physics. I write Dimensions with a capital letter when referring to my own categories to distinguish them from the dimensions normally discussed by geometry and physics.

Each of my own Dimensions appears to demand a further principle or principles absent from any previous Dimension.

Dimensions with a capital D

Dimension 1 — Matter

Matter is the lowest level of spirit-in-space. This Dimension includes space, as that term is *normally* used, and signifies both the distances between objects and the total physical environment in which objects exist. The Dimension of matter therefore includes gravity, magnetism, electricity, nuclear energy and all other such object-associated phenomena.

There is no suggestion at all here that matter is in any way a simple phenomenon. That we still have a great deal to learn about it is clear from recent discoveries like the 'black holes'. A black hole is a very large star that has collapsed in upon itself. So strong is its gravitational pull that all objects in the neighbourhood, including light itself, are inescapably drawn into it. Nothing, it seems, can ever escape from a black hole.

Matter, we observe, undergoes changes. These changes seem all to be in one direction with regard to normal time. Although a set of conditions can seem to *return* — as when a pond freezes over this winter just as it did last — the individual molecules of matter are not of course in the same position as they were the previous time. In fact, very few if any of the original molecules remain. Others have taken their place. As Socrates remarked, no man can ever step into the same stream twice.

Observing the output of an adding or counting machine, we might see the figure seven appear. Then it vanishes and an eight takes its place. Then a nine takes the place of the eight. Finally, the nine disappears and a seven appears. In common speech, and conceptually, we are inclined to say: 'Oh, it's gone back to seven now.' But the output has not *gone back* to seven: it has *gone forward* to *another* seven. There is no 'going back' in the physical world.

Some might want to jump in here to point out that leading physicists are now saying that some particles of matter *do* go back in time. This statement is true and not true. The position is well put by Fritjof Capra, who makes it clear that the notion is only a theoretical *possibility*, for which in any case a normal alternative exists.

> The mathematical formalism of field theory suggests that these [positron] lines can be interpreted in two ways; either as positrons moving forward in time, or as electrons moving backwards in time! The interpretations are mathematically identical.

My understanding of Capra's words here and elsewhere is that we are first not necessarily to assume a 'piece' of anything actually going back in time. Second, and importantly, an equally valid interpretation of this position exists, only involving *forward* movement in time. Third, we are talking in mathematical terms, where the 'impossible' (like the square root of minus one) is frequently used as a construct — and nothing more.

Most physicists today are saying that the interior of the atom seems to be largely emptiness — if not complete emptiness. This I do not find surprising. As I see it, the tiny 'particles' of the sub-atomic nucleus, most of which have a life of no more than billionths of a second in isolation, are the last remnants of spirit-in-space before we reach back to 'spirit' — for which we not only have no descriptive terms, but cannot even directly apprehend — and certainly not in objective terms.

In terms of the *complete* atom and upwards there is not the slightest suggestion anywhere that physical matter can move back in time. Nor in everyday reality at the level of visible objects do we ever observe it to do so.

The progressive changes which take place in matter give us

a measure of time. Many think that change *is* time. They suggest that if all the atoms in the universe absolutely stopped moving, time would disappear. Not only would there be no measure of time, there would be no sense of time.

I am willing to agree that change is a measure of some aspects of time, and even that some aspects of time are fully accounted for by change. In this sense time is 'matter' (just as light and gravity are matter, in my definition). But we can observe several aspects of time that are quite independent of matter. Most notably in association with organisms, time can reverse the direction of the material universe — it can flow backwards. Perhaps 'flow backwards' is an overstatement. But undoubtedly past time and past events that no longer exist in the present universe are *nevertheless available paranormally to human consciousness.*

Dimension 2 — Time

I describe time as the second Dimension. The time I refer to in this sense seems only to be found in the presence of organisms. As I just emphasized, 'non-existent' aspects of both the past and the future of the universe in which we live can be reached paranormally by human beings and other organisms. The possibility is therefore that this time-Dimension would continue to exist even if all organisms were to disappear.

I hope in the discussion of the first Dimension, matter, that it was clear that even Einsteinian time seems nevertheless only an aspect of matter. Although the passage of normal time slows down for an organism travelling at very high speeds, time still goes *forward*. The movement involved does not seem to be *reversible*.

With the paranormal, the position changes radically. A psychic individual can obtain information from or about another deceased individual *which is not known to any living person*. The qualification is important. If the information is known to some living person, even though not consciously and normally divulged by him or her, it remains possible that the psychic is obtaining it telepathically from the living individual. It is when we obtain information that nobody knows (as Swedenborg did in regard to the secret panel) that we apparently reach back through time into situations (or to consciousnesses) that no longer exist.

Some religious people would disagree here. They would say that the allegedly 'dead' individual is only dead as far as this world is concerned. He or she is at this moment living 'on the other side' and is sending the information across to us. Others, while discounting the spirit hypothesis, suggest that a dead individual's thoughts or personality are somehow impressed on the physical world. These traces linger on for a while, and can be picked up by sensitives and psychics. This explanation actually raises as many problems as it seeks to solve. Still, it neatly covers psychometry (from the *past*), and it is true that most psychics can only pick up information about the very recent past, so a trace-decay theory accounts for that situation rather well.

These objections (to death) and the other counter-proposals are, however, completely nullified by the further circumstance that psychic individuals can pick up events in the future, events which have not yet even happened. This form of 'time travel' cannot be accounted for by messages from the living dead, nor by events leaving traces of their passing. With paranormal knowledge of the future we demonstrate the escape from the limitations and rules of normal time — that is, of time as we understand it in relation to matter. Paranormal knowledge of the past is, then, evidently the same ability demonstrated in reverse. Not only can we run ahead of normal time, but it seems we can run back through time. Both past and future events are as if present with us (are synchronistic). We are therefore *outside normal* time, and so in some other Dimension.

Dimension 3 — Consciousness

I intend 'consciousness' to be synonymous also with 'organism' and 'life'. If there were a word which satisfactorily expressed all three at once, I would use it. 'Consciousness' is the third Dimension.

We can speak of evolved and less-evolved consciousness. We ourselves are examples of evolved consciousness. I consider that some form of rudimentary consciousness attaches to *all* organisms, even the most primitive and even the single cell. I believe also that this shows up as some form of (possibly electrical) field around all or part of the organism. The Kirlian aura was a failed attempt to demonstrate such a field (see pp.103—6). But we are sure that an organism in water generates a weak electrical field, for example. And certainly we can show electrical-field activity around the human brain. I am not necessarily implying that any of these particular fields *are* consciousness — only that these, and probably others unknown, are found in association with consciousness, with life.

Ultimately, I believe that the existence of such fields will be used to prove the presence of life, and their absence will prove either death (as with a dead cell) or non-living in the first place (as with a computer).

Consciousness, especially evolved or self-conscious consciousness, has the ability to apprehend and move within all aspects of normal three-dimensional space (my first Dimension) and to move to and fro in the time of my second Dimension. In this sense the third Dimension 'contains' all the attributes of the previous Dimensions. However, our ability to move about within the time of the second Dimension appears to be limited. Only a few psychics are able to so move with any kind of regularity. The majority of people seem never to experience even occasional spontaneous movement.

What does it really mean to be able to see future events before they happen, or past events known to no living person? In Jung's words, it looks as if the future events already exist, and the past events still exist.

Actually, it would be enough that they exist *potentially*, in the following sense. It will be remembered that the letters 'a' and 'b' written on a flat sheet of paper and separated by the length of the paper could be brought together by folding the paper in half. They always *could* have been brought together potentially, before I actually folded the paper. Their coming together was always possible, even though they were completely separated in two-dimensional space, *simply by virtue of the existence* of the three-dimensional space, through which I eventually folded the paper.

Similarly, the past and the future in human terms must

always be potentially capable of occupying one and the same instant — that is, 'now' — otherwise they would never do it even on one occasion. Human consciousness, it seems, is only rarely able to do the necessary folding. None the less, to do the folding *at all*, consciousness must by definition somehow be *of* and have access to a further Dimension.

There is still one other problem. It does seem as if our ability to reach into the past and the future is limited. We do not know, for example, where Ug buried Og, husband of Nig, after he killed him. No echo of such distant human events seems to reach us. Similarly, it does not seem as if clairvoyants can tell us what is going to happen in the year AD 3000. Why are there these apparent limitations? Why cannot we reach infinitely far forward into the future and infinitely back into the past? Perhaps a more highly-evolved consciousness will be able to reach further. (It would meanwhile be of considerable interest to have a frequency graph of the actual distances into past and future reliably achieved by clairvoyants.)

The suggestion that psychics may one day be able to see further into the future and the past is not entirely speculative.

Nostradamus, a scholar and psychic who lived in the sixteenth century, wrote a long series of prophecies covering the future until 'the end of the world'. Nostradamus claims to have deliberately confused the order of these to avoid prosecution as a magician. Aside from this drawback (or deliberate subterfuge) there are a large number of prophecies which so far seem meaningless. Nevertheless, a few are extremely striking, and appear to be more accurate than even a blunderbus technique of many attempts can fully explain. For example 'near the harbour and in two cities will be two scourges the like of which have never been seen' does strongly suggest the atomic holocausts of Hiroshima and Nagasaki; while a quatrain numbered 49 states: 'the parliament of London will put their king to death'. Charles I was executed in 1649 — and this is the only occasion on which the British have carried out a death sentence on their king.[13]

Still more impressive, this time in respect of apparent distant paranormal perception of the *past*, is the vision of George Fox, a great religious teacher in England in the seventeenth century (for knowledge of whom I am indebted to Colin Wilson[112]). Fox writes:

> As I was walking with several friends, I lifted up my head and saw three steeple house spires, and they struck at my life. I asked them what that place was; they said 'Lichfield'. Immediately the word of the Lord came to me, that I must go thither . . . As soon as they were gone, I stept away, and went by my eye over hedge and ditch until I came within a mile of Lichfield; where, in a great field, shepherds were keeping their sheep. Then I was commanded by the Lord to pull off my shoes. I stood there, for it was winter, but the word of the Lord was like a fire in me. So I put off my shoes and left them with the shepherds; and the poor shepherds trembled, and were astonished. Then I walked about a mile, and as soon as I got within the city, the word of the Lord came to me, saying: 'Cry: Wo to the bloody city of Lichfield.' So I went up and down the streets, crying with a loud voice: Wo to the bloody city of Lichfield. It being a market day, I went into the market-place, and went up and down in several places of it, and made stands crying: Wo to the bloody city of Lichfield, and no one touched or laid hands upon me. As I went down the town, there ran like a channel of blood down the streets, and the market-place was like a pool of blood . . . so when I had declared what was upon me and cleared myself of it, I came out of the town in peace about a mile to the shepherds, and there I went to them, and took my shoes, and gave them some money, but the fire of the Lord was so in my feet and all over me that I did not matter to put my shoes on any more . . .
> After this, a deep consideration came upon me, for what reason I should be sent to cry against that city: Wo to the bloody city of Lichfield . . . But afterwards I came to understand that in the Emperor Diocletian's time, a thousand Christians were martyred in Lichfield. So I was to go, without my shoes, through the channel of blood, and into the pool of their blood in the market-

place, that I might raise up the memorial of the blood of
those martyrs, which had been shed above a thousand
years before, and lay cold in their streets.[25]

(What a marvellous example this is to psychics today simply
to go with their intuitive impulse.)

In all, then, it is possible that an organism creates a kind of
consciousness field in some sense supportive to the continued
existence of the consciousness of deceased individuals, and
conducive to the existence of future consciousness — whatever 'field' means here.

Dimension 4 — 'God'

'God' (with a small g) is that Dimension which contains the
other three. It is the highest level of spirit-in-space which
'spirit', as far as we are concerned, has as yet been able to
achieve. This Dimension has a rudimentary existence only.

I have to stress always that the spirit aspect of the actual
spirit-in-space equation or compromise (which is all we ever
apprehend) only resembles original 'spirit' in the most
tangential and indirect of ways. (Similarly, by observing the
space aspect of the spirit-in-space equation we gain only the
dimmest idea, if any, of the nature of 'space' in its own
terms.) So the Dimension 'god' does have *more* of 'spirit'
in it than the Dimension of matter. But the spirit element
of this Dimension, being as ever one more example of
spirit-in-space, is none the less significantly modified by
'space'.

As 'spirit' progressively transfers more of itself into 'space'
so it then undergoes a process of evolution — through the
Dimensions of matter, time and consciousness, to god and
beyond. Eventually at some point all of 'spirit' will be in
'space'. What that end-stage will consist of is impossible to
say, and what transpires afterwards we cannot know.

It seems to me essential that any theory of the nature of
the universe must have in it provision for some kind of
'dynamic directionalism' of this kind. And equally an
'evolving directionalism'. It is in this particular respects
that modern science is so notably and lamentably deficient.
Religion, by contrast, does not duck these issues. In fact

it makes of them its central platform. Herein lies the strong
appeal which religion makes to us.

More of these particular matters later — but I want to
emphasize here my belief that the Dimension 'god' arises
out of man (or any such similarly-evolved creature). Man
is the platform for god, just as matter was the platform for
man. 'Spirit' is the driving force behind the whole enterprise
from start to finish. 'Spirit' is not a Dimension — it lies prior
to all Dimensions, just as does 'space'. Dimensions as I
describe them arise as the result of the interaction of 'spirit'
with 'space'.

In a way the whole of our universe is a vast laboratory.
Experiments are taking place at a multitude of points. We
are one of those experiments. We may think of 'spirit' —
and here perhaps I can throw a bone, so to speak, to the
occultists — as the Alchemist of our universal laboratory.

PART IV

FIVE
The Physiology of ESP

For a good many years, as a young psychologist, I puzzled over the question of where the unconscious mind could actually be in relation to the physical body — that is, where it was *physiologically*.

As regards the conscious mind, a good deal of careful research by psychologists and physiologists had already shown that conscious human functions are located in that part of the brain we call the cerebrum — the wrinkled mass of tissue immediately visible on removing the top of the skull. The two cerebral hemispheres (as they are called) of this part of the brain seem to house such items as logical thought, volitional control of muscles, speech, memory, the human will and so on. We are sure about this, first because electrical stimulation of particular points of the cerebral hemispheres produces flashes of memory, jerks of the muscles and so on. Second, actual loss of particular parts of the cortex (outer layers) of the cerebrum tends to result in loss of a given conscious function or functions.

So where in all of this, I wondered, was the much-discussed unconscious mind? Stimulation of the cortex of the cerebrum never resulted in a dream, for example, nor did loss of parts of it result in loss of dreaming. In fact, animals with the cerebrum completely removed still show all the physiological movements and accompaniments of dreaming — including the rapid movements of the eyes which, as we now know, are actually watching the dream in progress.

Leaving the direct problem of the unconscious mind aside for the moment, we note that physiologists and psychologists divide the total human nervous system into two main parts. These two parts are called the autonomic nervous system and the central nervous system respectively. The word 'autonomic' means 'self-governing'.

The apex or most evolved part of the *central* nervous system is the cerebrum, which we were just discussing. So the central nervous system (or c.n.s. for short) is concerned with consciousness, with will, with thought, with logic, with being awake, with voluntary movement and so with the striped muscles. The striped muscles are all those muscles on such obvious view in body-builders like Mr Universe. The active human being that we see about his daily business is being run by his central nervous system — in fact he *is* his central nervous system, at that point.

The *autonomic* nervous system is concerned with quite other matters. It deals with digestion, with heart rate, sleep, body temperature, excretion, sweating, breathing and so forth — all the maintenance functions of the body. It has control of the smooth internal muscles, like those of the heart, and can also cause reflex movements of the striped muscles. All the glands, all hormone and chemical secretions, and the blood itself, are likewise under the jurisdiction of the autonomic nervous system (or a.n.s. for short). Importantly, sexual activity is also under the control of the a.n.s.

The autonomic nervous system is further sub-divided into two other systems. These, like the a.n.s. as a whole, are important in respect of paranormal phenomena. We will come to these sub-divisions later.

At some point the — in retrospect — obvious thought occurred to me that what the conscious mind is to the central nervous system, the unconscious mind might be to the autonomic nervous system. I was by no means the first to consider this possibility, of course. Freud, and others before and after him, had noted the strong connection between, say, unconscious guilt and sweating, unconscious conflict and indigestion, unresolved complexes and disturbed sexual behaviour, and so on. (As a broad generalization we can say that a neurotic person always shows evidence of a malfunctioning autonomic system.) From the point of view of neurosis, *but no less from the point of view of the paranormal*, dreams in particular play a very significant role. Sleep and dreaming are once again functions of the autonomic nervous system. So, again, the paranormal itself is probably linked to the a.n.s.

This is only one of many lines of reasoning which over and over in the study of the paranormal lead back to the autonomic nervous system, and conversely *away from* the central nervous system. As a further example, in magical ceremonies autonomic elements and states play a considerable part — blood, sexual activity, virginity, preparations made of removed sex and other internal organs, and so forth. There is a confirmatory *rejection* of consciousness, when, for instance, the practicants work themselves into frenzies or trances, or drug themselves, either literally, or by repetitive dancing and rhythmic music. The beat of such music, incidentally, seems to be clearly connected with the beating of the heart, as actual experimental studies have shown.

We ought to mention in passing also the fakirs and mystics of the East. As part of their religious or magical ceremonial they learn to control such normally unconscious and autonomic matters as heart rate, breathing, sensitivity to pain, need for food and so on. Such individuals can drive knives and skewers into their bodies without pain or bleeding and deprive themselves of oxygen for long periods. Though these matters are not paranormal in themselves in the true sense, they are very often found in close association with genuinely paranormal events and genuine paranormal powers.

However, in linking the paranormal with the autonomic nervous system, just as Freud linked neurosis with the a.n.s., the main question went, and goes, unanswered. *Where, physically, and what is the unconscious mind?* Neither Freud nor any psychoanalyst was able to answer this question. Jung, for example, was content to consider the a.n.s. as a whole as the seat of the unconscious. Hence — though also for many other reasons — psychoanalysis gradually fell into disrepute with orthodox scientists and psychologists. You speak of the alleged unconscious mind, they said, but you cannot show us where it is.

I myself saw the search for the *physical* location of the unconscious mind as the absolutely central issue in all the psychological and parapsychological questions with which I was preoccupied. I realized, too, that for me it was but another form of the search for the magical lands, Aladdin's cave, fairyland, the Lost World, the lands under the sea, which dominated my childhood even as late as the age of thirteen. (Though I am vague about most dates and chronologies of my childhood, I am sure of that one, because I remember that I hoped to win the friendship of a lad I knew in that year by finding a real magic carpet.)

So the search as a child for the magical world as an *actually existing place*, which had proved quite fruitless, was later transformed for me into the search for the unconscious. But it was not enough for me to enter and to understand the unconscious world in a psychological sense. Once again I wanted to know where the unconscious *really was*, physiologically. For it to have a genuine existence, I felt the unconscious mind must have some genuine physical base.

As I said earlier, Freud failed to find such a base. The question did not worry him unduly — or, at least, he never seems to admit that it did. His position was that the psychological events he was studying and reporting were valid in their own right. In this he was correct. Psychological events can never be *reduced* to physiological events (although certainly we ought always to be able to show physiological correlates of psychological events).

As for the autonomic nervous system, it seemed orthodox psychology was perfectly prepared to regard this as a kind of headless horseman. This system was just a collection of little self-regulating systems that managed their own affairs. Though collectively we might speak of them as the 'self-governing' system, nobody orthodox seemed to feel that this self-government demanded a governor.

But *I* wanted a governor. And it seemed the concept of a highly-evolved unconscious mind provided the necessary alternative government. After all, the unconscious mind must have evolved out of *something* — why not out of the a.n.s.? But yet this 'governor', if such he was, had nowhere to live. There was still no government house!

It was while I was actually preparing to write *Total Man* that the answer more or less literally exploded in my brain. The headquarters of the unconscious mind, its seat of government, must be the *cerebellum*.

In one instant it became clear to me that the dwarf, the moon, the hunchback, the cat — all the symbols of the unconscious — were actually descriptions of the cerebellum: while the magical worlds of Atlantis, fairyland and the Garden of Eden lay within it.

Cerebellum

What follows is necessarily a summary. Those wanting further physiological details will find these in earlier books of mine.

Figure 6 shows a vertical cross-section through a human head, with major areas of the brain marked. The cerebellum is situated at the lower rear of the skull, below the over-arching cerebrum. Its apparent size is about that of a clenched fist.

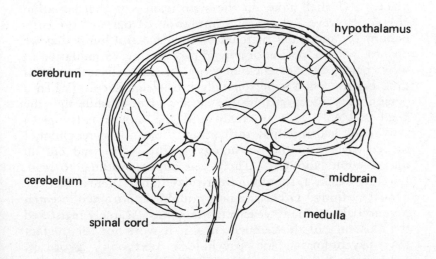

FIGURE 6 Section through the human brain

The summary facts concerning the cerebellum are these.
(1) It is far older, in evolutionary terms, than the cerebrum.
Though in a sense by-passed by nature at a certain point in
our evolution, the cerebellum has never ceased to evolve. It
reaches its highest point of development in man.
(2) The cerebellum is a relatively large organ. It weighs
more than the entire spinal cord. It is very complex. *It is in
fact the second most complex organ ever evolved by life on
this planet.* (A standard physiology textbook states: 'In
many ways the cerebellum is just as complex as the cerebrum.'[67]) Although by *weight* it is only eleven per cent of
the weight of the cerebrum, because of its complicated
folds and fissures the cerebellum is nevertheless *two-thirds
the size* of the cerebrum in respect of surface area. Surface
area is what counts.
(3) Like the cerebrum, the cerebellum has two upper hemispheres. These are covered with a layer of cerebellar cortex,
the equivalent of the cerebral cortex.
(4) The cerebellum receives extensive 'projections' from all
sensory systems. In the *cerebrum* such projections *are considered to be associated with consciousness.*
(5) Very little exploration of the cerebellum has taken
place. (I shall take up the significance of that situation
later.) However, electrical stimulation of parts of the cerebellum produces the twitches of the face and limbs that we
observe when a person or animal is dreaming. Stimulation of
other parts of the cerebellum produces the 'collapse' of limbs
that occurs when a person falls into deep sleep. (When a
person falls asleep sitting up, we see after a while that the
head suddenly lolls brokenly and the mouth falls open.)

When I had my first realization about the cerebellum, I
rushed eagerly to the physiology textbooks to find out all
that I could about it. There was almost nothing to read.
Looking back, I should have realized that there would be
almost nothing. Otherwise how could I, as a trained research
psychologist of many years' standing, have scarcely registered
the existence of the cerebellum — if it were not for the fact
that psychologists and psychology textbooks ignore it.

I believe that this is no chance omission. For the cerebrum
(consciousness) is paranoid about the cerebellum (the

unconscious). This same circumstance is, I think, the reason why we spend so much time and money exploring space, and so little exploring beneath the sea of our own planet, a much more vital source of information.

The moon (in magic and legend) is the cerebellum, because it is old and pitted and shines with less light than the sun (which, in symbolic terms, is the cerebrum). The moon shines by night, as does the cerebellum. (As I remarked in *Total Man*, we dream as if by moonlight.) The dwarf, again, is the cerebellum because he labours underground. He is smaller than a real person, as the cerebellum is smaller than the cerebrum. Fairy gold and fairy light (the consciousness of the *cerebellum*) vanish in the harsh glare of day (the consciousness of the cerebrum).

The labyrinths which the ancient Greeks built underground for their secret ceremonies — the word labyrinth is itself pre-Greek and we do not know its meaning — are, with their maze of confusing passages, models of the convoluted and folded cerebellum.

Labyrinths are underground and in darkness because the cerebellum is also underground, buried beneath the cerebrum. The cerebellum is the Atlantis of the nervous system (and Atlantis is itself a further symbol of it). The representative images and symbols of the cerebellum are always shrouded in darkness, buried below ground, or hidden under the sea.

How was it, then, that the cerebellum became buried by evolution and lost its own light?

The Evolution of the Cerebellum

In the developing human embryo, three brain structures flower from the brain stem. These are the fore-brain, the mid-brain and the hind-brain. (We believe, incidentally, that the human embryo, like the embryos of all animals, repeats in telegram form the entire history of its species, back into farthest time.) So it seems that at one stage of our very early evolutionary history — probably when our ancestors were still fish or primitive reptiles — the primitive brain possessed three sets of potentials. Of these three, however, that of the mid-brain was fairly quickly lost. The mid-brain survives in us today only as a small connecting stalk between the hind-brain and the fore-brain.

The hind-brain and the fore-brain of our early ancestors went on to develop into the cerebellum and the cerebrum respectively — just as they do in the growing human baby.

But there is more to this story. It looks very much as if nature's intention at one point was to wipe out both the mid-brain and the fore-brain, and to leave the hind-brain (the cerebellum) as the true headquarters of our being. This plan of making the cerebellum the dominant organ was partly followed through. Then, only, it seems that nature changed her mind and began rapidly to develop the fore-brain (the cerebrum). Yet the development of the hind-brain, the cerebellum, was not fully abandoned. It could have been, no doubt — as we see in the case of the mid-brain — but in fact it was not.

On the contrary, an astonishing situation arises. In association with the diminishing mid-brain and the cerebellum *many reptiles actually developed a second pair of eyes on top of their heads*! It was as if confused nature were carrying out two different plans at once. We are sure that this second pair of eyes was a fact, and the statement is found — though not *emphasized* — in the standard textbooks on the subject. To this day some primitive creatures (some lizards, the lamprey and the larvae of amphibians) retain a light-sensitive spot on top of their heads, an actual hole in the skull through which light enters and stimulates the gland that was once a pair of eyes.

This gland that was once a pair of eyes, on top of our ancestors' heads, is in ourselves today a single organ, buried in the middle of our brain. It is the pineal gland. (So it, too, is part of Atlantis.) But the wonders only begin with this statement. It is the pineal gland to which the Hindu mystics of 3000 years ago gave the name 'the third eye' — the 'eye' of clairvoyance and second sight.

The case for the cerebellum, in association with the vestigial mid-brain and the pineal gland, constituting the physical, physiological home of the paranormal is, as I hope is appreciated, already formidable. But we have not exhausted the evidence by a long way.

The Left-Handedness of the Cerebellum

By day, under normal waking conditions, the cerebellum functions as an auxiliary of the cerebrum. It works as a 'fine tuner' of movement and balance. Individuals who suffer damage to the cerebellum have difficulty when reaching for objects, tending to overshoot or undershoot with their hand. They often stagger in a drunken way when walking. These 'daylight' functions of the cerebellum are generally agreed, and I have no quarrel with them. (But, as we shall see, it is at night and certain other times that the cerebellum rouses from its daytime sleep, like the vampire — a further symbol of the cerebellum — and all the other creatures of legend and night, and takes its own share of life while the cerebrum sleeps.)

Some further well-established facts about the human nervous system are these.

When impulses from the organs of the body travel up to reach the *cerebrum* (the seat of waking consciousness), these impulses cross over before actually reaching the cerebrum, so that information from the left side of the body goes to the right cerebral hemisphere, and information from the right side of the body goes to the left cerebral hemisphere.

When information ascends to the *cerebellum*, however — which, incidentally, apart from sharing the pathways leading to the cerebrum also has ascending pathways of its own (it would seem in the cause of self-government) — these impulses do not cross. Messages from the left side of the body reach the left cerebellar hemisphere, and messages from the right side reach the right cerebellar hemisphere.

The direct result of this situation is that when efferent messages travel from the cerebellum to the cerebrum, these now have to cross over en route to take account of the existing arrangements of the cerebrum. The net outcome of all this as far as the cerebrum is concerned *is that the cerebellum is left-handed.*

The position I am suggesting becomes clear if we consider ourselves, as a first step, standing opposite and facing another human being. My right hand is nearest to his or her *left* hand and my left hand is nearest to his *right* hand.

Now consider what happens when we look at ourselves in a mirror. Our right hand has *become* a left hand and our left has become a right! When I move my right hand, the mirror-image (the 'other person') moves his left, and when I move my left he moves his right. In short, our mirror-image is left-handed. The functions of our two hands have crossed over.

The cerebellum, to spell this out, is therefore the mirror-image of the cerebrum. The same crossing over of function that happens metaphorically when we look at our own reflected image occurs *literally* between the cerebellum and cerebrum.

I believe that unconsciously we fully appreciate this situation in the nervous system. First, the cerebellum is literally left-handed — so that left-handedness, in the eyes of consciousness, becomes both evil and magical. (As most people know, the words for 'left' in the languages of the world always mean also something bad. In Anglo-Saxon *lyft* means weak, worthless, womanish. In French *gauche* means also awkward. In Italian *mancino* means also dishonest, and so on.) Second, *our own mirror-image* acquires the reputation of being magical. So a mirror, or a reflecting surface of water, is an entrance to the magical world. So the vampire and the ghost show no reflection in a mirror — because, I suggest, they *are* the reflection!

In medieval portraits, the Devil always steps from the magic circle, the pentagram (which is again a symbol of the cerebellum, though also of the vagina) with his left hand outstretched.

Dreams and Trance

We saw earlier how nature by-passed the cerebellum, intended originally it seems to be the true headquarters of the nervous system, in favour of the cerebrum.

The cerebellum could have been phased out completely at this point as was, effectively, the mid-brain. Yet for some reason the cerebellum was retained and continued to evolve.

In the same evolutionary period as brought the cerebrum to dominance, the cerebellum more than doubled its own size.

To describe what I consider happened in connection with the continued evolution of the cerebellum, I have to resort to human metaphors. I am not at all trying to suggest that nature herself conceives matters in this way — I am only trying to describe the underlying processes in a readily appreciable way.

As the cerebrum began to rise to power, the cerebellum, literally and metaphorically, went 'underground'. As far as possible without actually vanishing, it offered no threat, no challenge, to the cerebrum. It took a back seat, behind even the spinal cord, and completely away from the main trading routes between spinal cord, the lower and higher brain centres, and the cerebrum. It camouflaged itself in various ways. In appearance it mimicked the cerebrum ('look, I'm just like you') in the way some animals mimic attributes of animals that hunt them. So alike are these two brain organs that cerebellum actually means 'little cerebrum'. It made itself small by complex folding of its surface, so that although so tiny its surface area is actually two-thirds that of the cerebrum. So good is the functional camouflage that psychologists have completely overlooked the cerebellum, although it is on full view in the dissected brain.

The cerebellum also made itself useful, even indispensable, to the cerebrum. It said: 'I am completely at your service. I know that I am not pretty, but I am very useful. And I don't take up much room. I don't need much from you.' (The cerebellum is like the hunchbacked dwarf who assists the — often mad — scientist in his laboratory in horror novels and films, who gets no wages, sleeps in the corner, feeds on scraps. Indeed, the little hunchbacked assistant *is* the cerebellum. In this symbolic picture the 'madness' and overweening pride of the scientist are also relevant points, as we shall see.) Like the baby Moses in the bullrushes — yet another symbolic story of the cerebellum — this 'baby' in its basket can safely be brought into the palace. But then we see what the 'baby' can do! Or again, when Aladdin's lamp is rubbed, or the magic word spoken, the genie (the unconscious mind) of the lamp (the cerebellum) appears in all his power.

It is while the cerebrum sleeps that the cerebellum can live, up to a point, the life which evolution has denied it. So at night the sleeping vampire rouses for his brief spell of existence. Our dreams are the direct expression of the life and consciousness of the cerebellum.

Here now is a very significant aspect of cerebellar life. Like the vampire who sucks blood from the living, the cerebellum also lives *parasitically*. Though it generates a consciousness of its own, the cerebellum nevertheless *lives through* the cerebrum.

When we fall asleep, the electrical activity of the cerebrum, which has already slowed down and dwindled as we became drowsy, now shows predominantly long, slow waves. This is true, deep sleep. Then, about an hour after this condition of deep sleep has set in, suddenly the cerebral cortex is activated again in a manner very similar to that displayed in the waking state. But in fact the organism is more asleep than ever! The muscles of the body are not only slack — they are literally paralysed with slackness. What is happening is that dreaming has begun. The eyes now move beneath the closed lids, watching entranced the activities taking place in the cerebrum.

At this point the cerebellum is *using the contents of the cerebrum* for its own quixotic purposes. It is 'dressing up' in the contents of consciousness. It is play-acting in the storeroom, or the factory, closed and abandoned for the night. The cerebellum is *haunting* the cerebrum. Weird and insubstantial beings, parodies and grotesque distortions of what they are in real life and in real meaning (for the cerebellum does not understand the true purposes of consciousness) live out their ghostly lives on the silent, deserted stage.

(The toys which come to life at night, in *Coppélia*, *La Boutique Fantasque* and *Petrouchka*, are further symbols of cerebellar life.)

Yet the cerebellum and its consciousness do not only work at night in our dreams. I believe they are also at work *in all the various trance conditions we discussed earlier* (pp.76—82) — in mediumship, in hypnosis, under the influence of drugs, in love, in women especially and in children especially. Women have larger cerebella than men. Women dream more than men. Women are more superstitious than men. Children have more active cerebella than adults. Children dream more than adults. Children are more superstitious than adults. The reasoning is perfect here.

Trance conditions arise when cerebellar consciousness is called into being without waking consciousness having been fully abandoned (deliberately so in all magical ceremony). At this point 'ghosts' and real life become confused together. People see visions, hear voices, have hallucinations.

Yet a further dimension comes into play here, that of human evolution. Asiatics and Eastern peoples have larger cerebella than Westerners. (Do they dream more than Westerners? We do not know. I believe it will be proved that they do.) 'Hippies', artists and drop-outs dream more than conventional individuals.[46] (Do they have larger cerebella? We do not know. I say it will be proved that they do.)

As I have tried to show in the *Total Man* trilogy, we (modern man) are a hybrid creature, a cross between the Neanderthal and Cro-Magnon varieties of early man. Neanderthal man had an active religious life (see p.232) and we believe that Cro-Magnon took over many of Neanderthal's religious practices — though I believe he in no way had the same control over actual paranormal phenomena. *Neanderthal had a larger cerebellum than Cro-Magnon.*

Though the blood of Neanderthal and Cro-Magnon runs in each one of us, in modern world society there are some individuals with a greater dash of Neanderthal and others with a larger element of Cro-Magnon. Those individuals with a greater element of Neanderthal will be more religious and superstitious than their fellow-men and, importantly, more genuinely endowed with paranormal powers. Mediums are examples of this situation.

Evolutionary Purpose

What has life or nature really been doing in this matter of cerebrum and cerebellum? Again, the answer is something I have to express in man-centred, unscientific terms.

I believe that nature decided her plans for a cerebellum-dominated organism were premature. Perhaps nature or the life-force ('spirit', of course) saw that life on this planet was too hazardous for so 'spiritual' a creature, that she had under-estimated the real, objective dangers. It was necessary for nature first to enable man to deal with the physical world, to make them masters of the world of matter *in matter's own terms*.

So 'spirituality', or paranormality, was shelved for the time being and the go-ahead was given for the production of an objective, reality-centred brain. (No explanation is ever given in religious and occult accounts, incidentally, for the strong evolution of the cerebrum and reality-consciousness in man.) Nevertheless, as we have seen, the 'spiritual' brain was by no means entirely abandoned. Work on it continued as far as circumstances allowed.

Two points here. In *birds*, it seems, nature organized a pilot run of a possible cerebellum-dominated creature. Although the cerebellum reaches its peak of *absolute* development in man, it reaches its *relative* peak of develop-ment in birds. Birds are among the creatures that have long been felt by man to have a rather special relation to the paranormal. As Jung and others have noted, the gathering of a flock of birds in an unexpected place or way seems often to be a warning of death. I am myself more impressed by the following circumstance. Although the cerebellar develop-ment of birds has proceeded to the detriment of the develop-ment of the cerebrum — the seat apparently of all rational activities — nevertheless the only examples of the use of spontaneous, meaningful language I have been able to find in many years of research are in respect of birds (see Appendix II 'The Conceptual Powers of Animals').

The second point is that in Neanderthal nature seems to have gone some way towards the production of a cerebel-lum-dominated form of man. Not only is there strong circumstantial evidence of Neanderthal's involvement in religion and the paranormal, but there is good evidence that he was nocturnal — as the large, round eye-sockets and the large ear-cavities seem to indicate. There is further strong cir-cumstantial evidence that Neanderthal man was left-handed.

I myself consider that left-handedness (apart from the forms of it that are sometimes caused by brain damage at birth and during pregnancy) is brought about by an unusually powerful and permanent influence of the cerebellum on waking consciousness. Many men of outstanding ability — of genius in fact — are left-handed, far more than their maximum ten per cent share of the world population would allow: Michelangelo, Leonardo da Vinci, Goethe, Beethoven, Nietzsche, Holbein, Chaplin are only a few examples.

So nature by no means put *all* her evolutionary eggs in the one cerebral basket. And then, around 35,000 years ago, by crossing genetically the Neanderthal and Cro-Magnon forms, she made sure her cerebellar work was not wasted. There is good evidence (see my earlier books) that the Neanderthal element in the population is on the increase. Very many of the active social and revolutionary movements in the world today and of recent times are examples of what I call the 'Neanderthal backlash' — Christianity, Communism, the Romantic Movement, Spiritualism, Psychoanalysis and Women's Liberation. All of these, we notice, both literally and metaphorically, *rise up from below* — from an inferior social position usually, and from the unconscious mind always.

Large-Scale Evolution

Cerebellum and cerebrum, Neanderthal and Cro-Magnon, female and male are all aspects of a still larger process. This is the interaction of 'libido' and 'aggression'. Libido is Freud's name for the energy of the unconscious. Aggression requires no special definition. These two forms of energy seem to run side by side through all life, even in a rudimentary sense in single-celled organisms. Libido is always concerned with inward affairs (rather like the autonomic nervous system) and aggression with external affairs (like the central nervous system).

In man, both libidinal and aggressive impulses are initially unconscious and instinctive, but seem even in the unconscious always to remain separated. Freud energetically argues this, dividing the two energies of the primal unconscious into libido-instincts and ego-instincts. Libidinal energy is 'sexual' energy in the broadest sense of the term. In man libido evolves variously into emotion, religious feeling and spirituality. Aggression evolves ultimately into intellect and objectivity (both of which retain clear features of the initial aggression — see my earlier books and Chapter 6 of this book) just as religion retains traces of sexuality.

It can be asked: if religion and sexuality are closely related, and if aggression and intellect are closely related, why does religion so strongly deny sex and intellect so strongly deny aggression? The brief answer is that any surge of basic libido — 'sexuality' — swamps and for the time being puts out of action the fine tuning of the more highly-evolved aspects of the intuitive mind. And similarly, any surge of anger swamps for the time being the more finely-tuned and highly-evolved aspects of the cognitive mind.

In the terms defined in Chapter 4, libido is closer to 'spirit', while aggression is closer to 'space' — though, as ever, both remain examples of spirit-in-space. Spirituality is, however, *not* a more highly-evolved form of consciousness. It is merely another form. In ourselves actually it is a *less* well-developed form of consciousness than intellect.

A useful general term for the consciousness of libido (of the cerebellum) is 'Self', and a useful general term for the consciousness of aggression (of the cerebrum) is 'Ego'. These two terms respectively embrace all the psychological aspects of the two evolved energies of man.

The Sympathetic and Parasympathetic Systems

As mentioned earlier, the autonomic nervous system subdivides into two sub-systems, known as the sympathetic and parasympathetic nervous systems respectively. The two are very closely interconnected. Some functions of the one are always involved in some functions of the other. Nevertheless, the separate emphasis of each is clear and in many ways the operation of the two sub-systems is mutually antagonistic.

The names which scientists have given to these two subsystems are not specially good ones, but we are stuck with them. The sympathetic system, then, is concerned with anger and aggression, and violent emotions of this kind. It *spends* the body's energy resources, often quite recklessly. The parasympathetic system, conversely, is involved in states of quiescence — digestion, resting, sleep, the general conservation of resources and body repair; and, importantly, with sexual activity.

Although the two major systems, the autonomic nervous system and the central nervous system, have diverged away from each other in their evolution, becoming always more separate, at primitive levels it seems clear that the *sympathetic sub-system* of the a.n.s. does make a contribution to the evolution of the Ego and so to that of the central nervous system generally. We could say that anger is a 'useful' emotion to the Ego (in moderation at any rate). The states of passivity and receptivity (aspects of the *parasympathetic* sub-system) are of no use to the Ego. To use Freudian terminology again, anger and aggression are therefore primitive *ego-instincts*.

It will probably already be clear that I consider paranormal powers, although a property of the unconscious generally and of the autonomic system as a whole, to be specifically far more closely associated with the parasympathetic system. For once language is kind to us here and gives us an easy way of remembering: the *para*sympathetic system is the main source of *para*normal activity.

Now we can understand why the states of loving, receptivity and passivity are at the heart of the world religions: and why aggression (along with the Ego as a whole) is banished from them. Unconsciously man has long realized that it is his parasympathetic system, and the physiological and psychological states associated with it, which are the true doorway to the paranormal and the non-material Dimensions.

Once we begin to look in this way, the evidence is on all sides. During eighty per cent of dreaming time, for example, the male has an erection. (We can observe this easily enough in the household dog — the penis is erect during the twitchings of the face, eyes and limbs that denote dreaming.) It is in the state of love — between human lovers, between parent and child, between owner and pet — that spontaneous

paranormal events often occur. As we saw, the power to
attract animals paranormally also resides in the loving,
'religious' nature, as exemplified by St Hugh of Lincoln.
The professional medium when 'sitting' chooses a situation
of calm and quiet, puts aside all active thoughts, drinks a
glass or two of water (to activate digestive processes?),
closes the eyes and passively surrenders himself or herself to
the 'psychic influences'. The general practice of meditation
involves a similar surrender to the parasympathetic system.
What one is doing essentially is approaching the state of sleep
without actually sleeping (though in fact many meditators do
fall asleep!).

Conversely, the vast majority of psychics and mystics are
united in considering that states of anger and hatred are *not*
conducive to paranormal events. (A possible exception to
this general rule is poltergeist phenomena, assuming these to
be genuine. So we cannot leave the sympathetic sub-system
out of account completely. Poltergeist phenomena may be
the result of unconsciously blocked libido — that is, blocked
sexual impulses — or alternatively of blocked aggression.) I
myself consider that so-called 'black magic', presumably
deriving from states of aggression, is actually far less effective than so-called 'white magic', deriving from states of
receptivity and self-surrender. We recall that the psychic
healer who cured the tumours in one group of mice was
unable to make the tumours *worse* in the control group.
Despite all the blood-curdling novels and films based on
'black magic' there seems in actuality to be very little of it
around indeed. There are, of course, plenty of half-wits
prancing about naked in churchyards at midnight, but the
amount of paranormal activity they generate is, I suggest,
practically, if not absolutely, nil.

I hope we can now see that, translated, the figure of god in
religion is the parasympathetic system and that the devil is
the sympathetic system. It is these two sub-systems of the
total nervous system which, ultimately, give rise to these
archetypal (or, as I call them, archestructural) figures. In the
Christian and most other religions it is good which is stronger
than evil, god who is stronger than the devil. Translated,
this tells us what we have already established — it is the

parasympathetic system which is the major generator of the paranormal, not the sympathetic system.

Pseudo-Physiology

In India, China and elsewhere we find esoteric accounts of alleged aspects of human physiology, neither generally known, nor generally accepted in the West.

Indian mysticism speaks of seven major 'chakras' (though actually some say eight or nine). These are body centres into or through which spiritual energy flows. Various authorities mention a great many more minor chakras. None of the chakras, major or minor, can be seen, as it were, with the naked eye. They are invisible, aspects of the 'subtle anatomy' of man. The main chakras are arranged in ascending order from the base of the spine and the sexual organs, up the spine, to the top of the skull. Some of them are associated with specific known physical organs — the seventh and highest, for instance, being the pineal gland (the 'third eye'). Others are much more vaguely associated. The solar-plexus chakra, for instance, is associated with the pancreas, stomach, liver, gall bladder and nervous system — a motley collection, hardly inspiring any confidence in precision! The confusions mount as we proceed.

One of the main purposes of yogic studies seems to be to activate the chakras, so that spiritual energy can flow more readily. There are, however, considerable differences between, for example, the Hindu and Buddhic accounts of these matters. Lama Anagarika Govinda writes: 'It is, therefore, not permissible to mix up these two systems and to explain the Buddhist practice of meditation as if it were based upon or derived from the teachings and the symbolism of the Hindu tantras.'[38] Hindu yoga also speaks of the energy of 'kundalini', which after many years of yogic training and self-discipline can suddenly flow up the spine to burst in the head, in the form of a dazzling white light. (I suspect that kundalini is an aspect of libido, and that what is activated is perhaps the cerebellum.)

We cannot dismiss out of hand such esoteric theories concerning the possible 'subtle anatomy' of man, even though we see in them a great deal of confusion, a great many undefended assumptions and very little in the way of a practical outcome. For the realization of the evolutionary history and purpose of the pineal gland by the ancient Hindus was an astonishing piece of intuitive detective work. So we must be careful what we discard.

A further case in point here, however, is the Chinese theory and practice of acupuncture. Based on a *very* different view of the alleged subtle body of man from either the Indian or the Tibetan views, acupuncture is nevertheless a valid method of treating illness and of removing pain, simply by the process of inserting tiny silver needles in what are to us strange parts of the body, like the ear-lobes or the toes. Though pooh-poohed for centuries in the West, acupuncture has now been tested by Western doctors and found, by and large, to work. (It seems less effective on Caucasians than Asiatics, however.) Western science currently has no explanation as to how acupuncture works. But, on the other hand, is the Chinese *explanation* of acupuncture valid? We certainly know that the practice is. Possibly the explanation is not.

The crucial point I am trying to make is, how are we to stop things getting out of hand in esoteric physiology? Given that I have said there are aspects of life in the universe that can best, and in my opinion only, be explored intuitively, how are we to separate genuine intuition from phoney or mistaken intuition? What are the checks?

In general, my feeling is that we should abandon *conventional* physiology only when we are forced to — that is, only at the point where conventional physiology proves inadequate as an explanation. Despite its outlandish flavour, I think my own account of the cerebellum *is*, in principle, assimilable into the body of normal physiology.

First, an instance of what seems to me a clear case of intuition getting completely out of hand. This is the esoteric teaching of Alice Bailey, as currently purveyed by David Tansley and others. It is based on the Hindu and Buddhic teachings we were discussing, and a sample of this teaching, rendered by David Tansley, is available in *The Frontiers of Science and Medicine*. Tansley has also written books of his own.[98]

Apart from reading the texts concerned carefully, I have also attended a number of public lectures at which I have put questions. I have also discussed these matters with students of the subject. Nevertheless, I regret to say that I have not been able to make one word of sense of any of it. Despite many hours of work, I still do not know what a Buddhic permanent atom is. I do not know what the three fold monad is. I do not know what the solar angel is. I do not understand the plane of the second logos. I cannot grasp the first cosmic ether. Far from that, I cannot even see the reasons for postulating these concepts in the first place. It seems to me, on sad reflection, that most of this subject matter is intriguing, complex and beautiful — misconception.*

So what checks and balances, then, can we apply to intuitive thinking to make sure it does not fly completely off the handle? How can we stop David Tansley's esoterics, for example, going everywhere except somewhere? Bringing the question still nearer home, how can I personally show that my own theories are not just another wild free-for-all?

It seems to me that cosmologies and macro-theories of life or of the universe must nevertheless somewhere and somehow touch the smaller framework of the objective universe and of day-to-day life. First, all phenomena are continuous in some sense. Life, while reaching beyond it, is nevertheless rooted in the physical universe. The physical body, especially, is very much part of the physical universe. Macro-theories *must* therefore at least occasionally nod in the direction of the objective, material universe. When they do not, we must suspect them of being either inadequate or deliberately framed in such a way as to avoid having them put to the test. Their inventors are then guilty of conspiracy (as defined on pp.45—6). Major aspects of macro-theories of life will certainly lie beyond the scope of scientific testing — but minor ones should not.

---

* I ought to say more on these matters — but this would take us too far into this specialist area. I shall be discussing all these points in detail in a later book, *The Religious Impulse.*

A good general theory, whether it is intended to or otherwise, will generate what are called testable hypotheses. For example, the concepts of repression, sublimation and projection in Freudian psychoanalytic theory have been shown to operate under controlled experimental conditions. Jung, for his part, devised the standardized word-association test both to prove and to harness the Freudian view of free association.

My own theory of the paranormal generates a good many testable propositions (and I have for some time now been actively engaged in interesting research organizations in their investigation). For example, in my view the incidence of left-handedness ought to be much higher among mediums than it is in the general population.

I was discussing this last proposition at one point with a group of acquaintances, all of whom were psychic, some highly so. One of them expressed strong doubts about my suggestion. I then pointed out that of the eight people present, six were left-handed, one was ambidextrous, and only one right-handed (myself). The incidence of left-handedness in the general population is around ten per cent — one in ten.

I have also proposed that cats as a species, perhaps the most mystical animal of all (and the witch's cat or familiar, I suggest, again symbolizes the cerebellum), will be shown to have larger cerebella than dogs.

It follows very much from my theories that human individuals with strong psychic powers will have larger (or in some definable way more active) cerebella than non-psychic individuals. After putting forward this view in *Total Man*, I subsequently came across two individuals with noted psychic powers who reported *actual conscious experience of the cerebellum during their paranormal activity*. These two individuals were no less than Swedenborg himself, and Jerome Cardan, a sixteenth-century British physician.*

The Chinese — as the producers of the miraculous book, the *I Ching* — ought to have the largest and most active cerebella of all humans. Again after completing *Total Man*,

* See *The Neanderthal Question*, Chapter 7.

I came across actual proof of this in the book *Men of the Old Stone Age* by the anthropologists Breuil and Lantier. Modern Chinese, it appears, have the largest cerebella of all, 'very incompletely covered by the cerebrum'. I could not have asked for better experimental confirmation. Moreover, very recent research suggests that the incidence of left-handedness among Chinese is at least eighteen per cent — nearly double that of the West.[102]

So there is very much a practical side and a solid testable basis in objective fact to my general theory.

However, there is one hidden negative in this optimistic picture. The fact that a theory has a testable basis is no guarantee that scientists will actually undertake that testing. Wilhelm Reich, for example, was unable to persuade other scientists either to observe his demonstrations or check his findings. Here we clearly see the paranoia of the orthodox scientist, one instance of the general fear that the Ego (the cerebrum) has of the Self (the cerebellum).

For this reason you will look in vain in the indexes of modern psychology textbooks for words like trance or mediumship or telepathy or clairvoyance or left-handedness (except as a form of handicap) or love or spirit — or any of the terms and subject matter not just of the paranormal, but of the whole warmth and depth of human existence — in short, of the human experience.

I Ching

If we had no other proofs of the validity of intuitive, non-scientific exploration of the universe, the *I Ching* alone would suffice. The *I Ching* is a living, existing miracle.

I introduce this magical book at this point to show that not all esoteric accounts of the universe are as insubstantial as the Hindu and the Buddhic. As to the direct connection of the *I Ching* with physiology, the two halves of the yin—yang symbol, the dark and the light, seem to be once again the cerebellum and the cerebrum respectively, and of course female and male. I have also myself suggested that the solid and broken lines of the oracle are stylized representations of the male and female sex organs. Apart from such literal features, the *I Ching* in any case never moves far from living, breathing, here-and-now life.

Objectively speaking, this phenomenon is an ancient Chinese book of wisdom, and an oracle for telling the future. It is built around sixty-four patterns of solid and broken lines. Each pattern gives a different text reading. Added to each of the sixty-four main readings are six further small readings. And finally, in some circumstances a secondary main reading is also obtained. One method of consulting the book, the one I always use myself, is by throwing three coins in the air six times and allowing them to fall at will on the floor. The face and reverse of each coin has a numerical value which, when computed, yields the relevant readings.

In summary, the *I Ching* is an a-scientific statement of laws governing each individual's present and future life on this planet. Impossible, of course — but the proof of the pudding is in the eating. Somehow, by the controlled use of intuition, which appears to owe nothing whatsoever to science and objectivity, the composers of this book have hit upon laws, or relationships, which apparently govern the course of individual human life on this planet.

The book itself is very ancient. Its origins actually pre-date the existence of writing. It was initially a verbal tradition. In those far-off times, several thousand years ago, it seems that people had far more trust in and far more control over the intuitive faculty — they did not have science getting in the way, coming between them and their certainty! There once existed other books resembling the *I Ching*. All these were destroyed at the orders of the Emperor Ch'in Shih Huang Ti (clearly a paranoid Ego). Their loss is irreparable. The *I Ching* reveals to us just how inadequate are our own intuitive powers. I personally would not have the faintest idea of how to go about putting the book together from scratch — and neither would anyone else. But though a mystery, the *I Ching* actually works. What do I mean by 'actually works'?

I mean that, providing you obey the rules of the *I Ching*, you can by consulting it obtain a detailed analysis of your current problems, together with comment as to how these have arisen and how you can solve them — or an analysis and exposition of a *future* period or event — whichever you specify. The comments and analyses, I must emphasize, are not woolly generalizations or remarks that can be twisted to fit any set of circumstances. The statements are very precise and habitually, as it were, 'take the words right out of your mind'. The book will frequently use expressions to you that you have been using to yourself.

While as always with the paranormal there is no hope of convincing anyone else at second hand — necessarily you will have to make your own first-hand experience — one or two examples of the position may prove instructive. One such was given to me by the late Dr Manfred Lowengard, the internationally-known psychic.

He and some friends had been waiting in a private house for a lecturer, who was to speak to them on some aspect of the paranormal. The time of the lecture came and went. No lecturer appeared and there was no telephone call. To pass the time, Dr Lowengard suggested that they ask the *I Ching* what had gone wrong. They obtained a reading: 'The mule is stubborn. The mule will not go.' Eventually the lecturer arrived. On coming in through the front door he exclaimed: 'That damned mule of a motor-bike let me down!' After the roar of delighted laughter had subsided, and the position been explained, the lecturer said that he had never referred to his motor-bike as a mule before, and seldom used the expression in any context.

A mildly reproving example of my own is as follows. I had obtained a reading from the *I Ching* about my immediate state of affairs, with which I was thoroughly disgruntled. It told of all the things that I had hoped were not going to happen (and was, as events turned out, as accurate as usual). I was quite unwilling to accept the verdict of the *I Ching* on this occasion. In my mood of irritation and despair I told myself, not for the first time, that this was all nonsense. How could printed words on a page of a book umpteen thousand years old fix my future (and such an unwanted future, at that)? In contempt I asked the book: 'How now brown cow?', and threw the coins. The reading I got said, 'Care of the cow brings good fortune', and gave me a lecture on the virtues of patience.

On another occasion (at a very difficult decision point) I obtained what seemed to me a particularly meaningless and quite irrelevant answer. Deciding that there had been some mistake, I threw the coins again with the same question, though the rules forbid one doing this. I obtained exactly the same reading on the second occasion, a statistical event of rather astronomical unlikelihood. The next day, in despair, I decided to throw the coins an unprecedented third time, to force the issue. This time I got the reading that says: 'If the seeker is importunate, and asks the same question many times, the oracle will refuse to answer.' Small wonder that one feels the *I Ching* is not a book, but a living being.

One further recent example. In 1976 I was sent a new translation of the *I Ching*, by Wildwood House, for whom I act as reader. I was at first very suspicious of the book, being a devoted admirer of the Richard Wilhelm translation. However, the more I studied the new book, the more I liked it. The upshot was that I decided to recommend it for publication. Then it occurred to me — why not ask the Richard Wilhelm translation what it thought of this new one? Alas, I did not have my own *I Ching* by me at the time. I decided to throw the coins anyway, and look up the reading later. Then a further thought — why not ask this present *I Ching* what it thought of itself? At this point I had, incidentally, already thrown the coins.

The reference I obtained was number 48 — which is named 'I Ching' (the well), from which reference the book as a whole takes its name. So the book was saying yes, I am the real *I Ching*. The secondary reference obtained on this occasion was number 46, 'New Growth Out of Maturity'. What answer could have been more appropriate and more confirming than this?

I duly recommended the book for publication and included all the above events in my report also.[86]

How indescribably different this 'illogical' position is, and how incomprehensible to the laws of science and causality. With the *I Ching* one experiences a living, alive, changing relationship, as with another person.

The inner structure of the book, I repeat, remains a mystery

to me. The outer structure can of course be described —
a series of patterns of continuous and broken lines. But
this tells us *nothing* of why or how the oracle works. It
seems that the ancient Chinese had the justified confidence
and a powerful intuitive capacity that enabled them to say
simply, 'This is so.' And it *is* so.

I believe anyone can convince himself of the efficacy of
the *I Ching*, providing he obeys the rules and approaches the
book in the right spirit. The rules are these. You can only
ask the oracle the same question once. The answer you get
is *the* answer. (The rule of one question, one answer, has
applied in the magical world down through the ages. The
famous oracle at Delphi always only gave one answer to
each individual.) How sharply and diametrically this attitude
contrasts with that of science — which insists upon repeatability.

There can be no testing of the *I Ching* as science understands testing, because you can never seek to get the same
result twice. I have never sought to test the *I Ching*
objectively in this sense and I think all thought of that should
be put out of one's head. In practice, of course, a form of
testability does arise — you either find the answers meaningful and helpful or you do not. At unusually difficult times
in my life I have adopted the following procedure. First I
asked for a statement about the next six months (I have
never been bothered about what happens in the more
distant future). Then, at the beginning of each succeeding
month I asked for a specific prediction concerning that
month alone. Thus I had six statements within one large
statement. Not only was each individual prediction accurate,
but the six small readings were congruent in terms of the
overall long-term prediction. So this usage was, in practice,
a kind of testing.

I personally think one should not approach the *I Ching*
lightly or frivolously, or even frequently. There have been
times when I have not consulted the oracle almost for a
whole year. I did, however, in fact obtain a reading for the
six months in which I wrote this book, before starting to
write. I obtained the reading 'Integrity'. I think integrity is
a fair summary of the concerns of this book. At any rate, it

is for me.

Never forget that the reading is for you *personally*. You must not necessarily expect it to seem relevant or accurate to another person. I can promise, however, that it will startle you with the sense of a presence in the universe beyond normal space and time.

Do we have any other formalized means of contacting or sensing the presence — aside, that is, from the flashes of the spontaneous phenomenon? I think probably the answer for the moment is no — but there are perhaps one or two partially successful and partially formalized approaches. I have sometimes seen Tarot cards and ordinary playing cards used with striking effect. Margaret Morton seems to me to have a genuine gift in the use of cards, for example. What I am unsure of, however, is whether the cards harness the psychic abilities of the reader of the cards, or whether the cards themselves are an independent statement in the way that the *I Ching* is. If they are, we unfortunately lack the complete code. We must interpret the cards — whereas the *I Ching* interprets its symbols for us. We do indeed have a long way to grow into the intuitive.

SIX
The Knowledge that is not Science

The chemical and, ultimately, mathematical descriptions of the biochemical processes which take place in every organism are not the same item as the conscious experience of those processes and their consequences. It is astonishing actually that one has to make such a self-evident statement — but many scientists do not in fact accept it. They consider, certainly for all scientific purposes, that chemical descriptions and conscious experience are one and the same.

To a limited extent we can reproduce or duplicate simple aspects of an organism's biochemical and bio-electric processes outside the organism, and in the laboratory and the test tube. But in no way can we remove and examine an organism's consciousness. (For this basic reason — although also because of the complexity of consciousness — even purely psychological experiments, let alone the parapsychological, are only rarely repeatable. Only the most stereotyped reactions, which heavily involve permanent circuits of neurones, can be repeated with any degree of reliance.)

Somebody once remarked that while everybody else had a small, roughly-spherical object on top of his shoulders, he himself had a universe.

The universe takes place in our heads. This statement holds good even though many of the events which trigger the experiences of consciousness are outside our head and have their own independent, objective existence. Paranormal experiences, however, both first and last *only* exist in our heads. In the absence of human beings and other organisms, I suggest, the paranormal entirely ceases to exist, as far as the external physical universe is concerned.

Organisms are a bridge between the paranormal universe (whatever that is) and the objective, material universe. As human beings we have a foot in both camps — we have a physical body that obeys the laws of the material universe, and a consciousness which, at least sometimes, does not.

Material events can only move forward in time, at a speed (or rate of change) dictated by the material forces operating on them. Consciousness can run ahead of time (of the moment of material 'now') into time not yet; and back through time into time gone.

Or at least, that is how these matters are usually expressed. But I myself would prefer rather to say that consciousness is in touch with a dimension *where all events that ever were or will be exist simultaneously*. This is really a much better way of describing the position — and enables us to begin to understand a book like the *I Ching*. The *I Ching*, it seems, taps the dimension of eternity, where serial time and spatial separation are annihilated.

This last is a difficult, but not an impossible idea to grasp. Two analogies or illustrations of it are these.

In a one-dimensional world (using the word dimension in the conventional geometrical sense) the following 'events' — in the three parts of Figure 7 — are two sets of straight lines running parallel to each other.

FIGURE 7a

But then I am given some further, two-dimensional information — in Figure 7b — and I realize that what I thought were a number of short, straight lines are actually aspects of a much more complex situation.

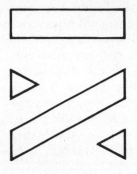

FIGURE 7b

But now I am given yet more, three-dimensional, information — in Figure 7c — and find that the actual situation is more complex still.

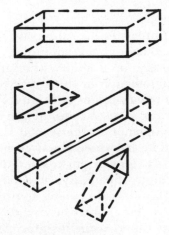

FIGURE 7c

The lesson here is that extensions in other dimensions show us aspects of situations, which we could otherwise not guess at — or at any rate could not confirm.

A second analogy is a little nearer what I am trying to say about the dimension of 'timelessness'. To print this page you are reading I could produce one letter at a time, one after the other, as I do with a typewriter. Or I can take a plate on which all the letters have been previously assembled and print the whole page in one movement — as with a printing press. The end result is in both cases identical although the paths to them were very different. But suppose, further, that in the case of the typewriter, as each new letter appeared, so the one before it vanished. Then we would have something like the notion of a moving (and annihilating) 'now', which also could not see the future. By contrast, the full printed page, where 'past' and 'future' letters were united in an enduring 'present', is then the dimension of timelessness.

The two examples given are only analogies — but they do help us to understand the idea of dimensions which supersede the limits and limitations of any or all dimensions currently available.

Science

The scientist approaches his subject by three stages. First he observes a phenomenon, perhaps initially in a state of nature, then more closely in a more structured framework. In placing the phenomenon in this framework he has probably already made a few decisions as to what is important. On the basis of his various observations, he arrives at an understanding of the phenomenon — the second stage. Then, to make quite sure that he has understood correctly, he undertakes the third step. He now begins to manipulate the situation he has observed and, apparently, understood in a series of experiments. His aim is to be able to produce and to modify the results to order. When he can do this time and time again, and when others using his procedures can also achieve the same results, the job of the scientist in respect of that particular phenomenon is complete. His findings can now be added to the body of scientific knowledge.

I have no objection in principle to these three stages of science — observation, understanding, control — being applied to the study of the paranormal. The objection lies rather in the many prejudices which science brings to the task. For the scientist thinks, for example, that control involves giving orders. He cannot understand that it may involve taking orders.

As I remarked in the section 'Bye-Bye Science' — pp.167—71, having dethroned the medieval god of superstition, science has now set itself up in the dethroned god's place. In tones scarcely distinguishable from those of the Old Testament prophets the scientist declares: 'Thou shalt have no other god beside me.' The religion of science, as I have said, is measurement and its law is causality.

Science is also quite unable to tolerate the idea that the relationships and interactions of paranormal events may not be causal. Quite on the contrary, it is very much in favour of the idea that paranormal events, like material events, can necessarily be broken down into ever-simpler stages, until we discover the basic building blocks or 'atoms' of the paranormal.

These attitudes and assumptions, I must emphasize, are prejudices. That is, they are prejudgments. There is therefore no willingness on the part of science to approach the paranormal with a genuinely open mind.

Freud, incidentally, encountered similar problems with scientists when he began to study dreams. 'How can you study dreams?' he was asked. 'They are so fleeting and indistinct.' To which he replied: 'As to the indistinctness of that is a characteristic like any other. We cannot characteristics.' But the scientist of the paranormal. He seeks to cs.

led, are entirely clear that the herwise unbreakable laws of the s back into time gone, and forward al matter, however, can only move ange *onward* — and is moreover the own present. That is, it can only be it at any particular moment permit

ome other organisms) are not entirely resent and they are not entirely the ical universe. They pass from it, momentarily, into some other universe of events — or, as I have defined it, some other Dimension.

The above comments do not exhaust the evidence for the inadequacy of science in its approach to the paranormal, or to other aspects of life and consciousness. The experience *of being*, as I have already partly suggested, itself lies beyond the reach of science. Nobody can measure the fact that I know that I know. To quote R. D. Laing again, existence is 'primary and self-validating'. The condition of being, of existence, of knowing, and knowing that one knows, all these *are*, both before science comes and after it is gone. They are independent of the regard of science and objectivity.

I hope the point is clear. I am raising no objection whatsoever to a scientific, objective study of physical or material aspects of life. Much good comes of that. The damage begins when science maintains (for instance) that a *description* of life is the same as *being alive*.

One piece of lunacy which follows from the scientific standpoint on this topic is that a clockwork toy which mimics the movements of a mouse is considered to be the *equivalent* of the mouse. If the clockwork toy is so designed that it avoids obstacles or increases its speed in the presence of a cat, it is said to be exhibiting intelligence!!

Therefore a computer is held to be the equivalent of a human being. A heap of lifeless junk is held to be the equivalent of a human being.

Of the radiant sense of existence, the fire of being blazing at the heart of every human, and every organism, nothing is said.

(It would be appropriate here to comment on some of the differences observed between synthetic vitamin C and naturally-occurring vitamin C demonstrated by Justa Smith and others — but I will keep those comments for the next chapter.)

In the section 'Synchronicity and Coincidence' I described the view, forcefully demonstrated by Gestalt psychology, that for human beings a whole is more than the sum of its parts. The tendency to organize parts into meaningful wholes, which then have properties not predictable or derivable from a knowledge of the parts in isolation, is extensively present in the human psyche and, by inference, in the psyche of other organisms also. Gestalt building (the creation of meaningful wholes) is possibly a property of the Dimension of consciousness, but not a property of the Dimension of matter, as these were defined earlier. The 'wholes' of matter are perhaps completely derivable from the properties of the parts. The whole can then be broken down into its constituents without essential loss. Gestalts or meaningful configurations, I suggest, cannot be so broken down. If this is in fact so, the main tool of science — reduction — is useless.

The view I am putting forward here is not really new, except in some points of detail. Many thinkers have questioned the validity of the reductionist approach of the scientist when applied to human affairs. Reductionism is, in my opinion as a professional psychologist, an approach of very doubtful value in any area of human psychology. In respect of parapsychology it is of no use whatsoever.

In this event, we are faced with the question, how do we approach the paranormal? How do we study it? How can we demonstrate the validity of any concepts we generate in respect of it, if scientific analysis and scientific testing are ruled out?

I believe that we have to generate a new kind of study and to develop a new form of knowledge. I shall be calling this new branch of knowledge Subjectivity, written with a capital letter to distinguish it from more everyday subjectivity, which nevertheless is itself included in the larger term. The principle underlying Subjectivity I shall call synchronicity, after Jung. Subjectivity and synchronicity are contrasted with Objectivity and causality. 'Objectivity', capitalized, includes science and the sciences; but it further includes those attitudes of mind and emotions which make up the human Ego (as defined in Chapter 5) and from which normal objectivity is derived. It includes, therefore, a certain quality of aggression, which most scientists think they do not have; but they do.

Subjectivity will also include all those attitudes and emotions which make up the Self (as defined in Chapter 5). An important element here is 'receptivity'.

Science (Objectivity) proceeds by mastering the events it

studies. Subjectivity, I suggest, proceeds by yielding to the events it studies. Subjectivity works by direct perception — which I shall refer to as intuition. This is the 'it is so' response of religion and mysticism. Objectivity works through indirect perception, and derives its information empirically. That is to say, Objectivity *deduces* its facts. It is by no means incorrect to say that Subjectivity induces its facts.

Aside from some shades of meaning which I have deliberately added, much of the above is actually respectable enough in philosophical terms. The differences between deductive and inductive *reasoning* are well-enough established. From one point of view, nothing I am proposing is really new. For the religious mind has always proceeded along the general lines I am now urging for Subjectivity. What is more, we have to say quite openly, this line of approach has led religion into a veritable morass of contradictions and general nonsense. It was for this reason — that is, by reason of the complete lack of any coherent progress — that the early scientists abandoned the intuitive faculty in favour of objectivity and empiricism — with the spectacular results we see all around us.

In trying to resurrect an outmoded and discredited approach — that of 'intuition' — it will be my task to show how further monumental failure is to be avoided and success achieved. I shall have to try to disentangle the uses from the abuses of subjectivity — and hopefully to incorporate the former only into my Subjectivity.

The Abuses of Subjectivity

The abuse of subjectivity lies (1) in the application of subjective judgments to objective events and (2) in attempting to force your own subjectivity on someone else, so denying the equal validity of another's subjectivity.

The first category involves, for example, intervention by religion in the affairs of science. In my own opinion, subjectivity has no direct part whatsoever to play in the study of the Dimension of matter. The physical universe must be left in the hands of the scientist, whose domain this properly is.

Imagine this little scenario. A Buddhist student is taken to a steelworks, where he is shown the production of nickel steel. 'Ah,' he says, watching the cascades of sparks in admiration, 'the eternal dance of Shiva's spirit. How well my religion has expressed these matters.' The furnace foreman puts a question to him. 'How much of this essence of Shiva do we need to add to this other essence of Shiva, and to what level of celestial activity (or degrees centigrade) must the mixture be raised?' 'I have no idea,' replies the student.

We can readily replace the Buddhist with a Catholic priest or a Baptist minister or whatever. As we know, not one single fact of any value about the material universe has ever come from the religious view.

The second category — denying the validity of another's subjectivity — is a far more serious business. It is not simply of no use (as subjectivity is of no use in the making of steel). It is catastrophically destructive of life, property and human potential. It is the generator of endless human misery.

Various subjective accounts of the nature of human life are utterly irreconcilable. The Hindu belief that life goes through a series of different incarnations on its path of development, for example, cannot be reconciled with the Christian idea of one life only. The Christian notion of the survival of personal identity in an after-life not too dissimilar from this one (except that not one of our present organs will be required!) cannot be reconciled with the Zen concept of the Void to which all life returns. Again, the Greek, Roman and Nordic ideas of a multiplicity of gods cannot be reconciled with the one god of the Judaeo—Christian tradition, nor the three-in-one god of Christianity with the one true god of Judaism. Further, the details of the religions of ancient Egypt bear no relation to anything that has so far been said in this paragraph.

Protestants fought Catholics in the Thirty Years' War, *each* side convinced that it was specifically fighting god's cause. Similarly, in the First World War, both Germans and British devoutly believed that god was on their side, and fought and prayed on that understanding. On both sides weapons were blessed before battle!

The present Pope considers that Mass should no longer

be said in Latin (an everyday language like any other, just a bit out of date). A priest in France thinks it should. Both imagine that the god of the universe is concerned about this situation.

With that we have already catalogued enough of the sillinesses of subjectivity for our purposes — though the list is in fact endless.

So is subjectivity, or Subjectivity, ever going to be any use for anything? Can we ever make any general statements about it, or through it, that will carry any genuine conviction — that is, in some sense be true or universal? The answer, I think, is yes in both cases. Moreover, Subjectivity happens in any case to be the only route by which we can approach the paranormal.

Before getting down to brass tacks, a word is necessary on the nature of opposites.

Opposites

There are, in my opinion, two principal reasons why opposites play such an important part in occult and religious symbol and practice.

Our recent ancestors in evolutionary time were two types of man known respectively as Neanderthal and Cro-Magnon man. We are only concerned here with one aspect of their differing lives. We know that Neanderthal man was 'religious' in many senses of the term; and we believe that Cro-Magnon man subsequently took over these practices rather than generated them for himself.

Neanderthal man, at any rate, buried his dead, often with ceremony and feasting, frequently incorporating 'grave goods' along with the body. Such procedures argue strongly for a belief by Neanderthal in life after death. Neanderthal built altars of animal skulls and set out symmetrical arrangements of stones in caves, often again in association with burials, that suggest ritualism. Neanderthal also removed and probably ate the brains of some dead individuals through the base of the skull. Since such cannibalized skulls are found only rarely, we may assume the practice was for occult reasons rather than for sustenance.

I have also argued (in *The Neanderthal Question*) that the instinctive responses of Neanderthal happened, more or less by chance (though perhaps not unsynchronistically), to be the opposite of those employed by Cro-Magnon. When modern man submits to a superior foe, for example, or when paying respects, he faces the other person and lowers his head. It seems that Neanderthal faced away from the enemy, crouched down and raised his buttocks. As it happens we find traces of this practice still among primitive peoples today and in ancient religious ceremony. Presenting the buttocks to the altar is, of course, also an element of the Black Mass. When about to fight, a modern man instinctively raises his chin and squares his shoulders. The purpose of raising the chin and squaring the shoulders seems to be to cause the beard to stick out and to make oneself larger and more menacing. It seems, however, that Neanderthal, when ready to fight, lowered his head and hunched his shoulders — and, eventually, charged like a bull. Finally, Cro-Magnon was tall, Neanderthal was short; Cro-Magnon probably had straight hair, Neanderthal curly hair; Cro-Magnon was probably light-haired and light-skinned, while Neanderthal was dark-haired and dark-skinned. Most important of all perhaps, Neanderthal was predominantly left-handed, while Cro-Magnon was right-handed.

If one blindfolds a left-handed person and gets him to walk ahead in a straight line, he will in fact veer to the left. A right-handed person in the same situation veers to the right. Hence, I suggest, a 'widdershins' (anticlockwise) movement was employed in Neanderthal religious ceremony — along with buttock-presenting and so forth — all of these things being perfectly natural for Neanderthal. As we know, the widdershins or anticlockwise movement is today character-istic especially of black magic, and the phrase 'the left-hand path' is applied to most occult studies.

The above brief account details one source of the oppo-sites and reversals to be found not only in occult ceremony and symbolism, but in religion in general. For example, Christians say that though one's sins are as scarlet, they will be washed white as snow. The holy colour of the Christian religion is white, while magic is synonymous with black magic. Man is finite, but god is infinite — and so on.

A still more significant source and type of oppositeness arises, I believe, from our intuitive awareness of the nature and functioning of the cerebellum (see pp.201—4). As we saw, as far as the cerebrum is concerned, the cerebellum is 'left-handed'. Impulses from the cerebellum to the cerebrum cross over at a mid-point to reach the opposite side, the opposite hemisphere, of the major organ. As we also discussed, when the cerebrum 'looks at' the cerebellum, its 'right hand' becomes its 'left hand', just as ours does when we look in a mirror. So the *magic* image or person is the mirror-image, and a major entrance to the magic world is through mirrors and the reflecting surface of water.

I believe that in all 'trance' conditions (dreaming, hypnosis, mediumistic trance and so on) the cerebellum takes control of the total organism and the cerebrum in particular. Most especially, I believe that paranormal experiences actually arise in or are mediated by the cerebellum. Hence there results a strong unconscious association of opposites, and oppositeness, with the paranormal generally.

Subjectivity: a New Branch of Study

Quite early on in my studies of the occult and the paranormal it occurred to me that 'oppositeness' might be truly fundamental to the whole issue, in this sense. Could it be, I wondered, that the paranormal in some way *reverses the very laws and properties* of the normal, physical universe?

It further occurred to me that general subjectivity — leaving aside the paranormal — is not only a kind of conceptual opposite of objectivity, but also in some ways literally reverses the position taken up in objectivity. We need only think of such pairs of words as 'private' (subjective) versus 'public' (objective), or 'belief' (subjective) versus 'proof' (objective). 'Female' and 'male' are again conceptual opposites, but there is once more a very literal side to the proposition. The male sex organ extends outward, the female organ extends inward. The male organ hardens in intercourse, the female organ softens. 'Hard' and 'soft' are also more general attributes of the two sexes. Males as a group are bonier and more muscular. Females are generally softer also by reason of a layer of sub-cutaneous fat, apart from items like the breasts as such, which are entirely fluid, and the fuller, softer lips. Men are taller on average than women. Women habitually and instinctively seek a partner taller than themselves, just as men instinctively seek a shorter one. And generally speaking, women are closer to the subjective and to the paranormal than men, who are closer to the objective and scientific.

Men and women (that is, male and female) seem to me therefore, as of course they do to many occultists, to be embodiments of two (I would say *the* two) forces or principles in the universe of appearances.

At a less literally physical level (that is, less completely in the 'matter' Dimension) further embodiments of opposite-ness are the pairs Self and Ego, subjectivity and objectivity, and my own suggestions of Subjectivity and Objectivity. All of these pairs are representations of spirit-in-space (see Chapter 4). I consider that the female, the Self and the Subjective represent more the 'spirit' side of the equation; the male, the Ego and Objectivity more the 'space' aspect.

We return to my earlier question. Is it the case that the laws and properties of the one side of the total equation *reverse* the laws and properties of the other? I believe this to be so.

There now follows (on the right) a list of some character-istic properties of objective science. These are reversed, on the left, to give us some of the 'laws of Subjectivity'. Explanatory comment follows some of the examples during the full list.

	Subjectivity	*Objectivity*
(1)	a private, personal matter	a public, impersonal matter
(2)	need not be proved (to others)	must be proved (to others)
(3)	applies individually	applies universally
(4)	all cases are unique	all cases are typical

In respect of the left-hand column, I hope the reader will

already have begun to recognize a description of such essentially-human and humanly-meaningful experiences as a love affair or a friendship. Every love affair is unique, every friendship is unique.

What, however, do I mean in respect of Objectivity when I say that instances of it are always universal and typical? For instance, sugar coming out of solution will always form crystals of sugar. A known gas will always diffuse into a vacuum at a known rate. At the most basic level, salt is always salt. As long as it remains in existence as sodium chloride, it will behave like sodium chloride and never like anything else. Fritjof Capra tells us:

> In the air, for example, atoms collide millions of times every second and yet go back to their original form after each collision . . . An oxygen atom will always retain its characteristic configuration of electrons, no matter how often it collides with other atoms. This configuration, furthermore, is exactly the same in all atoms of a given kind. Two iron atoms, and consequently two pieces of pure iron, are completely identical no matter where they have come from or how they have been treated in the past.

Human beings and organisms of course are *not* completely identical 'no matter where they have come from or how they have been treated in the past'.

(5)   is not repeatable   is repeatable

As we have seen, repeatability, under controlled conditions, is one of the hallmarks of scientific method, while on the other hand a love affair can never be repeated (just as an individual can never step into the same stream twice). Even when a dream repeats — though such repetition is a very rare event in itself — the second and third dreams are not identical in all aspects. Whatever else, what psychologists call the *affect* of the dream will differ, as well as various small details.

(6)   we look within ourselves   we look outside ourselves

Here we begin to touch upon some very interesting features. It is almost a truism to say that there is as expansive a universe within our heads as the one outside it. Inner space, many writers believe, is no less infinite than outer space. However, I am taking the matter one stage further. I believe that when we look within we are in one sense gazing back along a continuum which, ultimately, leads to 'spirit'. In each of us, so to speak, is one of the tiny springs through which 'spirit' bubbles continuously into 'space'. That is one sense. But there is another. In looking within (that is, in entering the Self) we enter *literally* another universe. We have access to the paranormal Dimension of consciousness. Such access is in general denied to the Ego (though, of course, being itself an example of consciousness, Ego is *of* the Dimension of consciousness in a way that matter is not and cannot be). The route to the paranormal, then, is *within*, not without — not outside ourselves.

So many fairy tales and legends describe this situation. The secret door at the bottom of the old garden, which leads into the magic world, the mirror or surface of water through which we step into the universe of opposites, the magic spectacles which enable us suddenly to see the secret world — all these are symbols and metaphors of our *inner* and secret powers, the inner door of being, which organisms alone (and we above all) possess. These *do not exist outside of ourselves* or in the material universe.

The upshot of the position I have just described I am afraid dramatically upsets the apple-cart of generally-accepted paranormalism and occultism, certainly of its terminology. For we now have:

(7) 'in the body'   'out of the body'
     experiences   experiences

The point is that we reach the paranormal by going *into the body* — that is, into our psyche. Of course, we *then* 'pass out of the body' into a non-physical dimension. But the inward direction of the journey has to be insisted upon. What literally lies outside us, all around us, in the immediate and strictly here-and-now physical sense is the objective universe.   So science, in a way, is the real '*out* of the body' trip!

(8)   wholistic, associative and   linear, sequential and
      synchronistic   causal

The term 'wholistic' need not have any paranormal implications.   When I perceive a picture wholistically, as I do, the picture is in the here-and-now world of physical events.   'Gestalts' or meaningful patterns exist in the Dimension of matter at least when an organism is perceiving the events concerned.   But Gestalts, as I have suggested, may also extend into time, and further, into paranormal time. Both past and future events, which have no existence at all in the Dimension of matter, may then form parts of synchronistic wholes.

That there should be a normal everyday level to the occurrence of meaningful wholes and Gestalts is important. For we can then link these to the 'associationism' of academic and Freudian psychology, as well as to the non-paranormal Gestalts of Gestalt psychology.   Our paranormal hypothesis has a firm basis in non-paranormal fact.

(Associationism, in passing, is one undoubted way in which aspects of our memory are organized, in addition to the conscious, logical sequences of thought.   Dreams, for example, are best interpreted and understood through the 'association of ideas' in them.   An early school of psychology named itself 'Associationism' — but its theories were not very good at accounting for conscious, rational behaviour.   They were and are, however, in my opinion, very useful in understanding unconscious processes.)

Association, Gestalt perception and synchronicity can all be understood to be aspects of an organism-generated patterning of events, in one or more Dimensions.   Certainly once we proceed beyond the Dimension of matter, I suggest it is likely that Gestalts and synchronistic wholes are an in-built property of the Dimensions themselves.

Apart from there being synchronistic events and clusters of events, we now therefore elevate synchronicity to the status of the general principle of Subjectivity.   It is to

Subjectivity what causality is to science and Objectivity.

(9)   synchronicity   causality

Earlier comments on associationism, Gestalt psychology and synchronicity enable us to justify the next proposition.

(10) cannot meaningfully be   can meaningfully be
     broken down into its   broken down into its
     parts   parts

We now also appreciate, in respect of the last statement on the left, the intuitive truth of Wordsworth's 'we murder to dissect' and 'the meddling intellect'. Science and objectivity, the processes of breaking down the phenomena of the paranormal (and the Subjective generally), destroy that which they are seeking to understand. This is what is meant also by the 'breaking of the spell' in fairy stories. (Objectivity — the Ego — not unnaturally describes this event as the release from an *evil* enchantment. The evil, however, is only that the rules and the rule of Ego, of Objectivity, were suspended.) The breaking of a mirror (the magic world) also brings 'seven years' bad luck' — which, I suggest, indicates the self-imposed absence from and denial of the magical. 'Magical' here, I must emphasize, includes the living wonder and warmth of normal life. Thus, in respect of love, men speak of a woman's beauty as 'bewitching'; she is 'enchanting'. We are 'under her spell'. The magical qualities of love are properly assigned mainly to woman (though let us not forget Svengali, for instance) because woman and the 'female principle' are nearer to the paranormal, to the Self and, ultimately, to 'spirit'.

(11) yielding/receptive   aggressive/acquisitive/
                                   inquisitive

The attributes here go back on the 'female' side to the human sexual situation; and to fighting and hunting on the 'male' side.

In the sexual encounter it is in general the female who is

receptive to the male, and not merely in the physiological sense. She is alert to the relationship in a far more intuitive and wholly preoccupied way. She (despite Women's Liberation) accommodates herself to the male, rather than the other way about. As an evolved human being, woman then brings these same qualities to her relationship with the universe.

The attractiveness of the male for the female derives initially, back in the evolutionary past, from his dominance over other males in the social situation. Fairly early on in our evolution, aggression between males *outside* their own social or tribal group evidently became a factor of great importance. (Only by this supposition can we adequately account for the enormous amounts of aggression human society both generates and tolerates.) Inter-tribal conflict, together with the ever-growing importance of hunting, turned the male's attention, in an *objective* sense, to the world outside and beyond him. To be a good warrior and a good hunter, it was necessary to study the movements and the potentials of other tribes and of other organisms — likewise the lie of the land, the time of day and the time of year. So, unlikely as the idea perhaps at first seems, the seeds of objectivity (which were ultimately to develop into science and logic) came from the battle and the hunt.

Many, many fighting and hunting metaphors do survive in the language of apparently entirely intellectual pursuits. I have gone into these matters in detail in earlier books. Briefly, we attack or tackle problems, master or wrestle with difficulties, crack cases, shoot trouble (as in trouble-shooter), fight boredom, beat a deadline; we pursue inquiries, we have production targets, speak of the aims of science; we have tobacco barons and cotton kings, we make a killing on the Exchange and we corner markets. This is only one kind of evidence. There is more of a directly physiological nature. For example, intellectual learning is easier when the muscles are tense than when they are slack — and for this there is conclusive experimental evidence. Also, when learning is taking place in the head, the electrical potential of the fingers changes, as if one were *doing* something. All in all, I have been brought to the position of stating that intellect is only highly-evolved muscle; while emotion and intuition for their part are highly-evolved glands and viscera.

A pair of attributes now, intended to summarize and include matters not dealt with in full in these notes:

(12) 'female principle'   'male principle'

When approaching a matter objectively, we try to detach ourselves from the phenomenon as much as possible, to stand away from it and to quieten our emotions completely. (Although we never succeed in doing this entirely. We cannot really turn ourselves into machines — and 'objectivity' remains still, whatever else, a human behaviour.) The reverse rule is true when we approach a matter Subjectively. Here we seek to involve ourselves with the phenomenon and to experience it not in a detached, cold way, but more as if the phenomenon were a person to whom we were relating. Even that is not quite enough. The aim in Subjectivity is to *become* the phenomenon we are studying! I will try to make this idea clearer — but of course we have already met the actual position in several paranormal cases. Rider Haggard, notably, was 'one' with his dog Bob — but also in the case of Wyndham Hewitt, Grindell-Matthews, Méry's friend and their cats (see Chapter 2), owner and pet were in some sense *together* at the moment of the animal's death, somehow each part of one Gestalt or experience that embraced man, dream and animal. The gaps between them in space and time were annihilated.

The religious individual will, I think, at once have understood what I am driving at. When a religious person seeks contact with god, or with the infinite, he or she defines the contact as a union, a one-ness with god. God, the holy spirit, grace (or whatever term we use) then *pervades* us. God becomes immanent within us. (By definition, god is of course immanent in all things. But Western religionists hold that man has been granted — by god — the right of excluding god, of being separate from him, if they so wish. We must choose, or not, to admit god into our lives.)

Poets often speak of being 'at one' with nature. Lovers are 'one' with each other.

This fusion with, this experiencing of an (actually) separate phenomenon as if it were an *extension or part of oneself* is the purest manifestation of Subjectivity.

Now we can attempt a definition. Objectivity is the separating of oneself (as far as possible) from what is studied. Subjectivity is the extending of oneself (as far as possible) *into* what is studied. The objective student *observes* his material: the subjective student *experiences* his material.

So we have a further pair of attributes.

(13) experience   observation

Experience, as I hope is now clear, is *a tool*, and in fact the principal tool, of Subjectivity — just as observation is a tool, and the principal tool, of Objectivity.

Subjectivity, then, is a personal, private way. It is *your* own way and not necessarily or even at all anyone else's. Mystics, in particular, will recognize the relevance of this statement to the practice of meditation generally and to the karmic idea that each of us has a personal, unique path of development. Psychoanalysts too, I hope, will realize that in Subjectivity I am also describing the nature and basis of psychoanalysis.

Perhaps so far so good. Yet a critic or sceptic might well put the following questions:

(a) What is the *point* of Subjectivity?

(b) What checks and balances are there in its application — is it a case of 'anything goes', more in fact of the wild free-for-all that this book has so far roundly condemned?

(c) Finally, are there not serious dangers of a very real kind (as you yourself have said) in the procedures you are recommending?

My attempts at answers to these questions are as follows:

(a) There is more than one point to Subjectivity. There is, for example, the matter of getting to know oneself — which, whatever else, will probably produce the benefit of better managing oneself. There is the point, too, of experiencing life more fully, of feeling more alive, of developing one's sensory awareness, perhaps seeing a flower properly for the first time — and the enriching of all one's life relationships. For myself, however, and for the purposes of this book, the main point of Subjectivity is the exploration of the paranormal. Subjectivity, in my opinion, is actually the only possible pathway into the supernatural. Science cannot take us there.

(b) The checks and balances of Subjectivity are, appropriately enough, subjective ones. It really all boils down, on the one hand, to honesty. Only you know whether you are telling yourself, and telling others, the truth about your subjective experiences. There is nothing to stop anyone lying — and, in my opinion, many people do lie about their subjective and paranormal experiences. But camouflage is rarely perfect. People who lie in general about everything (and I have very much in mind here also those whose whole way of life can be seen to be a lie, who manifestly do not practise what they preach — say, the rich Christian and the wealthy Socialist) are likely to lie about their Subjective experiences. People who are generally truthful can more readily be trusted to be truthful about their inner life also.

Lying to yourself is *your* problem — but as long as you are being honest with yourself about your own experiences and sensations, you will be able to compare these experiences with the accounts given by others, and in the long run sense a concordance or a discordance. It is true that I said that everyone's experience of Subjectivity is always in some sense unique. But we are nevertheless all members of the same species and possess the same kinds of potential.

What I am proposing generally becomes clearer if we consider two other areas of subjective experience — sex and gambling. The most obvious example is the man who assures you he is making a great deal out of his gambling, but is wearing a threadbare coat and worn shoes. Less clear is the case of the man who says he can make love six times in a night. He is almost certainly lying — but here we must weigh up his general character. If the man is also a spendthrift, a boaster generally, a heavy drinker and so on, the probable lie is fairly definitely confirmed. In the circumstances we must and should ignore his claim. But if on the other hand the man in question is quiet-spoken and generally reasonable — and confides the information about his sex life not as a boast but in some appropriate situation, say, to a doctor or a marriage-guidance counsellor — then we are probably getting the truth, and for the time being annotate it as such.

There can, however, be no full or final independent, objective test of Subjective experience. If I tell you of a dream I allegedly had, there is no real way you can establish whether I had it or not. Subjective experience, by its very nature, is not directly testable by a second party. *That is one of the characteristics of Subjectivity.* It is no good scientists bemoaning or criticizing this situation. We may not dictate to things their characteristics.

In the longer run, I think the true characteristics of the paranormal will emerge with a good deal of clarity, providing we proceed initially with firm personal honesty. I will elaborate on this position in the next chapter.

(c) Are there dangers attendant on the pursuit of Subjectivity and the paranormal? Yes, there are.

These dangers can be summarized as the losing of one's grip on objective reality — in extreme cases on the very sense of belonging to or being a part of the normal world. (But there are equal dangers in the pursuit of the Objective — the loss of the warmth and richness of human life, of the sense of *being* an organism.) Legend and fairy tale over and over again warn us of this danger inherent in the 'magical' world.

The loss of objective reality is exemplified by the mystic who stands holding his arm outstretched for years, until the use of the arm is lost: or who sits staring at the sun until he goes blind. This behaviour is supposed to serve some mystical purpose. We have a good word for it in the English language — stupidity. Such notions and actions are, in my opinion, complete rubbish, and the behaviour itself mentally deranged.

The mystical question, what shall it profit a man if he gain the world and lose his soul? is certainly a valid one. But so is the reverse — what shall it profit a man if he gain his soul and lose the world? In these questions I myself take 'soul' to mean the Self and the unconscious; and 'world' to mean the Ego and normal consciousness.

We can again see deranged behaviours in those who seek to pursue the Subjective path through the use of drugs, be these marijuana, L.S.D. or heroin. Not only can the ability to deal with real life be seriously or fatally impaired by such means, but actual brain damage and other irreversible physiological harm can occur. Even as yet unborn children can in consequence be affected. Those who advocate the responsible use of some of these drugs insist that initially the mildest possible doses only must be taken, and then always in the presence of those not taking the drug at all. Even so, drugs remain a path of real danger. In my opinion they should never be used.

When we comfort a screaming child during the night with the words 'it's only a dream', or in a cinema with the words 'it's only a film', we again have a situation where subjective experience has (temporarily) undermined the hold on objective reality. In young people the unconscious and the Self are stronger, and the hold on objective reality correspondingly weaker, than in most adults.

When we penetrate deeply into the subjective Self and its farther reaches, we may re-experience similar childhood terrors. During my own psychoanalysis I once or twice had dreams which haunted me for days at a time, and which caused me to telephone my analyst out of hours, so great was my fear. In one of these dreams I was by a lake dark as pitch, with the dusk surrounding me. I knew something was about to emerge from the lake. Finally it did so — a misshapen head on a great, weaving neck. This dream represents the terrors that consciousness often experiences in approaching the unconscious. Once again, many legends, perhaps particularly those of the ancient Greeks, warn of the dangers that lurk for the traveller voyaging to the far reaches of the mind.

On another occasion, in broad daylight, I experienced complete geographical amnesia. I had in fact just emerged from Oxford Street Underground station. Suddenly I no longer knew where I was. I was not, as it happens, panic-stricken — but as I looked around me there was no building that I could recognize. I was in no place that I had ever been in before. The disorientation faded gradually in the course of a few minutes. This experience shows how the unconscious (symbolized perhaps by the Underground) can radically change our view of the conscious world.

Trance mediums often warn beginners in trance ventures of the dangers of 'sitting' alone, that is, of allowing oneself to be controlled by 'spirits' without another person being present. They say that otherwise one may be taken over by malevolent spirits, who will refuse to go away (like the old man of the sea). The advice is sound, though the notion of 'evil spirits' (and the whole notion of discarnate spirits, in the traditional sense) is one that I do not entertain for a single second. That which 'takes over' is an aspect of one's own mind, and nothing else. Nevertheless, a person may get stuck in that take-over, and this basically is what I consider occurs in schizophrenia and psychosis.

I personally quite often 'sit' alone, just for the fun of it, to hear what my own personality has to say to me at that moment. Similarly, I sometimes engage in what is known as 'speaking with tongues'. In this condition one speaks with unintelligible but fairly coherent and structured sounds, as if speaking some foreign language. The language is actually gibberish, despite various claims made for it by the unqualified. But the experience *is* a useful and therapeutic one. I feel much more relaxed and generally cheerful after a brief session — it somehow releases an inner tension.

At any rate, we can already see that in general the Subjective path is beset with quite real dangers. In particular, some personality types do not cope well with Self experiences — certainly not without a long period of gradual training and acclimatization. This is no area to enter either lightly or quickly. Influential thinkers such as R. D. Laing are at fault, in my opinion, in recommending a deep and perhaps rapid immersion in the Self to all and sundry, and in arguing that this positively must be a therapeutic experience.

Be that as it may, if you wish to experience the paranormal in particular, the path through the Self and the unconscious is the one that must be followed.

Peace with Honour

I hope it will be fully realized that my proposals in respect of Subjectivity offer to both the religious-minded and the scientific-minded the opportunity of peace with honour.

There are gains and losses for both sides, but no humiliation for either.

The gains for the religious-minded are these. We have established a fully autonomous and valid study and discipline, termed Subjectivity, into which important aspects of what was hitherto called religious experience and religious knowledge at once fit. There is no longer the slightest question of a religious devotee having to go cap in hand to the scientist to ask if what he is doing is acceptable – the position we have virtually reached today, and which is actually the mirror of the former equally ridiculous situation, where the scientist had to go cap in hand to the priest to ask if what *he* was doing was acceptable. Many of the current practices of the religious-minded person can continue unchanged, if the individual concerned finds them to be of value – prayer and meditation, for instance. Many of the practices – but not all.

The loss for religion is that of empire-building. There is no longer any question of evangelism and conversion to a *particular* faith. All faiths are equally valid – or equally invalid, if an individual chooses to disagree. Not only is every religion as good as every other, but the personal religion which Joe Bloggs invents for himself is automatically better than *any* other – for him, and as long as he thinks so.

Straight away, really, the whole superstructure and formalized edifice of conventional religion collapses. This is not to say that religious individuals cannot or should not share their experiences with each other. But the coming-together no longer requires to be formalized or in any way sanctioned. Individuals find their own way – with others if they wish, or alone, if they wish. There is probably something to be said in favour of coming-together specifically in respect of the paranormal. For there is good evidence that a group can achieve more than an individual in isolation, rather along the lines of a battery composed of several cells.

Conventional religion should not complain too much about the changes I am proposing – because they are coming about anyway. Established religion is crumbling throughout the world. The empty, derelict churches are sufficient evidence in themselves. Even the Catholic church is undergoing 'rapid contraction'. Four out of every ten young people born into Catholicism now drop out before confirmation, and the level of new converts is down to forty per cent of the level observed in 1911. Fifty per cent of all Catholics marry out of the faith.[95]

Young people today increasingly turn to whatever religion appeals to them — the religions of India, the Far East, the North American Indians. Or perhaps more often still they put together a religion entirely for themselves, some patchwork of pantheism, shintoism, spiritism, nature-worship, moon-worship and whatever. This is excellent. The religious spirit is diversifying into the 'many mansions' which are its true expression — as contrasted with the single edifice of science and objectivity.

Dogma, however, is at an end. All religious views are, as I said, equally valid or equally invalid. Jesus is the Son of God, if you think so. Or not, if you don't.

Not everyone is going to find this state of affairs satisfying or reassuring, especially at first. They hunger for certainty (though there never *was* any in the past either). 'What is the *truth*?' they ask. I am afraid there is no answer to that question at present and perhaps there never will be. At best the Subjective enterprise I propose is the beginning of a voyage of discovery. We do not know where it is heading.

What of science? What are *its* gains and losses?

As to loss, science must abandon the idea that it is god (that is, the anti-god) and that it has all the answers to all the questions. This is actually not a *real* loss, for science never was those things, even when it thought itself to be. Science is 'losing' a spurious possession — and I personally would consider that a gain. Science must now concede the existence, and the validity, of Subjectivity in its own full right. The territories of Subjectivity lie absolutely outside the jurisdiction both of science and the objective method.

Where is the outright gain, if any, for science? The gain lies in the re-affirmation that the world of physical matter is solely under scientific jurisdiction. Religion and other Self activities have no direct part whatsoever to play here, and have neither call nor right to interfere. The physical universe is Caesar's domain and no one else's.

A 'New Age' Aspect?

A great deal of talk is heard these days of the New Age which is allegedly just beginning. This New Age, again allegedly, will be intimately involved with the paranormal.

In a few ways, though by no means in all, I go along with such talk. I certainly feel that all previous ages are played out once and for all. I certainly feel that unless we can not only devise, but actually implement a radically new way of running our lives, then humanity is doomed as of now. And finally, I certainly consider that any way ahead must be through the paranormal.

In this general context I want to propose one final reversal of the laws of the physical universe. This particular proposal concerns telepathy only (the passing of information paranormally from mind to mind), not clairvoyance or any other of the paranormal faculties — and hence I have not included it above under my general laws of Subjectivity.

It may be that telepathy is a force *whose strength increases over distance.* That is to say, the *further apart* two minds are geographically, the *better* may be their chances of making contact telepathically. The forces of the conventional universe, of course, *weaken* as distance increases.

Theorists have often been puzzled why ESP abilities generally have not been gradually reinforced in the course of time in at least some if not all species of animals, just as is any other favourable characteristic, along normal Darwinian lines. The answer, in respect of telepathy, may be because in nature parent and offspring, individual and pack, habitually remain rather close to each other. If telepathic powers do come into play only when a very great distance exists between the individuals concerned, then the ability could not hitherto be demonstrated. Powers which do not come into play can confer no survival advantage. It is only with the advent of modern man that parent and child, or dog and 'pack leader' (that is, the human owner of the dog) become separated by the large distances possibly required. *Now* perhaps the dog can register the death of his distant master, or the parent realize that a beloved son or daughter has died, and so on.

If any of this is true, then telepathy seems designed *par excellence* for a space age with its vast separations. The paranormal generally — especially clairvoyance and knowledge of the future — might also truly come into its own when creatures (i.e. man) venture into a habitat which they are in no way naturally equipped to deal with — deep space.

We might begin to discover the truth or otherwise of these speculations if we could put a psychic on the moon.

SEVEN
The Psychic Universe

The 'psychic universe' is made up of those Dimensions that lie beyond the Dimension of matter — beyond, that is, the normal, physical universe (see Chapter 4). There seem to be three such Dimensions. They are: (some aspects of) time; consciousness; and 'god'. Throughout this chapter references to 'god' as a Dimension are written in quotes, to distinguish my special use of the word from more normal use.

Where does man stand in respect of these Dimensions, these 'alternative universes'? With the question we hit the nub of the problem. Man, like all living organisms, exists in more than one Dimension at once, and in fact, at least potentially, in all four. Our basic, physical body is principally in the Dimension of matter. It is not only composed mainly of matter, but we eat matter in order to sustain it. That we do need to feed upon matter to live is clear evidence in evolutionary terms of our origins *in* matter.

The nature of man's consciousness, especially in its relation to time and notably to paranormal events, convinces us that consciousness cannot be fully equated with matter. Consciousness breaks the rules of the Dimension of matter — and yet these are rules which cannot be broken! So we are obliged to add at least one further Dimension to our original base in order to resolve what would otherwise be a paradox.

Similarly, as we have seen, normal geometry resolves insuperable problems and paradoxes in normal *two*-dimensional space by resorting to *three*-dimensional space. The letter 'b', for example, can never become the letter 'd' in two-dimensional space, no matter how we twist and turn it. But if we turn the letter 'b' *over* — that is, move it through three-dimensional space — the 'b' does become a 'd'. The appeal to further dimensions to resolve the problems of a given dimension is perfectly respectable. Einstein himself also appealed to a dimension of time to resolve otherwise insoluble problems of space.

The four Dimensions of my own model of the universe are:

(1) matter   (that is, all properties of physical matter, including space itself, and including also Einsteinian space—time)

(2) time   (those aspects or functions of time — or perhaps the *absence* of time — which consciousness makes use of, or has access to, when reaching paranormally into the past and paranormally into the future)

(3) consciousness   (the living, experiencing, non-matter aspects and functions of all organisms)

(4) 'god'   (that level or Dimension towards which consciousness and life seem to be evolving)

The concerns of those who wish to involve themselves with psychic matters lie really with Dimension 2 and beyond. Again, if we are specifically concerned with the purpose of life and evolution, our attention should be with Dimension 2 and beyond. However, anyone concerned simply with the *maintenance* of life will be devoting most attention to Dimension 1.

The last comment has a very direct bearing on the question of psychic healing.

Defining the Psychic Universe

I have just firmly stated that the individual interested in psychic phenomena need not concern himself with Dimension 1, the Dimension of matter. In very many ways the physical universe is irrelevant, a blind alley as far as psychic events are concerned. Not only should the interested individual address himself directly to psychic phenomena, but his very first step should be to obtain paranormal experiences of his own. I will come back to this point.

I intend now to say something probably rather disconcerting. I am going to suggest that so-called paranormal physical phenomena, and psychic healing, and a number of other items still *are not psychic at all*, in the true sense of the term.

I am saying, just to make this quite clear, *that so-called paranormal physical phenomena are not actually paranormal or psychic phenomena.*   They seem to belong firmly in Dimension 1, the Dimension of matter. They are certainly very unusual events — but they are not paranormal.

Hauntings and Poltergeists

The reader will probably recall certain rather odd questions that I have put from time to time. One of them was whether haunted houses are haunted when there is no one present to witness the haunting.   I now want to ask two other such questions.   Do we ever get ghosts from the future; and do *poltergeist* events ever occur when no one is present?

Hauntings range from sightings of ghosts unaccompanied by any other activity, through ghosts accompanied also by clankings of chains, moanings and whatever, to noises and movements of objects without, however, any accompanying sighting of a presence.

In my opinion, as given earlier, figures of ghosts are merely 'hallucinations of the sane'. They are no different in principle from the hallucinations experienced by lunatics, or by persons under the influence of drugs. They are an aspect of trance-work (see pp.78—82).   They are made up and projected for us by our own unconscious minds. Hence they wear the clothes of the past — because nobody yet knows what the clothes of the future will look like! There is at very best only a one-way traffic in ghosts, from past to present — and one-way traffic is the hallmark of the physical universe, not of the paranormal. I am personally satisfied that there is no literal 'traffic' at all.

Ghosts, then, in my opinion, do not appear when there is no one to see them, because they are purely a product of the mind, a figment of the imagination, of the person who sees them.   How can I be sure?   My sureness comes partly from the fact that *poltergeist* phenomena do not occur when no one is present. Moreover, these do occur *only when a particular individual is present* — the person who, it seems quite clear, is generating the phenomena. If he or she is *not* present, the presence of the remainder of the family or of strangers does not result in the occurrence of the happenings.

Assuming poltergeist phenomena to be genuine — and the evidence is after all fairly strong — we can consider these to result from an extension and, most importantly, a purely *localized* extension of some form of living energy projected by the nervous system. A case extensively investigated by W. G. Roll and J. G. Pratt established that most of the physical phenomena occurred within ten feet of the individual responsible for them. Some light objects were also occasionally moved at a distance of twenty-two feet.[77]

But as we know, the truly paranormal is no respecter of distance. The paranormal annihilates spatial separation. Yet, poltergeist phenomena are always localized. In this respect at least they do not seem to bear the stamp of the paranormal.

Psychic Healing

In standard psychic healing the practitioner lays his hands on the afflicted area indicated by the patient. Remission of pain and/or accelerated healing result from this treatment. No faith-healing is involved — no faith on the part of the patient, that is — for more than one healer has demonstrated his or her abilities in respect of animals and plants under laboratory conditions (see pp.107—10). Healers of course themselves believe that a power flows from them out of their hands into the patient.

This notion of an individually-generated, localized power, causing changes in the nearby physical environment, is very similar to the descriptions of poltergeist phenomena — except that 'healing power' is controlled, directed and beneficial, whereas 'poltergeist power' is uncontrolled, random and harmful. None the less, there seems no conceptual reason why the basic power involved should not be the same in both cases. (It is, I have suggested, the Freudian libido.) Looking at healing and poltergeist phenomena we can compare electricity docilely illuminating a bulb — or wildly exploding a fuse box and starting a fire.

What of psychic healing at a distance — so-called absent healing? First, I am by no means persuaded that this actually occurs. There is no experimental support whatsoever for this effect. (Perhaps Estebany and others could be persuaded to try to provide it.)

Even if individuals do occasionally improve as a result of the prayers of an absent healer, we could look for other explanations. In the vast majority of cases, the sick person knows that the healer is trying to help. This knowledge may have psychological effects on the course of the illness, including of course the remission of unconscious hysterical symptoms, such remission actually being the hallmark of what is known as faith-healing. It is really for bodies like the National Federation of Spiritual Healers to demonstrate that 'absent healing' is a reality *in the same way* that healing by laying-on of hands is a reality — preferably that it occurs also when animals are used as subjects.

The theoretical problems do not end there, however. Why is it necessary for the healer ever to lay his hands on an afflicted person actually present — if he can cure him just by thinking about him from a distance? *Does* the power flow from his applied hands or does it not? The circumstances in the two cases are after all very different. Assuming that psychic healing at a distance actually works, which is not so far proven, must these not be two quite different forms of healing? Or if not, and if absent healing is simply much less effective, then we would clearly have a diminishing of power over distance. So then we would seem to be squarely back in Dimension 1 — for it is characteristic of the Dimension of matter that its effects *weaken over distance*. In respect of telepathy and other genuinely paranormal events, increases of distance appear to make *no difference whatsoever*.

Acupuncture

The practice of acupuncture lends considerable support to the notion that psychic healing involves an unusual form of energy, but one nevertheless in principle acceptable to the physicist and demonstrably part of the Dimension of matter.

As already indicated, in acupuncture small silver needles are inserted at key points in the patient's body — the ears, the lips, the toes and wherever. In consequence certain other parts of the body become anaesthetized, to the extent that major surgery can be undertaken without pain being felt. Alternatively, the application of the needles can in itself be therapeutic — causing indigenous pain to diminish and healing to accelerate.

The practice of acupuncture is today very well documented and accepted as genuine even by most Western doctors. It does look rather as if each of us has an 'energy body' or bodies associated with the more grossly physical body. Acupuncture perhaps causes adjustments in the energy body to take place. Possibly the psychic healer uses his own energy body to affect the energy body of his patient.

This highly-unusual and unorthodox possibility of the existence of an energy body, hitherto unsuspected by Western medicine, still leaves us nevertheless in Dimension 1. These unusual effects do seem fairly definitely to be part of the here-and-now physical world.

In passing, the fact that acupuncture is generally admitted to be more successful among peoples of the East than peoples of the West is in line with my view that the actual nervous system of these 'Neanderthal' types of modern man, notably the cerebellum, differs from that of 'Cro-Magnon' types. As we saw in Chapter 5, Asiatics do have larger cerebella, longer intestines and so on, than Caucasians.

Control of the Autonomic Nervous System
Along with such matters as acupuncture, we find that peoples of the East are generally far more adept at controlling their autonomic nervous systems than Westerners generally are. (Although, by definition, the autonomic system is supposed to be outside our conscious control and self-governing — see p.196.) So we find individuals in the East able to drive skewers and nails through their flesh, apparently without pain and certainly without bleeding or infection. They are able to walk over hot coals with naked feet. They can increase and decrease their heartbeat rate at will — some can even stop the heart, briefly.

Some individuals in the West have also developed similar degrees of control. Two well-known examples are Jack Schwarz and Jan Merta. Jack Schwarz can drive a knitting needle through his limbs with no bleeding, leaving only the tiniest of marks. If he allows a wound to bleed, he can cause it to stop bleeding instantaneously. He can push his hand into live coals without burning the flesh. Similarly, Jan Merta can stub cigarettes out on his tongue and hold red-hot irons in his hand. The physical medium D. D. Home (see p.150) is also credited with being able to hold red-hot coals in his clenched hand for minutes on end.

Here, now, is a link of considerable interest. Jack Schwarz, Jan Merta and D. D. Home exhibit a high degree of control over their autonomic functions. *Merta and Home also apparently produce physical phenomena.* Can this therefore mean a close link between the autonomic nervous system and *physical* phenomena?

What would be of the greatest interest would be for Jack Schwarz, Jan Merta and Matthew Manning (another physical medium) to attempt to produce psychic healing in animals, as demonstrated by Estebany. Should these three — who do not consider themselves to be psychic healers — produce the healing effect, we would begin to have some very tight reasoning indeed for *one* basic ability with several facets.*

Gellerism

Uri Geller's alleged abilities to bend forks and the hands of watches, to fracture metal and in general to sabotage the physical universe have received wide publicity. They may or may not be genuine, though, as I have said earlier, I myself discount them entirely on the grounds of Geller being what the legal profession calls an unreliable witness.

As for Professor John Taylor's 'psychic children' my regretful feeling is that they managed to deceive him. I am disinclined also to accept D. D. Home's alleged ability to levitate himself and the chair he was sitting in, or rumours that Sister Agatha used regularly to float off the ground during Communion. (Yet I do agree that once we accept

---

* This might well also include dowsing.

poltergeist phenomena — the movement of objects without their being touched in the normal way — we thereby automatically admit the possibility of levitation. As established under the laws of thermodynamics, any object moved by another object or force offers an initial resistance, which must be overcome. If the initial resistance is greater than the force applied, the would-be moving force is either neutralized or redirected. So a large stone travelling towards a sheet of glass overcomes the small resistance of the glass and passes through, losing only a fraction of its energy as it does so and dragging the pieces of glass after it. But a tennis ball hitting the glass may well rebound from the glass. In this same general way, the psychic exerting a force against a large object or specifically the floor may be lifted off the floor. In fact levitation is, or would be, proof that we are, despite appearances, dealing with an aspect of the normal physical world!)

However, I absolutely do not accept that a psychic healer can dematerialize his hands and cause them to rematerialize within a patient (p.56). I also do not accept that there is such a thing as an apport — an object materialized out of thin air, or transported paranormally in an instant across hundreds of miles and through walls and mountains. As I remarked earlier, coincidentally or otherwise an apport is always an object of a size that can readily be concealed under one's coat. Possibly the exaggerated claim of the apport arises from the fact that in poltergeist situations objects sometimes move towards the agent.

I am ready to accept that there may well be truth in some accounts of physical phenomena, especially, perhaps, those of poltergeists. But I have never yet personally experienced what I would call a satisfactory instance of any of these items.

Assuming that some Geller-type phenomena do occur, there still seems no difficulty in any case in describing them as a function of Dimension 1 — although, like life itself (a truism, of course), they always occur exclusively in the presence of organisms. They seem to be one further aspect among the many aspects of organisms that are definitely of the basic, physical, here-and-now world.

Findhorn

The members of the Findhorn farming community in Scotland have apparently caused crops to grow with great vigour in an otherwise inhospitable soil and environment. The result was not achieved through artificial fertilizers or intensive cultivation in any scientific sense. It was achieved, apparently, simply by the loving interaction of these people with their plants.*

There have been whispers of man—plant interactions of this kind for many hundreds of years, but Findhorn certainly provides the most spectacular evidence to date. I do not myself object to the idea that the community members have somehow 'spiritually' encouraged the growth of the plants. After all, Estebany has done precisely the same thing under controlled laboratory conditions.

It is the community's 'explanation' that there are nature spirits or fairies living at Findhorn on the non-physical plane that I must reject. This explanation is just another instance of trance-work (as discussed in the section 'Trance States' and elsewhere). The trance-work is, objectively, meaningless as an *explanation*. It is, certainly, the subjective means (or by-product of these means) which enables the community workers to exercise their own latent faculties for stimulating plant growth.

At least a majority of the community members seem to generate appreciable quantities of the energy (or energies) which we have been discussing in the last several pages. The fact that there are a number of individuals working *together* gives us once again the 'battery' effect, which I have already mentioned, and which we traditionally see operating in the seance circle.

It would be of great value theoretically if the members of the Findhorn community would try also to produce their remarkable effect *at a distance* — say by 'adopting' some ordinary, run-down farm a couple of hundred miles away, currently being worked by ordinary farm-workers. Best of all would be, of course, if they kept the identity of that farm

* See *The Findhorn Garden*, The Findhorn Community, (Wildwood House, London, 1975).

a total secret during the experiment, especially from the farm-workers involved.

I personally doubt that the community members would produce any effect in this way. I believe it is essential for them to be on the spot and in the actual physical neighbour-hood of their plants. If so, then once again we need have no hesitation in assigning the admittedly unusual results of Findhorn once again to the normal, here-and-now physical world of Dimension 1.

In summary, two points which provisionally seem basic to all the various physical manifestations we have been discussing:

(1) They all take place in the here-and-now — that is, not in the past, not in the future, but in the present.

(2) They all take place locally, not at a distance; and they seem tied to the particular presence of a particular individual (or perhaps battery of individuals).

The two basic statements — proximity (not distance), here-and-now (not past or future) — seem to me absolutely to remove physical phenomena from the realm of the paranormal. These appear to be normal, though unusual, attributes of the body. Objects do not move without being touched, as is claimed — for they *are* touched, but by the energy field of the human being concerned. John Taylor has always argued this, and on the basis of the evidence I would agree with him.

Some Deficiencies of Science

If the physical phenomena of the paranormal are, after all, of Dimension 1 — and so not paranormal in the true sense, but merely unusual — then, clearly, they lie in the undisputed province of the scientist. These territories and their investi-gation must therefore be handed over to science.

However, the position is not simple. (Few things ever are.) The normal 'hard-line' approach of science will *not* serve in this area, just as it already fails to serve in the complex ques-tions of ordinary human psychology. We are here dealing with organisms and the properties of organisms. Man, like every living organism, is always more than the sum of his parts, even when considered in a physical frame of reference.

So 'reductionism', the practice of breaking phenomena down into their component parts, one of the main tools of science, is going to play at best only a limited role. It will at all times have to be used with the greatest caution.

The physical phenomena we have been talking about are not even found, in any appreciable quantity, in association with all organisms or even with all people — only with a few extremely fragile and sensitive human beings. One cannot just put such people 'through the mill' and expect results. A psychic or sensitive is like an athlete, or still more an artist. He does well when 'in form' and under the right conditions. Otherwise he does badly. An athlete's failures not only do not cancel out his winning performances, but the individual can never guarantee a good performance. The same comments apply even more to the artist, composer, poet, actor or whatever. His great performances cannot be forced — they can only be encouraged and hoped for. So it is, even more again, with the psychic.

The scientist, in investigating the strange, elusive qualities of paranormal or so-called physical phenomena, must accommodate himself to the psychic or sensitive — and not the other way around. The psychic must be left free to work when he chooses and under what conditions he chooses. Any experiment must be so designed as to meet this requirement (without, naturally, ceasing to be a good experiment). Dr Norman Shealy, Dr Bernard Grad, Dr Justa Smith and others have shown us that it *is* perfectly possible for psychics and researchers to work successfully together, with the personal dignity, integrity and methods of the sensitive left intact.

A still more important point is missed by the large majority of scientists and the scientific establishment. This is that objectivity is an emotional attitude. It is certainly true that objectivity demands the absence of all *other* kinds of emotion. But, as we have seen, objectivity has, in evolutionary terms, developed out of aggression and curiosity. More importantly, and as a further confirmation, objectivity, like all emotional states, exercises a compulsive, blindfolding quality in respect of other possibilities of the total situation which it views. So love is capable of blinding us to another's defects, anger of blinding us to the rights of others, hope of blinding us to reality. The dangers that follow from the blindness of objectivity, the blindness of science, have been well shown by Dr Justa Smith.

In what follows we are not speaking of the paranormal (except in the sense that life is an aspect of the paranormal), but of items that should in no way have escaped the attention of the scientific establishment. The reason why they have escaped it lies in the blinker effects of being 'possessed' by objectivity, in the same way as we are possessed by anger, fear or whatever. The extreme form of such possession is seen here in the objective denial that life is dramatically different from non-life.

Dr Justa Smith is a biochemist at the Human Dimensions Institute in New York. She and her colleagues have succeeded in duplicating work pioneered by other scientists (such as Dr Ehrenfried Pfeiffer) but hitherto dismissed by the scientific establishment.*

One part of this work was the demonstration of crucial differences between naturally-occurring and synthetically-produced vitamin C — substances which orthodox science and medicine consider to be identical. The proof of the difference lies in the production of chromatographs ('coloured pictures') which are obtained by means of impregnating prepared filter paper. Synthetic vitamin C produces a circular uniform staining of plain concentric circles. Natural vitamin C produces an exquisite stain, with fluted edges and spikes radiating from the centre. These are shown in Figure 8.

To us, the natural vitamin C stain is aesthetically superior. But even in cold scientific terms there is no denying that the pattern of the natural vitamin is intricate and structured, while that of the synthetic product is simple and uniform.

Justa Smith considers that we have here a picture of the 'life-force' and I myself agree with her. The scientific establishment, however, seems unable to tolerate the idea that the product which science makes is not as good as the product that life makes.

* Published in the taped version of the May Lectures, but not included in the book version.

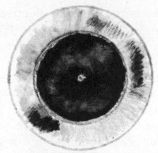

Synthetic Vitamin C   Natural Vitamin C

FIGURE 8 (reproduced by permission of Dr Justa Smith)

Further research by Dr Smith demonstrated that natural vitamin C also contains enzyme and protein. Neither of these is present in synthetic vitamin C. Quite independently, other scientists have demonstrated that animals fed on synthetic vitamin C show a greater tendency to haemorrhage in the small blood vessels — that is, bruise more easily — than animals fed on the natural product.

Life

That life is a fundamentally different phenomenon from non-life has been the intuitive conviction of religious and other individuals all down the ages. Hard evidence to this effect has in the main been wanting, although the work of Justa Smith and others is now making up this deficiency. Even so, that is, even in the face of such evidence, I am sure that many scientists and materialists will still want to claim that the difference between, say, a stone and an apple tree is only one of complexity. They will still want to argue that no firm dividing line can be drawn between life and non-life, no line between organic and inorganic matter. They will point to the enzymes — those tiny fragments of matter that in some ways behave like chemicals and in other ways like organisms. The enzyme seems to sit mid-way between matter and organism, being both and neither at the same time.

This view I emphatically wish to dispute. My own feeling is that living organisms will be found to be characterized by the presence of a 'life-field' — an activity, possibly electrical in nature, emitted by and surrounding the organism. This field would disappear when the organism (or the cell) was dead.

I am not disputing that life in a sense evolves out of physical, inorganic matter, and I have said as much. Our bodies and the bodies of all organisms are obviously built of the same basic materials used in the construction of the rest of the universe. In very many ways these materials in us go on obeying the laws of the physical universe. Our bodies are subject to the pull of gravity, for example.

My proposal is that organisms are in some sense receivers, as that term is used with respect of radio. I suggest that when matter — that is, clusters of the more complex molecules — reaches a certain level of organization or complexity it becomes able to receive 'emissions' of some form of energy — *emissions of organizing information* — which now enable it to organize further. Such 'emissions' must of course exist at all levels (including at the stage of pure matter) — but there are crucial stages and plateaux. The reception of 'higher' emissions constitutes an evolutionary leap — in this case across the divide between non-life and life. (It seems likely that the evolution of ourselves from the general primate group constitutes another evolutionary leap — to an organism now capable of receiving crucially higher emissions of organizing information.) Objectively speaking, any reception occurring in any alleged life-form will be shown by the presence of a life-field.

What then of the enzyme? Is it a life-form — that is, does it show a life-field? My proposal is that primitive creatures such as enzymes are sometimes alive and sometimes not! They are alive on an occasional basis.

How could this be possible?

Pursuing the analogy of a radio receiver, I questioned Professor Ernest Hutten, Professor of Physics at Holloway College, about the nature of a simple radio. The earliest radios, as most people know, were crystal sets. They consisted of a natural crystal that was, literally, tickled by a cat's whisker. The cat's whisker was moved around the surface of the crystal until a point was found where reception of broadcast waves occurred. I asked Professor Hutten whether, in principle, the receipt or non-receipt of a signal could depend on the alignment or non-alignment of a single atom. (In practice, naturally, many atoms are likely to be involved.) He said that in principle this was indeed the case.

Remembering always that I am using the primitive radio as an analogy and not necessarily as an exact model of what occurs, I believe that enzymes sometimes act as receivers and sometimes do not — depending on whether their inner structure is 'in phase' or not. Necessary evidence for my view would crucially require the demonstration of oscillation, of the coming-and-going, of the life-field which, I have suggested, will always be found in association with living organisms.

While I must be the first to emphasize that hard evidence for my view is lacking, the theoretical model I propose is able not only to provide a firm definition of what constitutes life (and how it differs from non-life), and not only to deal with the difficulty of phenomena such as enzymes — but it can also explain how human beings who are clinically and briefly dead can come to life again. While we are not supposed to kick television sets and radios when they do not function, we all do kick them, and a kick sometimes does start them up again. Similarly, the jolting of a coffin has more than once brought a dead body back to life.[108]

It will be clear without my saying it that the 'broadcaster' in my analogy of the receiver is 'spirit'.

Bridgeheads

The initial explosion of what I call 'spirit' into 'space', perhaps that described by science as the big-bang origin of the universe (see p.180) established a bridgehead for 'spirit' in the form, apparently, of atoms of helium and hydrogen only. These atoms of helium and hydrogen seem to be the lowest level of 'spirit-in-space' — though presumably science may one day give us reason to change our minds about that.

Where science so utterly and lamentably fails is in not offering us any *reason* or explanation why these atoms of helium and hydrogen should ever evolve into an incredibly complex organism (ourselves) with the attributes of thought and feeling and self-awareness. Not content with its failure to offer us reasons, science considers the 'why' of the universe totally unimportant. Concerning our own existence — that which by very definition and by our feeling in the matter is the most important thing to us in the universe — science has nothing to say. It seems, moreover, proud of that position.

To others (and, in all fairness, to some scientists also) it seems self-evident that some driving, in principle evolutionary, force or forces are at work in the universe. This is not simply human vanity — an attempt to say that 'I personally' must mean something. It is a conclusion forced upon one by the contemplation of the events on display. This rabbit, and this buttercup, were, it seems, once merely hydrogen and helium atoms floating in an inconceivable emptiness of space. Surely we cannot think that the hydrogen and helium atoms as such took matters into their own hands? It would seem far more reasonable to suppose that *they* were taken in hand by forces acting upon them: that they themselves were also the product of those forces in the first place.

Even supposing that complex matter evolves from simple matter in some purely mechanical way — how then do life and meaning arise?

A process akin to statistical chance just might be sufficient to account for a certain amount of the shuffling around and combining of primordial matter. But statistical chance cannot account for what human beings understand as meaning. Meaning, we must insist, is as much a fact as any atom. As we saw in an earlier section (pp.151—62), chance attempts continually to leap upward to reach the level of meaning, but *always* falls short, and infinitely so.

As I have put the position, the atoms of primordial matter constituted the initial bridgehead of 'spirit' in 'space'. From this base 'spirit' was in a position to advance further. The first stage of advance (the first Dimension) was completed when all the various atoms and molecules, including the complex molecules that are the building blocks of living matter, were in existence.

I hope I have emphasized enough that I consider the progress of 'spirit', the gradual growth of spirit-in-space, to be a fumbling and experimental one.   Progress today I believe to be of the same variety — experimental and uncertain.   The frontier of evolution (at whatever stage) is always chaos.   Only *behind* the front line is the relative calm of an understood position — understood by us, but more importantly by 'spirit' also.

With the creation of life, 'spirit' takes a huge step forward. It can now operate at an infinitely more meaningful level. It is now in a position (as ever, from outside 'space') to upgrade its broadcast transmissions — the transmission of itself into 'space'.   Far more complex and more purposeful messages now become possible.

Clearly, there is an assumption in my model that 'spirit' is somehow sentient and somehow aware, as we ourselves understand these terms — but any further or more detailed attempts to define the nature of 'spirit' seem to me to be impossible.   'Space' I consider to be non-sentient and non-aware, as we understand those terms, but not therefore inert or powerless.   As I have suggested, 'space' forces compromises on 'spirit' at every stage.

With the bridgehead of organisms as such in existence, 'spirit' is then able to proceed with the evolution of consciousness, ultimately of self-conscious consciousness, such as we ourselves possess.   I will say more about self-conscious consciousness under the heading 'The Purpose of Evolution'.

The stage beyond self-conscious awareness is 'god', and the discussion there forms another sub-section in its own right.

Some further comments first on trance-work.

Trance-work

Briefly, trance-work is the imaginings of the Self or, if preferred, the 'thoughts' of the unconscious mind. I have already discussed the concept of trance-work, but several points remain to be emphasized.

I cannot stress too strongly that the trance-work is very largely (if not entirely) meaningless in an objective sense. Its meaning lies (1) in its personal significance for the individual concerned, (2) in its role in elucidating certain aspects of life and the universe not accessible to objective consciousness and (3) in the fact that it contains occasional fragments of genuinely paranormal material. The trance-work is a means to an end, not an end in itself in the way that science is an end in itself. Its purposes are self-knowledge, self-awareness, the appreciation of existence and the direct, intuitive perception of the paranormal Dimensions of life.

So strange is paranormal nature in particular that any vision of the paranormal tends always to remain only personally valid, and not universally valid for all human beings.

A man looking at a heap of mud and rocks might exclaim: 'Ah, so that's gold' (or iron, or aluminium, or whatever). He would be corrected: 'No, that is the material from which we *get* gold.' The trance-work, then, is best understood as the ore from which we mine the paranormal; that strange stuff of the universe which lies above the Dimension of matter.

All religion is trance-work. Religious dogma therefore has, by definition, *no objective value or existence*. So there are no spirit-doctors helping the medium on the other side. The Holy Trinity is not sitting in heaven. No god spoke to Moses, any more than Zeus appeared to Io. These are all simply figments of our imagination. They are the personal ramblings of the unconscious mind. It would make as much (and as little) sense to believe the world is a cardboard box resting on the back of a giant flea. It does not really matter *what* one imagines is happening. The trance-work in itself does no harm, and may do much good, *providing it is never confused with objective reality*. Trance-work is a means to an end. The means has no value, except as a bridge; while the end does have.

The very most that religion can do is to provide a path for each of us personally to explore his or her own being and the nature of being. Religion is *just like* your dreams. It is one part of the process by which the unconscious mind attempts to communicate with consciousness.

In my opinion only one fact can be sifted from the drifting ashes of all the world's religions — and even then it is only the paranormal which clinches the matter. This is that some aspects of life, some aspect of man, is non-physical, non-material, and is not bound by the laws of normal time and space — perhaps therefore not even by death itself.

The Purpose of Evolution

Taking the short view, the purpose of evolution at any one point is to produce the following stage out of the present stage. But taking the longer view, it seems that looking back we can discern stages which have been consolidated and then in a sense abandoned — though as with a coral reef, the new growth relies upon the old, abandoned growth below for its own very existence. Looking at ourselves and our own present we see the stage evolution has currently reached. Ahead of us we glimpse the faint outlines of the next stage. Beyond that, nothing.

Coming down to details, what we see all around us is a physical system, a physical universe, which has been in existence a very long time. It is extremely complex and there is evidence that the complexity evolved slowly over very long periods. Although this next is an organism-centred view, it looks as if the architect of the physical universe was building himself a very elaborate stage (or laboratory) on which to enact or produce the drama and miracle of life.

So at a particular point life is formed. There is not the slightest reason for us to suppose that this event is special to our planet. The likelihood is that experiments with life are taking, and have taken, place all over this galaxy and in all the other galaxies.

Looking at life on this planet (the only example available to us) we can see (because the early steps are still in position) that life began with primitive single-celled creatures. Even if there were only one kind of these to begin with, soon there were thousands of kinds. Single-celled self-reproducing organisms then gave place to multi-celled organisms. Early along the way we have a still more crucial development, that of the two sexes, male and female. Both sexes are henceforth essential to the process of reproduction. All biologists agree that the evolution of two sexes occurred in the interests of greater diversity and development potential. Whereas the self-contained organism, by dividing itself in two, reproduces only a carbon copy of itself — and for *change* must rely on the infrequent and dangerous effects of mutation — the two sexes, working together, produce an organism that is different from either, and in fact unique. Each parent gives the offspring only a part of his or her own endowment. The two semi-endowments then combine in the child to form a brand new, full endowment.

Two-sexed organisms themselves multiplied and diversified. As discussed in Chapter 4, the long-term purpose of these experiments seems to us to be to produce consciousness, and ultimately self-aware consciousness. I agree that we are once again talking in a man-centred way and not a scientific way. It is not only right to do so, but I think essential to do so. For we shall not make sense of anything, other than by the use of the sense we have.

Each long stage of preparation and experimentation seems to be followed rather suddenly by a breakthrough, followed in turn by a period of rapid development. Once the new gains have been exploited, progress again slows almost to a halt, while the gradual search and preparation goes on for the next breakthrough and the next stage. Finally, and suddenly, we have man. His progress, from the time of his actual beginning, is a breathless sprint.

This is not just a metaphor. Sudden is scarcely an adequate word. If we consider the whole existence of life on this planet as a single day, then man appears on the scene only a few seconds before midnight. In those few seconds he achieves all that we see around us. There is no other organism that begins to compare with him, in any sense at all.

Each succeeding stage of evolution seems to move and mature more rapidly than the stage before it. The overall process, that is, seems to be steadily accelerating. The stage to follow consciousness (and which I refer to as 'god') may therefore in fact not be all that far ahead, as evolution reckons time. That is, of course, assuming we are going to make it at all. I feel, and I cannot suppress this point, that there is a better than even chance that we are not going to make it, that we are going to prove one of nature's (or 'spirit's') failures. We may very well end in destruction and madness, of one kind or another.

On a purely intuitive basis, I feel that none of 'spirit's' experiments in the life process anywhere in the universe has yet succeeded in reaching the 'god' stage. Without doubt there must have been thousands, even millions, of experiments in life in different parts of the galaxies. Many more must also coexist with us. Yet I feel that once any life-form achieves the 'god' stage, the life-force will dwindle in any forms anywhere that are left. The next stage will have been achieved.

After all, we can see how the emphasis, and the initiative, has left *other* life-forms on *this* planet, now that we are here. There is no way any other form could now catch up with us — assuming, always, that we do not destroy ourselves.

'God'

The evolutionary stage which is to follow the achievement of self-aware consciousness I term 'god'. The nature of this stage must necessarily be speculation, since we have not yet reached it. It is, nevertheless, a coming event which casts its shadow before. In my earlier book, *Personality and Evolution*, I have tried to show how *all* events of evolution are pre-formed, before they are actually moved into and occupied.

Obviously, my use of the term 'god' implies some connection with the normal meanings of the word god. But there are also some very crucial differences between these terms.

First, I consider that writers and thinkers on religious and occult themes are confusing aspects of god with aspects of what I term 'spirit' — the prime, sentient awareness that exists before the manifestations of the spirit-in-space of which we are one instance.

'Spirit', situated outside 'space', but progressively shifting ever more of its being into 'space', is that energy or force or presence which continually fuels the evolution of the universe as we know it. Evolution, both that of matter and that of organisms, moves on because of the push from within that 'spirit' gives it. I have already said that each of us has within us a tiny spring of the primordial energy I call 'spirit' (just as every atom carries within it a minute fragment of that same force).

So we are not being drawn up to god or heaven — we are being pushed there! And we are not *going* to heaven, we are going to *become* heaven. God (conventional god and heaven) is our future, our own evolutionary future which we somehow discern on the far horizon.

This 'god', this advanced state of man (if he makes it) will possess some of the attributes which religious thinkers have visualized — timelessness, loss of the physical body and so on. Unlike many religious individuals, I do not think that man will then have lost his reason and intelligence! They will be yet stronger. These aspects of 'god' remind us somewhat of Nietzsche's vision of *Übermensch* (superman).

The suggestion of the loss of the physical body is a daunting one. Yet is it more daunting than the idea that physical matter could evolve into life? And *that* miraculous development, at least, we know did take place. Also, we do know that consciousness can already operate to some extent independently of the physical body. In respect of our mind's ability to reach clairvoyantly into the past, for instance, we either have to assume that the consciousness of dead individuals somehow persists after the death of the body, so that we pick up that consciousness, or that our own consciousness can somehow move back in time. Our minds can also certainly travel into future time, as when we foresee the not-yet clairvoyantly.

But perhaps, in any case, it is not a question of our losing the body altogether, but more a question of its becoming less and less important. Or, possibly, it might become less and less damageable. For example, full control of our own autonomic nervous systems (see Chapter 5) might enable us to avoid all illness and to postpone physical death almost indefinitely. These possibilities, at least, are far from being fantastic.

I am in my own mind absolutely certain that the 'hereafter' does not consist of each of us personally living on as we are now, attending glorified vicarage tea parties. The idea that the endless miseries of life on this planet, the apparently unending horrors of Belsen, the Kolima, Northern Ireland and so on — to say nothing of organized crime — are gone through in order that we should reach a Sunday School teacher's idea of heaven — this idea is enough to send one insane on the spot.

The further idea that the unintentional — an earthquake in Turkey that renders thousands dead, maimed and homeless; a blast furnace that explodes showering molten metal on the men around it; the Soveso chemical disaster that led to the disfigurement of the living and the deformity of the unborn — the idea that these are designed ultimately for our own good, or because we have done something obscene — *this idea itself* is the ultimate obscenity.

It is what comes of taking the trance-work literally, in imagining that the imaginings of our own minds are *literally* the instructions of some god. *In that sense* there are no such instructions. We are on our own, as far as dealing with the problems and difficulties of the here-and-now are concerned.

The false view of the trance-work as *reality* and the notion of god (as opposed to 'god') leads also on the one side to the torture and death of the Christian at the hands of the 'barbarian', on the other to the torture and death of the barbarian at the hands of the Christian, in order in both cases to force the change to the view which the other holds 'in good faith'.

As for the 'meaning' of the many horrors of this planet and this life — there *is* no meaning, in the sense of excuse. The blind fumbling of 'spirit' venturing ever further into 'space' is, I think, simply unable to avoid these events — just as we, making our way in the dark through an unfamiliar room, knock over and break what we cannot foresee, and so cannot avoid.

Above all, it is abundantly clear that life does not care about individual lives. Any more than I, tearing my way out of a burning building, care about my fingers — or driving to avoid a flood have any compunction about ruining an engine. There *are* some grounds, however, for considering that life cares about *life* — for in general organisms fight to go on living to the bitter end, blindly; in our own case often long after hope and reason are gone.

Though I cannot myself consider that when we die we go forward or upward to any heaven, I do imagine that the life energy released reverts to the main body of 'spirit' outside 'space'. There it is put to re-use — not reincarnated in that sense, but certainly recycled. (Here, I think, the notions of Zen Buddhism come nearest to the actuality.) This view can give us some personal comfort, I think, about the processes of the universe as a whole — some sense of being part of something 'meaningful' and continuous. But I do not think this circumstance gives us any real day-to-day instructions or pointers about how to lead our lives.

We have, surely, been equipped with self-awareness and the power of reflection in order to use them. The failure to use them will result in the failure of this whole planet for us personally, and beyond that of experiment XYZ, in the on-going universal series.

Conclusion

In any discussion or enterprise involving the paranormal, it must never be overlooked what a very small part the paranormal plays quantitatively in the everyday affairs of this world. (But as with the infinitesimal amounts of radium in each ton of pitchblende, the importance of this tiny quantity must also not be underestimated.) The large majority of individuals, however, do not seem to have one genuine paranormal experience during the whole of their lives, certainly not any of which they are conscious. Others have perhaps one paranormal dream. Even in the case of mediums and other psychics, paranormal activity can scarcely comprise ten per cent of their total experiences. Of course, neither the trance condition of the medium, nor the ramblings of the alleged spirit guides are themselves paranormal. But embedded in these activities are usually a few fragments of paranormal perception.

The first step we must take in an exploration of the paranormal by non-scientific means (since the scientific approach is of no value here) is to get down to the bedrock of it. The sham and the doubtful must go. The wild claims and the fantastic stories must go. At present the hull of the paranormal is encrusted almost out of sight with barnacles from the seas of nonsense through which it has sailed.

Paranormalists need above all to renew their grip on common sense and on reason. They must put their house in order, instead of leaving themselves open to be the laughing-stock of the uncommitted and the butt of the scientist. Paranormalists should not mourn the loss of the fake and the worthless (like the Philippine healers). There are quite enough genuine wonders to occupy and satisfy us.

These steps of putting the paranormal house in order must precede any new programme of development. We cannot possibly go anywhere, least of all ahead, as matters stand at present.

The cornerstone of the edifice of Subjectivity can only, in my opinion, be laid by those who, whatever their other qualifications, have themselves had first-hand, personal experience of the paranormal. The ideal candidate is the *strong* psychic who is equally endowed with normal intelligence.

Already a few such individuals are available and active. There is Robert Temple. Aside from having a degree in Classical Languages, he is a Fellow of the Royal Astronomical Society, a writer of distinction, and of course himself psychic. Jan Merta, quite apart from his outstanding psychic gifts, is a trouble-shooter for an international organization in the physiological problems of deep-sea diving. He has himself logged many hours at maximum depths in the North Sea and elsewhere, and is consultant in respect of the most recent monitoring equipment. (He has also just completed his doctorate in Psychology.) I myself was for some years Senior Research Psychologist at the National Children's Bureau, wrote the first of Longman's *Studies in Child Development* and hold degrees in Modern Languages and Psychology. Marcel Vogel, Senior Chemist at I.B.M. and a notable psychic, would also make a powerful ally. He is, however, an ardent Catholic — but perhaps he might be persuaded to dissolve some of the narrowness — as I see it — of his position in the service of a greater whole.

I hope very much that individuals like Dr Lyall Watson and Professor John Taylor can be tempted back to what I myself regard as the true path — can develop the knack of being a little firmer with over-imaginative psychics, and with downright tricksters — but more importantly will actively seek to develop psychic powers in themselves.

The aim is to remove the study of the paranormal from the hands of scientists in general, from the hands of religious dogma in particular, and from the (I regret to say) dead hands of the organizations currently engaged in psychic exploration.

Even those who are only vaguely curious about the paranormal, but who have not themselves had any valid or convincing psychic experience, should seek such experience. They should not be content just to read books about it. The only genuine way ahead is through personal experience. Seek the company of psychic individuals, listen (by all means) to what they have to say.

It may well be, incidentally, that individuals who have difficulty in experiencing the paranormal for themselves may be helped by the concentrated efforts of a *group* of psychics. I would hope that psychics would see it as part of their work to provide *direct* paranormal experience for the less-endowed individual, if necessary by functioning in teams, as just suggested. The idea of attempting to give every individual a psychic experience by means of a number of sensitives concentrating on that person at once and functioning as a battery is, I believe, new — and should form a basic part of the work of any psychic group.

In recent times we have made great strides in our understanding of objective reality. I would wish with my whole heart that we could make equal progress in our investigation of the equally real, but yet far more elusive, subjective reality. I believe it offers our only hope of a future. For matter can never be more than matter — and our destiny is to become 'god'.

APPENDICES

APPENDIX I
Ready-Money Karma

The concept of ready-money karma was initially explained to me over the telephone by Richard Kirby, after I had told him of finding a £5 note (see below). In the hasty circumstances, my understanding of the concept was a little garbled. Richard subsequently straightened my ideas out and gave me some references. Here is how Ernest Wood describes the notion.

> There is common belief among the Hindus that we are each destined for a certain length of life, according to our karma, but this is generally considered to be alterable by means of our current activities. There is always present activity to be taken into account, and what has sometimes been called 'ready-money karma'. If in a busy town a man crosses the street against the red light, in defiance or through neglect of the traffic regulations, any injury he may sustain must be credited to his present action as ready-money karma, not to karma coming over from a previous life. Similarly, good deeds done now with a good heart may counterbalance or neutralise certain outstanding karmas, or offset karmas which are in store and have not yet begun to fructify.[113]

Nevertheless, my initial understanding of the concept was not all that far from the mark, and privately I have retained it. I understood that ready-money karma was the reward of present 'good deeds' or good living, by out-of-the-blue gifts of actual cash. This is certainly how the ruling (if there is any such ruling!) seems to apply in my case. (Actually, I don't personally subscribe to the Hindu view of karma.)

In isolation some of the events which follow may not seem especially striking, let alone paranormal, to the sceptical reader. Perhaps by the end of the section I shall nevertheless succeed in convincing, if only by the sheer volume of material.

All my adult life — but most notably in the last ten years since becoming a writer — I seem to have had the knack of attracting unearned income, and especially when matters were desperate — as they frequently have been. It is not therefore that I have not known financial hardship. On the contrary, I am afraid such hardship is the regular lot of the large majority of writers, artists, actors and other creative, self-employed individuals. Yet when things grew desperate it seemed I could always rely on rescue.

Starting at the most general level, the quantity of money I find lying about in the streets is phenomenal. I have the impression that other people must be simply flinging it away. Principally I find coins, as many silver as copper, sometimes several in the course of one day. Single £1 notes, however, are also quite common. Once I found three £1 notes lying spread out on the pavement in Chancery Lane, in the City of London, in full view of everybody. The largest sum I ever found was a £5 note. It was on a recent Saturday morning in Hampstead in north London. I was pondering the fact that I had only £1.50 to last the weekend and was ruefully deciding that once again eggs were going to form my staple diet, when a £5 note came dancing along the pavement towards me. On the hill up which I was walking there was no one in sight. A slight drizzle was falling, yet the note was scarcely wet. I hasten to add that (unlike Puharich) I do not believe the *existence* of the note was in any way paranormal. It could easily have blown out of a window of one of the houses.

This general finding of money blends with other circumstances and sources of unearned income. Let me give two instances that occurred in a strikingly *à propos* manner (like the incident of the *Guardian* in the film in Chapter 3). I am sure that these were genuinely synchronistic little events.

On the day I was setting off to London University Library in central London to write this Appendix, I was pondering the fact that I had not found any money for two or three days, and a little down-hearted that I would be writing in slightly inauspicious circumstances. I reached Swiss Cottage Underground station. In front of me, at the ticket office, was an American tourist, a woman. She said hesitantly to the clerk what I — and obviously the clerk — thought was 'Two . . . to Regent's Park'. In fact, as I realized subsequently, she must have said 'To . . . to Regent's Park', being, as a tourist, slightly unsure of the station.

The clerk took her £1 note and punched his machine. Two tickets appeared on the counter, and the change rattled into the change-cup. The woman scooped up her change without examining it, together with one of the tickets.

At this precise moment the telephone behind the clerk rang, and he turned away to answer it. Otherwise he would have noticed the spare ticket. I picked up the second ticket and ran after the woman. 'You forgot your other ticket,' I said. She looked at it and at me. 'I don't want it,' she said. 'You have it.' 'Oh — O.K., then.' I held out the money. 'No, no, don't bother,' said the woman. 'I've no time.' And she ran off down the escalator at the sound of an incoming train. Whether she understood that she had in fact paid for the ticket I do not know.

One more 'chance' ingredient in this little drama was that the woman, although going to a different destination from myself, also needed a 20p ticket. So her ticket was perfectly all right for me.

So there it was. I had made 20p out of thin air and in a set of circumstances that resembled the degree of contrivance of a Feydeau farce. I was of course hugely delighted — here I had a perfect item, to order, for my ready-money Appendix.

That was not the end, however. Here we come to another item (which I will discuss shortly), the getting of wrong change. On the afternoon of the same day I went into the student refectory for a cup of tea and a biscuit. I was the only person being served. There was not the slightest pressure on the woman at the cash-desk, whose only function was to take money. She looked at my tray. 'Ninepence', she said clearly. She took my 10p piece, rang up 9p — and gave me 2p change! I had 'made' another penny!

The amount involved is of course utterly trivial (though I hasten to say that I would not normally diddle a student refectory even out of 1p). In my 'triumph' I decided to keep the 2p coin as a souvenir. Here again was a little more grist for the mill.

It is the *frequency* of these incidents which is the real point. A day or two later, three events occurred in one day. I was going into town to see my publisher, but out of habit bought a 20p ticket, instead of a 30p ticket, as if I were going to the library as usual. Once on the train I realized my mistake. At Piccadilly Circus I went to the excess-fares clerk and gave him my 20p ticket and a 10p piece. The fare from Swiss Cottage to Piccadilly was and had been 30p for the last nine months or more. The clerk gave me an excess ticket for 5p and 5p change. I was about to remonstrate with him — but then in a flash decided to see whether the ticket collector would pick up the mistake, for I now had to give both tickets to the regular ticket man. I went over to him — he was currently completely idle, between trains — and gave him both tickets. He took them, examined both, and nodded me through.

Later, in the post office, I found an unused 20p stamp on the writing counter. There was no one else around, just one or two people queuing at one of the grilles. Then later again was an incident of the first type. I asked a street trader, clearly, for a pound of chestnuts. He began weighing tangerines. 'No — chestnuts,' I repeated. He weighed me a pound of chestnuts, said, 'Thirty pence', which was correct — and then counted 80p change into my hand from my £1 note. I was the only person being served and in fact the only other person around apart from the trader himself.

Street traders and ticket inspectors are in my opinion the *last* people to make these kind of mistakes. My experiences — still more to follow — incline me in the long run to believe I must exercise a paranormal effect on the individuals concerned in these, usually, one-to-one encounters.

(On the general point of being given wrong change — I was at one time a little worried about keeping such money, in view of the unfortunate consequences it might have for the individual making the mistake. In the end my own selfish worries about money carried the day. I did, however, make the rule that generally speaking I would only accept the wrong change in large department stores and supermarkets, where I cannot believe, with the volume of business involved, that any till ever balances. In small shops, as a rule, I give the money back.)

A few days subsequently I bought a pillow in a department store. I was again the only person being served at that counter. The girl said, 'Three pounds, eighty-five pence', wrote that amount on the bill in front of her, rang that amount into the till and took my £5 note. Then she solemnly mis-counted £1.90 into my hand (instead of £1.15) making the counting come out right! I stood looking at her in disbelief for this was no understandable mistake — waiting for the light to dawn. She returned my gaze, smiled and turned away. I walked off shaking my head in disbelief.

Two days after that I bought a bottle of spirits (a weakness of mine, usually more important than the rent) in a liquor supermarket. It was £3.86. I gave the assistant a £5 note. He carefully gave me back £2.14 — instead of the £1.14 it should have been. I held the money in my outstretched hand and stared at him — for I am not willing to have any stealth on my side of the transaction. He stared blankly back at me. I looked at the money in full view in my hand and looked at him again. He returned my gaze impassively. I picked up the bottle and left the shop.

I have really lost count of the times I have given an assistant a 50p piece, which the assistant correctly places on top of the till as a check (it being easy to confuse a 50p piece with a 10p piece) — and then counts into my hand the change from £1. A few days ago, while I was making a fair copy of this manuscript, the girl in the local stationery shop started to give me £1 change from a 50p coin. Then she stopped and looked at me strangely, as if to say, what did you do to me? She did not look at the 50p piece on top of the till, which would be the normal reaction to the realization of a normal mistake. (On this occasion I *would* have given the money back, as it happens, if only because I am a regular customer in the shop.)

Statisticians should find it remarkable that I cannot recall ever having been given *less* change than I should get.

Apart from finding money and being given too much change, people often send me unsolicited money. During an eighteen-month period a few years ago, for instance, I was sent £200 anonymously. The money came in three instalments of £100, £50 and £50. It was sent in used notes in registered envelopes. The back of the envelope carried a fictitious address. In the first was also a typewritten note: 'A small token of my regard for your work — a well-wisher.' The origin of the money remains a mystery.

On another occasion some two years ago I had been working as a packer for several months. My writing and research was considerably hampered. With a fair amount of despair I consulted the *I Ching* about what to do. The oracle counselled me not to worry, as help would come from the West. Two days later I received a letter from a woman in Wales. She inquired why my next book was so long in appearing — and was I in any kind of difficulty? I wrote back explaining the position. She then telephoned me and asked how much money I would need to finish the book on which I was currently working. As a result of the conversation this benefactor sent me £200 a few weeks later, and subsequently another £100.

Perhaps I ought to say that I regard such funds as an indefinite loan rather than a gift. However, I have become easier about accepting them in recent years, out of a growing conviction of 'karma'. I write the world 'karma' in quotes because, as I said, I do not accept the religious view on this matter — but as a believer in synchronicity I do accept that there are meaningful constellations of events, not entirely within our power to control (see Chapters 5 and 7). It seems more sensible (as well as more convenient) to move with them.

I will mention just one further gift. A well-known author sent me £50 out of the blue, on condition that I spend it 'only on luxuries'.

Now to rather different aspects. Like my father and grandfather before me, I have been a gambler all my adult life, but with this difference — my gambling has been as fortunate as theirs, alas, was unfortunate. I will divide these comments on gambling into two parts. The first consists of what one might call routine gambling — where, nevertheless, I am consistently more lucky than most. The second consists of what I would call paranormal gambling.

Anyone who gambles habitually will appreciate the remarkableness of the events I shall describe. The non-gambler, in attempting to evaluate them, should bear in mind the following. *Everyone who gambles loses money.* All the people one sees thronging betting shops and gambling casinos are steadily losing their money. They might as well make a standing order payment — and stay away. People do have occasional wins, of course, but these are more than cancelled out by their losses. An acquaintance of mine who began playing roulette a few years ago told me the other day that he had just won £80 — but added, with rare honesty, that he was still £500 out of pocket overall. Bookmakers have a saying — they never give anyone money, they only lend it. It always comes back.

Probably the high-water mark of my routine gambling career was achieving a seven-horse accumulator. This involves picking seven winners in a row, with the accumulating winnings automatically passing on to each next horse. This 5p bet paid £151 before tax. For those interested, the individual odds were 6:4, 7:2, 5:2, 9:2, 2:5, 3:1 and 6:4. What is called a 'yankee' bet (four winners in succession) is quite a commonplace winning bet for me. Many gamblers have never had one yankee in their whole career.

Of more interest to most people, I think, is my truly paranormal gambling.

It is not easy to define the terms of reference here. They involve intuitive judgments not only of how to bet, but when to bet. It is, of course, useful to try to define or describe the terms of reference, for here I think we begin to come close to the nature of the paranormal.

It seems, first, that I must never *plan* to bet. I must never say 'tomorrow I will bet' — unless, perhaps, through intuitive impulse. Still less can I say 'I need to win this and this amount', and never at all 'I *will* win'. These matters are not in my hands. (The situation generally here rather resembles

that of the believer who gives himself up to the 'will of God'
or the mystic with his fatalistic view of karma.) Instead, I
gamble only when an opportunity 'presents itself' and when
there are appropriate 'indicators'. These 'indicators' vary
enormously, so that it is hard to generalize about them.
They are really very similar to the little cues from the
environment that many superstitious people watch out for.
Unlike *their* superstitions, however, mine seem to work most
of the time. Perhaps the cues themselves are meaningless,
nothing more than further instances of trance-work. Possibly,
in other words, they are just the means by which the psychic
impulse manifests itself to consciousness. Let me give some
examples.

I was on my way to visit Simmona de Serdici — with
whom, as I have already indicated, I have a rather lively
psychic rapport. On the way it seemed appropriate to
drop in at a betting shop I was passing. I was in no great
hurry, and under no particular other pressure.

In the next race a horse was running which has the same
name as the road in which Simmona lives (I suspect the
owner of the horse must live there). Also running was
another horse with the name of the district in which the
road is — Hyde Park Corner. I put 50p to win on the horse
with the name of the road. Apart from straight bets, there
are others, like the forecast, where you have to name the
first and second horse. So I also combined 'Simmona's'
horse with Hyde Park Corner for a 10p forecast.

Simmona's horse came first at 20:1. Hyde Park Corner
was second at 14:1. For the win I received £10.50 (including
stake). For the forecast I received £15. So altogether my bet
of 60p produced £25. For the *cognoscenti* I will remark
that this was a twenty-three-horse race, in which Lester
Piggot, Pat Eddery and many other top jockeys were riding.
The result was a dramatic reversal of form with a degree of
improbability which the market odds in no way adequately
reflect.

Sometimes when I go into a betting establishment, the
name of a horse will leap out at me from somewhere, as if
someone were visually shouting it. This horse is usually a
winner — but other matters can be involved. Sometimes

the horse will break a leg or bust a blood vessel during the race. Or he may throw and injure his jockey. Sometimes again, the odds of the horse I am drawn to will tumble dramatically during the on-course betting — say, from 12:1 to 5:2. But the horse actually gets nowhere in the race. What I seem to be picking up at that point is the strong charge of emotionalism at the track and not a precognition of the result.

One morning, in the course of conversation with a medium I was visiting, I mentioned my interest in gambling. 'Oh, in that case,' she said, 'let me give you a horse.' She told me she could not do this for herself, but occasionally did it for others in deserving cases (!). She asked if I had a daily paper. She took it and glanced at the racing section. 'That one,' she said. The horse was Easby Abbey. It started favourite and won at 5:4.

In roulette casinos the hints take an altogether different form — and this is actually a totally different gambling situation, one based completely on chance and nothing else. Two (I regret to say, missed) opportunities were as follows.

On one occasion in a busy West End London casino, where twenty or more tables were in full swing, with a hubbub of noise everywhere, there was a sudden moment of almost complete silence. I heard a croupier at the far end of the great room say quite clearly 'twenty-eight black'. The next number on my own table was twenty-eight black.

Another time I had gone to play roulette in the afternoon (always the best time to play). I had been seated only a few moments. Then a woman standing across the table from me (a total stranger) looked at me and said abruptly: 'I've been playing for two hours on the number eight. It hasn't come up once and I've lost all my money.' With that she walked off. The next number was eight. The number after that was eight. And the number after that was eight. Three eights in a row — an occurrence of enormous rarity. I did not bet on any of them. I cursed myself after the first eight, thinking my chance gone. The second eight left me speechless. After the third eight I had no more heart, stopped playing and went home. I have never had such a clear psychic elbow in the ribs as on that occasion.

Like most gamblers, I still sometimes gamble compulsively, out of depression or boredom or whatever. On such occasions I then face much the same chance odds as everyone else, though still usually with a built-in 'lucky edge'. On a particular afternoon, having had lunch, instead of going home to do some more work, I walked the other way to a betting shop. In fairly short order I lost £4. I set out for home, thoroughly disheartened, and not feeling in the least like doing any work. About a hundred yards down the road I found a £1 note lying on the pavement. I was, of course, still £3 out of pocket. But it was as if life were saying to me: 'Well, you've always got your ready-money karma, haven't you?'

APPENDIX II
The Conceptual Powers
of Animals

Many people, especially those with pets of their own, believe that animals are extremely intelligent. Such is not usually the case. Before looking at instances of genuinely intelligent behaviour in animals, we need to look at two other types of behaviour which seem intelligent, but are not.

The first is conditioning, a mindless form of learning, found incidentally also in ourselves. We need not go into all the refinements of conditioning here, but roughly speaking, any action which an animal happens to perform, if followed by a reward in the shape of food or affection, will tend to be repeated in similar circumstances. By the means of rewarding desired behaviour in an animal, we can train a pigeon to play a long, complicated tune on a xylophone with its beak, or a pig to give the 'answers' to addition or subtraction sums by tapping its foot the correct number of times. Neither animal, however, has the slightest idea what it is actually doing. These actions are performed to order because each tiny action in the whole complex chain of response has been rewarded by the trainer many times in the past. In human beings, the *movements* involved, say, in typing or driving a car are conditioned responses, even though we ourselves of course understand the purpose of the movements. (We nevertheless go on doing the old movements on a different typewriter or in a new car, until new conditioning takes place.)

The second source of apparently intelligent behaviours in animals is instinct. Instinct can be defined as the predetermined inherited tendency to act in particular ways in particular situations. These tendencies are part of the genetic equipment of the animal and the species in question. The sheep dog — that apparently so intelligent animal — provides us with a fine instance.

Wolves, from which the sheep dog is descended, instinctively chase single animals that have become detached from a herd. (These detached animals, as it happens, are usually the weaker or older individuals.) The instinctive response of the herd animal (a sheep, for instance) on being chased or attacked is to run towards the herd. These two instinctive tendencies in the two animals make the basic work of the sheep dog possible. For the dog then to perform its instinctive action in response to specific whistles from the shepherd is simply a conditioning process overlaid on the instinctive response.

The essentially mindless and automatic quality of the instinctive response is seen in another action of the sheep dog. In hunting, the wolf attempts to drive the prey towards other members of the wolf pack, in principle towards the pack leader. So the sheep dog therefore has no problem in driving the sheep towards the shepherd. But it is extremely difficult for the shepherd to get the sheep dog to drive the sheep *ahead* of him, if the shepherd himself is *behind* the dog. This situation arises, for example, when the flock is being driven home in the evening.

In this situation the dog not only looks unhappy and anxious, but he is continually trying to slip past the flock and turn the sheep back towards his pack leader (the shepherd). The shepherd must continually block the execution of this unwanted behaviour by his conditioned whistle signals. But still he cannot stop the dog *wanting* to behave in his instinctive way.

We can begin to speak of reasoning and conceptual understanding only when animals perform actions not dictated either by instinct or by conditioning. The animal must at no time have been conditioned or trained to do the action. Ideally, what we need is a complicated piece of behaviour, a solution which the animal 'gets right' first time and which appears, therefore, to result from an analysis and a correct understanding of a situation — just as we use those words in respect of a human being. The solution to the problem in question may well involve an appreciation of a future event or outcome and of events not actually physically present in the situation to hand, but nevertheless affecting it — in other words, conceptualization.

Only if we can find such behaviours in animals do I consider that we have a basis for assuming that animals may have the ideas of 'somewhere else' and 'sometime else' which, it seems to me, are necessarily involved in the supposition of ESP transmission and reception in animals.

I have collected from many sources (these are given on p.294) a number of examples of apparent understanding in animals. Those that follow are a sample.

A dog which had been trained to carry objects in its mouth was given for the first time a basket of eggs to carry. Arriving at a stile, he pushed the basket of eggs under it with his nose, jumped the stile and then picked up the eggs again.

A retriever was observed to be collecting mouthfuls of hay and depositing them in a particular spot. On examination it was found that the dog was covering a rolled hedgehog. When he had covered the hedgehog, the dog picked the bundle up in his mouth and set off home with it.

A collie was lost from a farm and was missing for nearly a month. Another collie was observed to make off into the woods with a bone. The dog was followed for about a mile. It reached a disused well and dropped the bone in. At the bottom was the other collie, standing in about two inches of water. From the dog's condition it had obviously been well supplied with food. (A puzzle here is why the second collie did not deliberately lead a human being to the spot. The indication from such an 'oversight' is that the dog's understanding of the position was very fragmentary — only a dim perception that the other dog needed food, but nothing more — no concept of rescue, for example.)

A dog was badly stung by bees. This had happened to him on a previous occasion. Now he made his way straight to the vet who had treated him on the first occasion, without first returning home.

The manageress of a boarding house was awakened one morning by a cat pulling at her hand. The cat was the companion of a bedridden woman who lived in the house.

The manageress went with the cat to the woman's room. She was dying and in fact died just as the manageress arrived.

A ring-tailed coon in Paraguay was a household pet. Without any encouragement, he developed the habit of unscrewing the cap from a tube of shaving soap, and squeezing a gob of it onto his stomach, while lying on his back on the bed, propped up on the pillows. Then, spitting on the mixture from time to time, he would cover himself all over with it as far as he could reach. Then he would go down to the stream to wash it all off. (Coons, of course, do wash their food and are very fastidious animals.)

One day in Wales, during the severe winter of 1963, the worst since 1742, Thurlow Craig saw three buzzards circling. He went to see what was attracting the birds. A dead fox was lying spread-eagled, its jaws gaping wide. Craig assumed it had been shot by a farmer. Slowly the buzzards circled lower, then settled, and gradually hopped closer. Then one jumped on the fox's head and struck for the eye. Suddenly the fox was on its feet with the buzzard between its jaws.

A husky dog was brought from the Arctic to Edinburgh. This dog would set out pieces of meat and lie down next to them pretending to be asleep. When birds, or occasionally mice, came to feed he would pounce on them.

(Both these animals had apparently devised their behaviour under conditions of extreme hardship. As in man, necessity seems to be the mother of invention in animals also.)

An old grey mare on an *estancia* in Argentina was herself past breeding age, but liked to adopt new colts. All the horses were corralled and kept from certain pastures by means of fences. In these fences were 'gates' which would collapse if a loop of wire hitched around a post were lifted off. The old mare had taught herself to open these gates. But she would also take her latest young protégé to the gate, rub the wire noose with her nose, turn to the colt as if observing whether he were watching, and only then lift off the loop allowing the gate to collapse. She would then turn once again to the colt as if to make sure that the lesson was understood, and at that point only lead the colt into the forbidden area.

Mrs R. Lee reports on a number of parrots that apparently occasionally used words appropriately in meaningful situations.   One of these, whenever it had food it did not particularly care for, would call 'puss, puss' in appropriately endearing tones, and when the cat duly appeared, would drop the morsels to the floor below.

The ethologist Konrad Lorenz reared a raven as a pet. He called it 'Roah' — the name being an approximation of the call-note of the raven. However, it seems that the raven, far from understanding that this was his own name, thought it was Lorenz's own call-note. For one day when Lorenz was in a dangerous situation, the raven flew over his head, making the body and tail movements which instinctively cause other ravens on the ground to take to the air, *while calling the word Roah with a human intonation.* It was calling Lorenz's name.

(It seems that of all animals it is only birds which ever spontaneously use a *sound* as meaningful language — as it happens, a human word.)

A man owned a mongrel dog, Pierrot. This dog loved to forage in dustbins, for which behaviour, however, he was punished. The owner went out one day, leaving Pierrot apparently asleep in the study. A few minutes away from home, the man realized he had forgotten something. Arriving back at his front gate, he heard a noise that was unmistakably made by the garbage can being dragged along the kitchen floor. Going to the front door and opening it, he was amazed to see Pierrot 'asleep' on the couch in the *hall*. When he spoke to the dog, it drowsily opened its eyes and yawned. But the waste bin in the kitchen told its own story. Pierrot was a great actor — but a poor geographer and an indifferent logician. (Parents and teachers will recognize the similarity here to the behaviour of young children — they cover their tracks skilfully enough in one direction, without realizing how transparent their guilt is from another.) This same dog, if tied up, would slip its collar and go about its business. On its return *it would once again force its head through the collar*! Here the dog's logic was quite faultless.

A Newfoundland dog, Dandie, had been taught to take pennies to the baker who exchanged them for bread (a simple conditioning process). But the dog was then found to be hoarding the pennies and using them when he felt hungry. (For people who knew of the dog's party trick often gave him extra pennies in the street, hoping to see him perform.) Just to clinch the story, when the hiding place of Dandie's pennies was discovered, he then began hiding them in a new place!

Gustav Eckstein the biologist has two cases, rather too long to report in detail here, one of a blind canary in a laboratory that was apparently assisted by its sighted mate, and one of a dog that without any training whatsoever, at the age of four months, began habitually walking on its hind legs and using its forepaws as hands.

All the book references given below, from which these stories are taken, contain a very wide variety of informative anecdotes about animals. From these I have selected only those that meet my own rather strict definition of intelligence.

Bibliography

Archer, F.M., *The Soul of a Dog* (Church Publishing Co., London, 1931).

Barbanell, Sylvia, *When Your Animal Dies* (Spiritualist Press, London, 1969).

Craig, Thurlow, *Animal Affinities with Man* (Country Life, London, 1966).

Eckstein, Gustav, *Everyday Miracle* (Gollancz, London, 1949).

Ledesna, A.F. de, Letter, *New Scientist*, May 23rd, 1968.

Lee, R., *Anecdotes of the Habits and Instincts of Animals* (Grant & Griffith, London, 1852).

Lee, R., *Anecdotes of the Habits and Instincts of Birds, Reptiles and Fish* (Grant & Griffith, London, 1853).

Lorenz, Konrad, *King Solomon's Ring* (Methuen, London, 1952).

Méry, Fernand, *Our Animal Friends* (Rider, London, 1954).

APPENDIX III

Arthur M. Young and 'The Reflexive Universe'

After I had completed the first draft of my text I was given two books to read by Arthur M. Young — *The Reflexive Universe* and *The Geometry of Meaning*.

It is always a pleasure, for obvious reasons, to come across someone expressing similar views to your own — especially when that person is a scientist of considerable achievement. But pleasure aside — and more importantly — there is the evidential and supportive aspect. Arthur Young is a man who has been crucially and independently impressed by some of the same aspects of life and the universe that have crucially influenced me also.

Far from attempting here any general review of Arthur Young's work — except to say that he is aiming to produce a theory of the genesis of ourselves and our universe, in short a cosmology — I am simply going to list one or two of the more important parallels between his and my thinking (and trust that the reader will himself be motivated to take a first-hand look at Young's ideas).

(1) Young, like myself, is forcibly impressed with the 'one-wayness' of conventional time (what he calls 'time's arrow') which travels only in one direction, and never reverses. Even Einstein's relativity does not 'release' time from its one-way path. (See pp.175–86 of this book for my own views.)

(2) Young is convinced that ancient myths sometimes embody scientific truths about the universe that we have not yet discovered along our twentieth-century scientific path. Note the point here — he and I are not talking about 'philosophical truths' or wise sayings about how to live life.

We are talking about *scientific* factual truths, contained in mythical and legendary accounts. For example, Young suggests that the fact that Mars' mythical chariot is driven by two horses shows a foreknowledge of the two actual moons of Mars, only discovered by scientists in 1877.

At many points in my own books, for instance, I have myself argued that the ancient stories reveal a knowledge of brain functions that are *still* not known to science today — the function of the cerebellum, for example. See pp.199—204.

(3) Young makes a number of observations in connection with machines. For instance, he points out that one cannot ascertain the purpose of a machine by looking at its dismembered parts. You can only discover its purpose — that is, its purpose only *emerges* — when the machine is assembled or reassembled. This, then, is another and very clever way of demonstrating that *a meaningful whole is more than the sum of its parts*. Equally also, the dissection of an organism cannot tell us about the organism as a meaningful, operating whole. (And a dead organism cannot tell us what a living organism *is* when it is living.)

For my own comments on the differences between the parts and the meaningful whole see especially pp.132—4 of this book. For some of the differences between 'identical' dead and living structures see also pp.262—5.

But Young says still more here. He points out that *there never was a machine that did not have a purpose*. A machine is made *for* a purpose. Even if reductionists want to say that man, or some animal, is 'just a machine' they do not thereby escape the implications — the *purpose* — of that situation. Young poses another very interesting question by turning the position round. He asks 'Does purpose always require a machine?' — that is, what is the purpose for which man and all organisms are required?

On pp.151—60 of this book and elsewhere I myself have argued that *chance cannot by itself produce anything meaningful*. Chance cannot even spell a word of more than eight letters. Essentially mine is the same statement as Young's. For, coming closer to Young's analogy of machines, we can say that chance could never make even a simple utilitarian object like a beer bottle. *Never*, in all the tortured chemistry of evolving planets and boiling stars, could a beer bottle be produced. Natural glass? Yes, certainly. Strange shapes of natural glass? Yes, certainly. But a perfectly proportioned, tapered bottle, slightly and uniformly coloured throughout, having sides of constant thickness with a thicker bottom section, open at one end and having there a lip to which to attach the cap — no, never. Not ever, ever, ever.

(And what then of the label for the bottle?)

Let us hope that Arthur Young and I and the many others striving towards a genuine total understanding of man and the universe he inhabits will one day persuade 'otherwise reasonable scientists' (see p.166) of the self-evident truth of the differences between life and non-life, and between events due to chance and the clearly purposive event. The denial by science of organization and purpose in the universe I am afraid deserves a stronger word even than stupidity.

Bibliography

Young, Arthur M., *The Reflexive Universe* (Delacorte Press, New York, 1976, and Wildwood House, London, 1977).

Young, Arthur M., *The Geometry of Meaning* (Delacorte Press, New York, 1976, and Wildwood House, London, 1977).

Brief Glossary

clairvoyance The mental ability to obtain, other than by means of the normal senses, information about the past, present or future not currently known to any living person.

ectoplasm A substance allegedly exuded by some mediums in trance, which can also allegedly form itself into the features of individuals who have 'passed over'.

ESP An abbreviation for 'extra-sensory perception'. This is a blanket term covering all aspects of the paranormal except psychokinesis (see below) and physical phenomena (see below). But in casual use the term is often understood to cover these phenomena also.

paranormal That which lies outside or beyond the normal objective universe of cause and effect and outside normal time.

physical phenomena Paranormally-induced sounds, lights or voices, audible or visible to more than one person, the paranormal movement or breaking or meterialization of objects, the dematerialization of objects, the production of ectoplasm (see above), levitation, the alleged paranormal production of images on unexposed film, psychic-healing and so on. In all these alleged phenomena the *physical*, as opposed to the time, laws of the normal universe are apparently violated.*

* My own view is that some of these phenomena are only fraudulently produced and do not otherwise exist. Those that are not fraudulent will, I believe, be found to obey laws of the physical universe that are in fact perfectly normal, though as yet not understood. See main text, especially Chapter 7.

precognition   Paranormal awareness (that is, other than by means of the known senses, or by logical inference) that an event which has not yet happened will happen.

psychic (adj.) That which relates to the paranormal.

psychic (noun) A paranormally-gifted individual.

psychic healing   A curing of physical illness simply by the procedure known as 'laying on f hands' — that is, by the psychic healer holding or stroking the affected region.

psychokinesis The paranormal movement of objects without normal human agency, or through the effect of known natural forces. See physical phenomena.

psychometry   The practice of obtaining information paranormally about either the dead or the living, and the past, present or future, through holding an object belonging to the person concerned.

retrocognition   Paranormal awareness of a past event not known to any living person or in any way normally recorded.

Synchronicity   The name of a principle which links or connects events together, but which has no relation to the logical and scientific connections of cause and effect. The Chinese oracle that *I Ching* is based on an aspect of synchronicity.

telepathy The passage of information from one *living* mind to another, other than by any normal means of communication. (It is possible that a psychic individual may also *clairvoyantly* obtain information that, as it happens, is known to another living human being — but in such cases we are not able to distinguish firmly between these two phenomena.)

Bibliography

1. Bailey, Alice, *Treatise on Cosmic Fire* (Lucis Trust, New York, 1970).
2. Behrendt, H.C., 'Dr. Puharich and Uri Geller', *Journal of the Society for Psychical Research*, vol.48 (1976).
3. Behrendt, H.C., 'Uri Geller — Pro and Con', ibid., vol.46 (1974).
4. Berg, Charles, *Madkind* (Allen & Unwin, London, 1962).
5. Bestall, C.M., 'An Experiment in Precognition in the Laboratory Mouse', *Journal of Parapsychology*, vol.26 (1962).
6. Bleibtreu, John, *The Parable of the Beast* (Paladin Books, Granada, London, 1970).
7. Bozzano, E., *Manifestations Métapsychiques et les Animaux* (Meyer, Paris, 1926).
8. Brown, Beth, *ESP with Plants and Animals* (Simon & Schuster, New York, 1970).
9. Burtt, H.E., 'An Experimental Study of Early Childhood Memory', *Journal of Genetic Psychology*, vol.58 (1941).
10. Capra, Fritjof, *The Tao of Physics* (Wildwood House, London, 1975).
11. Carlson, Rick, *The Frontiers of Science and Medicine* (Wildwood House, London, 1975).
12. Castaneda, Carlos, *The Teachings of Don Juan* (Penguin, Harmondsworth, 1968).
13. Chettham, Erika, *The Prophecies of Nostradamus* (Spearman, Jersey, 1973).
14. Cummins, Geraldine, *Swan on a Black Sea* (Routledge & Kegan Paul, London, 1965).

15. Däniken, Erich von, *In Search of Ancient Gods* (Souvenir Press, London, 1974).
16. Dobervich, Carolyn, 'Kirlian Photography Revealed?', *Psychic*, vol.6, no.1 (December 1974).
17. Donahoe, James A., *Dream Reality* (Bench Press, California, 1976).
18. Douglas, Alfred, *Extra-Sensory Powers* (Gollancz, London, 1976).
19. Duval, Pierre, and Montredon, Evelyn, 'ESP Experiments with Mice', *Journal of Parapsychology*, vol.32 (1968).
20. Ellis, D.J., 'Listening to the Raudive Voices', *Journal of the Society for Psychical Research*, vol.48 (1975), p.763.
21. Ellis, R.S., 'Norms for Some Structural Changes in the Human Cerebellum from Birth to Old Age', *Journal of Comparative Neurology*, vol.32 (1920–21).
22. Evans, Christopher, *Cults of Unreason* (Harrap, London, 1973).
23. Evans, C., and Gooch, S., 'Science Fiction as Religion'; chapter in *The Significance of Science Fiction*, ed. Richard Kirby (Brans Head Press, London, 1978).
24. Ford, William, Report in *Light*, vol.41 (1921), p.569.
25. Fox, George, *Journals* (Cambridge University Press, Cambridge, 1950).
26. Freud, Sigmund, *The Psychopathology of Everyday Life*, Collected Works, vol.VI (Hogarth, London, 1966).
27. Freud, Sigmund, *The Interpretation of Dreams* (Allen & Unwin, London, 1954).
28. Freud, Sigmund, *Introductory Lectures on Psychoanalysis* (Allen & Unwin, London, 1933).
29. Fuller, John, *Arigo: Surgeon of the Rusty Knife* (Crowell, New York, 1974).
30. Gaddis, V., and Gaddis, M., *The Strange World of Animals and Pets* (Cowles Book Company, New York, 1970).
31. Glaskin, G.M., *Windows of the Mind* (Wildwood House, London, 1975).
32. Gooch, S., 'Alternative Persons: the Entities of Myth

and Science Fiction'; chapter in *The Significance of Science Fiction*, ed. Richard Kirby (Brans Head Press, London, 1978).

33. Gooch, S., 'Once More With Feeling'; chapter in *Pulsar I*, ed. George Hay (Penguin, Harmondsworth, 1978).

34. Gooch, S., *The Neanderthal Question* (Wildwood House, London, 1977).

35. Gooch, S., *Personality and Evolution* (Wildwood House, London, 1973).

36. Gooch, S., *Total Man* (Allen Lane, London, 1972).

37. Gooch, S., 'Re-Thinking to Some Purpose in Psychical Research', *Journal of the Society for Psychical Research*, vol.40 (1964).

38. Govinda, Lama Anagarika, *Foundations of Tibetan Mysticism* (Rider, London, 1969).

39. Grad, Bernard, 'Some Biological Effects of the "Laying on of Hands" ', *Journal of the American Society for Psychical Research*, vol.59 (1965).

40. Grad, B., *et al.*, 'The Influence of an Unorthodox Method of Treatment on Wound Healing in Mice', *International Journal of Parapsychology*, vol.3, no.2, (1961).

41. Grant, Joan, *Winged Pharaoh* (Methuen, London, 1965).

42. Grant, Joan, *Time Out of Mind* (Barker, London, 1956).

43. Grossman, S.P., *A Textbook of Physiological Psychology* (Wiley, New York, 1967).

44. Guirdham, Arthur, *Cathars and Reincarnation* (Spearman, Jersey, 1970).

45. Haggard, Rider, Report in *Journal of the Society for Psychical Research*, vol.11 (1904), p.212.

46. Hartmann, E., *et al.*, 'How Much Sleep and What Kind?' *American Journal of Psychiatry*, vol.127, no.8 (1971).

47. Hawkes, Jacquetta, 'In Pursuit of Strange Gods', *Sunday Times*, September 15th, 1974).

48. Haynes, Renée, *The Hidden Springs* (Hollis & Carter, London, 1961).

49. *I Ching* (The Book of Changes) transl. Richard Wilhelm and Cary F. Baynes (Routledge & Kegan Paul, London, 1968).

50. *Index of Possibilities* (Wildwood House, London, 1974).

51. Iverson, Jeffrey, *More Lives Than One?* (Souvenir Press, London, 1976).
52. Jacobson, Nils O., *Life Without Death?* (Delacorte Press, New York, 1973).
53. Jung, C.G., *Studies in World Association*, Collected Works, vol.2 (Routledge & Kegan Paul, London, 1969).
54. Jung, C.G., *The Archetypes and the Collective Unconscious*, Collected Works, vol.9 (Routledge & Kegan Paul, London, 1969).
55. Jung, C.G., *Synchronicity: an A-Causal Connecting Principle*, Collected Works, vol.8 (Routledge & Kegan Paul, London, 1968).
56. Jung, C.G., *Memories, Dreams, Reflections* (Routledge & Kegan Paul, London, 1963).
57. Kant, Immanuel, *Dreams of a Spirit-Seer*, transl. Goerwitz, ed. F. Sewell (Swan Sonnenschein & Co., London, 1900).
58. Koestler, Arthur, *The Roots of Coincidence* (Hutchinson, London, 1972).
59. Laing, R.D., *The Divided Self* (Tavistock Publications, London, 1959).
60. Manning, Matthew, *The Link* (Smythe, London, 1974).
61. Marshall, Brenda, 'A Telepathic Cockroach', *Light*, vol.96, no.3 (1976).
62. Merta, Jan, 'The Effect of Permanent Magnetic Fields on Avoidance Learning in Mice' (privately circulated research report).
63. Méry, Fernand, *Our Animal Friends* (Rider, London, 1954).
64. Metta, Louis, 'Psychokinesis in Lepidopterous Larvae', *Journal of Parapsychology*, vol.36 (1972).
65. Michell, John, *The View Over Atlantis* (Abacus, London, 1973).
66. Mishlove, Jeffrey, *The Roots of Consciousness* (Random House, New York, 1975).
67. Morgan, C.T., and Stellar, E., *Physiological Psychology* (McGraw-Hill, New York, 1950).
68. Morris, Robert L., 'Animals and ESP', *Psychic*, vol.5, no.1 (1973).

69. Morris, Robert L., 'Psi and Animal Behaviour', *Journal of the American Society for Psychical Research*, vol.64 (1970).
70. Morris, Robert L., 'Some New Techniques in Animal Psi Research', *Journal of Parapsychology*, vol.31 (1967).
71. Moss, Thelma, 'Dreaming Winners at the Races', *Psychic*, vol.2, no.4 (1971).
72. Onetto, B., and Elguin, Gita H., 'Psychokinesis in Experimental Tumourogenesis', *Journal of Parapsychology*, vol.30 (1966).
73. Ostrander, Sheila, and Schroeder, Lynn, *Psychic Discoveries Behind the Iron Curtain* (Abacus, London, 1973).
74. Pirsig, Robert M., *Zen and the Art of Motor Cycle Maintenance* (Bodley Head, London, 1974).
75. Playfair, G.L., Letter in *New Scientist*, November 14th, 1974.
76. Pratt, J.G., *Parapsychology: an Insider's View of ESP* (W.H. Allen, London, 1964).
77. Pratt, J.G., and Roll, W.G., 'The Seaford Disturbances', *Journal of Parapsychology*, vol.22 (1958).
78. Puharich, Andrija, *Uri* (W.H. Allen, London, 1974).
79. Randall, John L., 'Recent Experiments in Animal Parapsychology', *Journal of the Society for Psychical Research*, vol.46 (1972), p.753.
80. Raudive, Konstantin, *Breakthrough* (Taplinger, New York, 1971).
81. Regush, Nicholas (with Jan Merta), *Exploring the Human Aura* (Prentice-Hall, New York, 1975).
82. Renault, Mary, *The Bull from the Sea* (Penguin, Harmondsworth, 1973).
83. Rhine, J.B., 'A New Case of Experimenter Unreliability', *Journal of Parapsychology*, vol.38 (1974).
84. Rhine, J.B., 'The Present Outlook on the Question of Psi in Animals', *Journal of Parapsychology*, vol.15 (1951).
85. Rhine, J.B., and Feather, Sara R., 'The Study of Cases of Psi-Trailing in Animals', *Journal of Parapsychology*, vol.26 (1962).

86. Richmond, Nigel, *Language of the Lines* (Wildwood House, London, 1977).
87. Roberts, Jane, *The Seth Material* (Bantam Books, New York, 1976).
88. Roberts, Jane, *Seth Speaks* (Bantam Books, New York, 1974).
89. Rose, Ronald, *Living Magic* (Rand McNally, New York, 1956).
90. Rudaux, L., and Vaucouleurs, G. de, *Larousse Encyclopedia of Astronomy* (Batchworth Press, London, 1959).
91. Ryall, E.W., *Second Time Around* (Spearman, Jersey, 1975).
92. Schiller, Friedrich, *On the Aesthetic Education of Man*, transl. E.M. Wilkinson and L.A. Willoughby (Oxford University Press, London, 1967).
93. Schmidt, Helmut, 'PK Experiments with Animals as Subjects', *Journal of Parapsychology*, vol.34 (1970).
94. Smith, Justa, 'Paranormal Effects on Enzyme Activity', *Journal of Parapsychology*, vol.32 (1968).
95. Spencer, A., 'The Demography of Catholicism', *The Month*, April 1975.
96. 'Spontaneous Hallucinations of the Sane', *Proceedings*, Society for Psychical Research, vol.10 (1894).
97. Stevenson, Ian, *Twenty Cases Suggestive of Reincarnation* (University of Virginia Press, 1974).
98. Tansley, David, *Radionics and the Subtle Anatomy of Man* (Heath Science Press, London, 1972).
99. Tarver, W.J., Letter in *New Scientist*, October 24th, 1968.
100. Taylor, John, *Superminds* (Macmillan, London, 1975).
101. Temple, Robert, *The Sirius Mystery* (Sidgwick & Jackson, London, 1976).
102. Teng, E.L., *et al.*, 'Handedness in a Chinese Population', *Science*, vol.193 (September 17th, 1976).
103. Thouless, R.H., 'A Test of Survival', *Proceedings*, vol.48, (1948–9), Society for Psychical Research.
104. Tompkins, Peter, and Bird, Christopher, *The Secret Life of Plants* (Allen Lane, London, 1974).
105. Watkins, G., 'PK in the Lizard', *Journal of Para-*

psychology, vol.35 (1971).

106. Watkins, G., and Watkins, A.M., 'Possible Psi Influence in the Resuscitation of Anaesthetised Mice', *Journal of Parapsychology*, vol.35 (1971).

107. Watson, Lyall, *Gifts of Unknown Things* (Hodder & Stoughton, London, 1976).

108. Watson, Lyall, *The Romeo Error* (Hodder & Stoughton, London, 1974).

109. Watson, Lyall, *Supernature* (Hodder & Stoughton, London, 1973).

110. Wilson, Colin, *Mysteries* (Hodder & Stoughton, London, 1978).

111. Wilson, Colin, *The Occult* (Hodder & Stoughton, London, 1971).

112. Wilson, Colin, *The Outsider* (Gollancz, London, 1956).

113. Wood, Ernest, *Practical Yoga* (Rider, London, 1951).

114. Wood, T.E., 'A Further Test for Survival', *Proceedings*, vol.49 (1950) Society for Psychical Research.

115. Young, Arthur M., *The Geometry of Meaning* (Wildwood House, London, 1977).

116. Young, Arthur M., *The Reflexive Universe* (Wildwood House, London, 1977).

Index